FULFILLING THE POTENTIAL OF YOUR DOCTORAL EXPERIENCE

Mendeley -> for Research Search Database.

Sara Miller McCune founded SAGE Publishing in 1965 to support the dissemination of usable knowledge and educate a global community. SAGE publishes more than 1000 journals and over 800 new books each year, spanning a wide range of subject areas. Our growing selection of library products includes archives, data, case studies and video. SAGE remains majority owned by our founder and after her lifetime will become owned by a charitable trust that secures the company's continued independence.

Los Angeles | London | New Delhi | Singapore | Washington DC | Melbourne

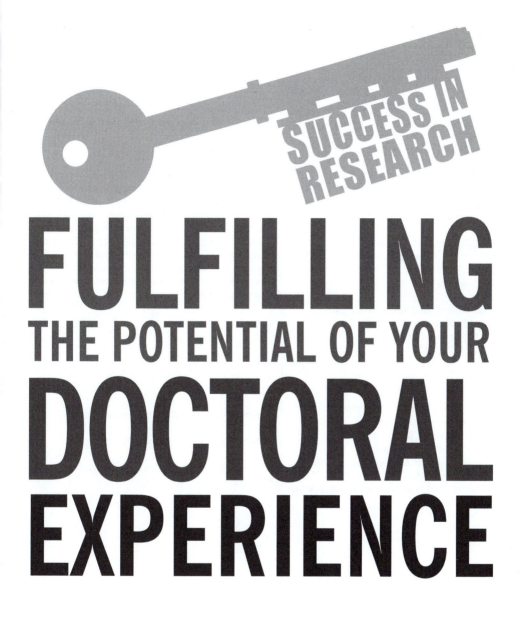

SUCCESS IN RESEARCH

FULFILLING THE POTENTIAL OF YOUR DOCTORAL EXPERIENCE

PAM DENICOLO  JULIE REEVES  DAWN DUKE

Los Angeles | London | New Delhi
Singapore | Washington DC | Melbourne

Los Angeles | London | New Delhi
Singapore | Washington DC | Melbourne

SAGE Publications Ltd
1 Oliver's Yard
55 City Road
London EC1Y 1SP

SAGE Publications Inc.
2455 Teller Road
Thousand Oaks, California 91320

SAGE Publications India Pvt Ltd
B 1/I 1 Mohan Cooperative Industrial Area
Mathura Road
New Delhi 110 044

SAGE Publications Asia-Pacific Pte Ltd
3 Church Street
#10-04 Samsung Hub
Singapore 049483

First published 2018

Editor: Jai Seaman
Assistant editor: Alysha Owen
Production editor: Ian Antcliff
Marketing manager: Susheel Gokarakonda
Cover design: Sheila Tong
Typeset by: C&M Digitals (P) Ltd, Chennai, India
Printed in the UK

Library of Congress Control Number: 2017937073

British Library Cataloguing in Publication data

A catalogue record for this book is available from the British Library

ISBN 978-1-4739-7478-4
ISBN 978-1-4739-7479-1 (pbk)

At SAGE we take sustainability seriously. Most of our products are printed in the UK using FSC papers and boards. When we print overseas we ensure sustainable papers are used as measured by the PREPS grading system. We undertake an annual audit to monitor our sustainability.

We would like to dedicate this book to every doctoral researcher, past, present and in the future. We hope this book honours your experiences from the true joy of idea creation and discovery to those moments of self-doubt and tainted thoughts of being an imposter. We, too, have had all these experiences and, through it all, we believe it is possible to 'thrive with style!' We also wish to dedicate this to those who passionately support doctoral researchers: the supervisors, mentors and support staff, who encourage, champion and stand with these newer researchers, helping them to fulfil their great potential.

CONTENTS

LIST OF FIGURES AND TABLES

Figures

Tables

LIST OF FURTHER RESOURCES

Activities

Information Boxes

Reflection Points

Top Tips

Voice of Experience Boxes

ABOUT THE AUTHORS

Pam Denicolo is an Emeritus Professor at the University of Reading, a chartered constructivist psychologist and honorary pharmacist, who provides consultancy on doctoral support and research methodology as well as examining doctorates in institutions worldwide. Previously she established, managed and developed the University of Reading Graduate School, providing a substantial contribution to its Research Methods, Generic Skills and Doctoral Supervisor training. Her passion for supporting graduate students and other early career researchers is demonstrated through her numerous successful doctoral candidates and her leading roles in national and international organisations such as the International Study Association on Teachers and Teaching, the Society for Research into Higher Education Postgraduate Network, the RCUK Impact and Evaluation Group, several working groups ofVitae including the development of the Researcher Development Framework (RDF), the QAA Doctoral Characteristics Advisory Group, and the UK Council for Graduate Education, all of which have resulted in many publications, presentations and workshops. Through these organisations she met up with Julie and Dawn who became inspirational collaborators on many projects, as well as valued friends. Pam edits and contributes to the SAGE book series: *Success in Research*, aimed at those in the early years of a research career, and co-edits and co-authors with former doctoral researchers a series with Sense, dealing with *Critical Issues in the Future of Learning and Teaching.*

Julie Reeves is a Researcher Developer and Lecturer of Academic Development (Research) at the University of Southampton. Prior to this, she was the Skills Training Manager (Faculty of Humanities) at the University of Manchester. She has been involved with the Roberts agenda since 2005, working with postgraduate and postdoctoral researchers and academic staff. Her academic background is in politics and international relations; her doctoral research was in cultural theory and international relations. Her newly acquired knowledge and understanding was put to practical advantage when she taught in Eastern Europe for the Civic Education Project, where she then learned much about differing pedagogies. She is a member of the *Chartered Institute of Personnel and Development* and the *Society for Research into Higher Education (SRHE)*. Julie met Pam through the project to create the Vitae Researcher Development Framework; they became co-convenors of the Postgraduate Interest Network of the SRHE and, then, they published *Developing Transferable Skills: Enhancing Your Research and Employment Potential* together in 2014. Julie met Dawn through Pam, SEPnet and the SRHE, as they provided workshops for newer researchers and their supervisors/PIs. Together they produced a literature review on researcher development for Oxford Bibliographies. All three have been 'partners in crime' ever since!

Dawn Duke is the Head of Researcher Development within the University of Surrey's Doctoral College. She leads the team that supports the transferable/employability skills of postgraduate researchers and early career researchers across all disciplines, as well as delivers supervisor training. Dawn received her neuroscience PhD from Imperial College. In 2008, she moved from researching and teaching neuroscience to concentrate fully on researcher development. She has worked to embed and normalise skills training to better prepare researchers for the variety of opportunities available to them. Through her work at Surrey and a partial secondment as Director of Graduate Training for the Southeast Physics Network (SEPnet), she has focused on bringing researchers together with employers from a range of sectors, integrating this wider range of expertise into training, creating spaces for discussion and experience sharing. Dawn believes that the world would be a better place if the amazing research that is done within our universities had an even greater impact on policy, society and the economy and is dedicated to enabling the next generation of researchers to take on this challenge. Dawn met Pam through a mutual friend at University of Surrey, and they soon became not only colleagues but also good friends. Then Pam introduced her to Julie and the fun truly began!

ACKNOWLEDGEMENTS

We three authors thank every researcher who has ever attended one of our training sessions or talks. We are grateful to everyone who has shared their thoughts, comments, concerns and fears about all aspects of the doctorate with us and contributed during our sessions, and thus covertly to this book. Without them, we would have little to say. We would also like to thank all the anonymous researchers, whose contributions of advice and experiences will help many others. We are especially grateful to the following people for their expert views, honest reflections and words of wisdom: (first and foremost) Dr Alison Yeung Yam Wah, Academic Writing Tutor, University of Surrey, for her superb contribution of Chapter 4. We thank you for your incredible patience and for allowing us to share your expertise with the doctoral audience.

Dr Carol Boulter – a science education researcher, for sharing her vivid dream and viva experience.

Dr Laura Christie – Educational Development Officer (Researcher Development) at Royal Holloway, University of London, for her experience with mentoring.

Dr Steve Clowes – Senior Lecturer in Physics, University of Surrey, for sharing his experience with impactful research and for general all-round support.

Dr Zoe Harris – Postdoctoral Research Associate, for contributing her experience of, and the concept of, 'Productive Distractions'.

Dr Elaine Hickmott – Development Director, EH Enterprises, for sharing her thoughts and top tips on career trajectory after the doctorate.

Dr Andrew Scott – Consultant, for providing an insight into the skills obtained and what employers want.

Catherine Stephen – Library Client Services and Academic Engagement Manager, for her advice on the incredible resources libraries hold.

Last, but not least – the amazing, sadly late, Maya Angelou, for inspiring us!

PROLOGUE: WHO WILL BENEFIT FROM THE BOOK AND WHY

Who is this book for?

This book has been produced in response to the profound changes that have taken place in the research community in recent years. The three main authors and our guest chapter author share a passion for supporting the work of researchers, especially **doctoral** and **early career researchers**. We have all worked for many years in various capacities to further that ambition, and in so doing have learnt much from researchers about what they find helpful and what they find challenging. We have also witnessed tumultuous change in doctoral education over the last fifteen years or so, including increasing diversity of doctoral candidates, types and titles of doctoral degrees, and the nature and scope of the doctoral research process. Thus, we recognised a need not only to provide an up-to-date resource for our newer researcher community but also to acknowledge that the community itself has transformed and requires a different kind of guidance to that traditionally provided.

The doctoral research community no longer mainly consists of full-time, funded, quite young PhD students but spans a range of ages and experience, including many undertaking a professionally based research degree, and those who study on a part-time and self-funded basis. What has so far remained consistent is that the community includes people from a range of national backgrounds, in whichever country their study is based and whichever geographical context provides the venue for data collection. Given that our audience is diverse in multiple respects, we have attempted here to provide useful general guidance and stimulating ideas for all but with some special advice for specific groups or circumstances, such as part-time researchers, whenever a significant difference emerges. To illustrate ideas and points, we have included the voice of researcher experience both from guest contributors and as generalised and anonymised comments from researchers whom we have engaged with over the years. This book is not, though, a substitute for all the available books on specific aspects of the doctoral process, such as reviewing the literature, writing a **thesis** or developing transferable skills, nor does it intend to make redundant other books about the general doctoral process. Indeed, we will recommend many of them, or at least some sections of them, for further reading of specified topic areas.

Instead, this book takes a distinctive stance which we think is more appropriate for doctoral researchers of today and tomorrow. Before we explore that stance, please note that we will continue to address our main readership as doctoral researchers in recognition both of the diversity of named degrees on which they may be enrolled and of the special status which we think they deserve in the academy. Others may also find this book informative, especially those professionals who support researchers such as **supervisors/advisors** and trainers, administrators and specialist providers like those involved in careers guidance and psychological/social support services. They will forgive us, we hope, for addressing the text to the main intended audience. Please note that from here onwards, we will use the term 'supervisor' rather than the term 'advisor', which is used in North America and elsewhere.

What is unique about this book?

We have acknowledged that there is much wisdom to be found in other books produced as guides for doctoral students. However, many of them start from the premise that they are 'survival guides' for those struggling in an alien context, while some address only the problems that may force themselves on the unsuspecting, rather passive student. We wish to dispel several myths in this book, one of them being this notion that doctoral researchers will necessarily 'suffer the slings and arrows of outrageous fortune' while engaged in their **project**, with relief coming only with its completion.

While, like Shakespeare's Hamlet, we seek to ensure that you are armed 'against a sea of troubles', we nevertheless go further and more positively: we want to highlight for you the huge potential inherent in a **doctoral programme**, including the enjoyment to be had as it progresses as well as future benefits to be gained. Undertaking a doctorate or any project that spans several years will mean dealing with uncertainty and becoming comfortable with it; whilst, over time, the research itself will be subject to change, we want to reassure you that this is normal and that if things do not turn out as you originally planned, this may prove to be a benefit and not a disaster. We want to dispel any paralysing fear of change. Instead, we want you to choose ways to manage your doctorate proactively to take advantage of the wealth of opportunities available to delight you along the way and enhance your prospects beyond the doctorate. In other words, we want you to get the most out of the doctoral experience by, among other things:

- Preparing for study at the doctoral level and recognising the step change required from your previous studies
- Managing the project and the people involved effectively, including managing your own expectations and reactions
- Understanding the implicit assumptions of colleagues and teachers within the academy and adjusting to the 'hidden curriculum' of doctoral education
- Gaining insight into the diverse range of successful communication and dissemination strategies so as to choose what is most appropriate for you
- Developing strategic plans to maximise the potential **impact** of your research, paving the way to gaining further research funding or impressing potential employers
- Using assessment processes as a constructive learning experience
- Highlighting and demonstrating the value of your project
- Elaborating your skills and personal development so that you can make innovative contributions to your chosen profession
- Establishing a network of support and source of professional and intellectual stimulation to last you a lifetime
- Recognising the global and interdisciplinary nature of research and the tensions that may exist between you as a researcher, the context or department/institution you are situated in, and the international setting, so that you can respond to these in productive ways

Thus, this is not a handbook that will tell you what to do in situation X because we know that you will meet situations that we and you have not yet dreamt of and for which there is no 'quick fix'. Instead, we present a range of options which you must tailor to your circumstances and to your growing confidence and competence. By empowering you with knowledge and greater understanding of the context, we hope that you will take control of the process and manage the key stages, knowing when and from whom to seek help, in a mature and professional way. In this way, we hope that you will experience less anxiety, despite the inevitable challenges that a research project entails, and constructively enjoy the whole process.

For those of you who are either re-joining higher education (HE) after a break or who are not familiar at all with the UK higher education procedures, we hope that our attempts to demystify the system will prove particularly helpful. For all readers, we hope to remove some of the arcane secrecy surrounding the doctoral journey.

How can you best make use of the book?

Unlike those books that take you through the doctoral journey step by step, perhaps from application to the post-viva activities, we have chosen to organise our story around a series of questions related to specific processes in which all doctoral researchers must engage. The questions themselves are arranged into three parts: Engaging with the process; Success is in the detail; and Progressing with confidence. Each of these has guidance or suggestions of relevance for all stages of the doctorate. Therefore, although you could read from beginning to end to gain an overview, we intend you to address specific issues as they arise or change in priority. We have chosen this structure because many, indeed most, issues thread their way throughout a research project or degree registration, evolving as they go. For instance, writing, reflection, relationship building and assessment are a few of the activities that should be indulged in from the first days to the last of your registration and beyond. A summary of the parts is provided below so that you can pick which topic is the most salient for you at any one time.

Part One, Engaging with the Process, starts with a discussion that makes a case for the general benefits of doing research within a credit-bearing degree such as a PhD, DLitt or Professional Doctorate. It explains the nature of the doctorate in relation to your previous studies and what qualities you can usefully bring to bear throughout the process. It also begins the process of identifying opportunities within doctoral studies that can help you, with advice on how to take advantage of them. We then focus on how you can set yourself up for success from the very beginning, avoiding ad hoc or emergency-driven responses by identifying resources, including sources of help, in advance, and by developing good habits and work routines whilst developing a flexible plan. We then shift the focus to putting that plan into operation: dealing with routine, setting goals, monitoring your own progress, managing developments as they occur. This is the process of becoming a research professional with inevitable changes to your relationship with knowledge and with significant people in your life such as your supervisors, family, friends, peers, work and home communities. This process often melds excitement with disappointment, stimulation with mundane but necessary activity, as you cultivate a self-aware stance with professional values to gain your own research professional voice. In essence, you are forming your identity as a researcher and becoming a professional researcher. Therefore, we include suggestions about maintaining your motivation and energy in the final phases.

Part Two, Success is in the Detail, begins with that critical activity of writing, particularly the process of developing a thesis. The thesis is your argument about why the topic was selected, how it was explored, what emerged from the research, what it means and why it is important. We provide some general suggestions about how to produce a good quality thesis, one that presents a coherent, concise and clear research story in a critically engaged way. We also include some of the most frequent critical responses from examiners. Practical advice about writing and curating data, reviewing the literature and referencing, using quotations and avoiding **plagiarism**, is woven into the chapter to help you develop a good research story. Complementing your writing activity will be the need to access resources and make the most of the myriad of opportunities and sources of support within your institution and beyond. We discuss how to identify and access courses, events, people and other resources, some of which you will need from early in your research. Some opportunities and resources will serve immediate project needs but many will also enhance your life and your career beyond the doctorate. Indeed, we discuss how you could balance your needs, expectations and responsibilities towards your project with building a profile for the future. The relationships you develop during your doctoral programme are crucial so we explore how to build effective professional relationships with supervisors and other influential academics and mentors. This includes managing supervision meetings, dealing with criticism and developing your own standpoints, eventually taking ownership of the research as your expertise increases. We remember that this complex process is turbulent, a roller-coaster of a journey, so another aspect we address is managing your emotional responses. We encourage you to be less emotionally dependent on your supervisor, so that you not only move towards intellectual independence but you increase your level of self-awareness to become, by the end of the process, self-directing. This is helped by building a network of friends and contacts who can provide feedback and support during the doctorate, while becoming professional allies in the future.

We then address the necessity of learning to be an assertive authority on your topic, an attribute that examiners are looking for in a viva. This leads to the prickly issue of assessment, which we address by providing an overview of what kinds of assessment to expect as a regular feature of the doctoral process and why it is a positive facet that can guide and support your progress. We suggest how to prepare for reviews, what they entail in general terms, what outcomes are possible and how you might respond effectively to them. The final assessment of the doctorate, which we outline in a separate chapter, takes different forms in different national contexts but there are many common criteria. We provide guidance on how you might prepare for that final process while addressing the criteria during the whole project process. For those who will experience a **viva voce**, we suggest ways to limit stress and, indeed, even enjoy the process. Finally, in this section, we discuss potential outcomes of the thesis examination and how to respond productively to any suggested amendments to improve your thesis.

In Part Three, Progressing with Confidence, we turn to facets of the research process that are particularly future-oriented, although they are developed throughout the doctoral programme. Few researchers would wish their research efforts to produce an insignificant outcome, yet there is debate in the sector about the pressure from government and funders for all researchers to be able to articulate and demonstrate the impact of their research. We introduce you to this debate and its consequences for doctoral researchers and future careers. Further, we discuss means of identifying potential impact to help realise the potential of your research, indicating a range of ways in which benefits can accrue from wide dissemination, including, for instance, public engagement and enterprise initiatives. You will undoubtedly need to develop several new skills and build your skills-set to achieve those ends beyond learning traditional research methods. Therefore, we present a range of attributes of successful researchers and examples of the approaches and techniques different researchers use and tailor to their own characteristics. We encourage you to reflect on your own experience, natural inclinations, discipline area and ambitions so that you might adapt them for your own use. Our message here is that it is to your advantage to be proactive, seeking out opportunities rather than waiting for them to emerge.

Throughout the book, we emphasise the personal growth that accompanies your intellectual development and furthers knowledge accumulation over the progress of your doctorate. In this third part, we discuss these as marketable attributes. We consider how you can recognise them in yourself and then promote them effectively to future employers, tailoring your CV appropriately to the target audience and learning to write and speak in registers different to that used within the doctoral research community. This leads to our concluding discussion, which focuses on transitioning beyond the doctorate to establish a new role. In the latter part of your doctorate, you can take advantage of opportunities that will help you move to new environments with different **cultures** and demands. Every organisation, including each school within a university and extending into commerce, industry and the public sector, has its own peculiar culture and requirements of its employees. You can prepare for this using some of the skills, of flexibility and tenacity to name only two, that you have acquired and/or developed during your doctorate and which are as important for your future career as the certificate and title itself.

Voice and vocabulary

Although we have all contributed to each chapter, in combining our expertise and experience of different disciplines and contexts to provide a range of perspectives and ideas, we have necessarily contributed different proportions to specific chapters. Thus, you may 'hear different voices' and encounter different vocabulary/jargon as you address different topics in the book. We hope this adds to, rather than distracts from, the content and your enjoyment. We will refer to the process of sharing your writing with others in the chapter focused on thesis writing, drawing on our experience of providing each other with constructive feedback while writing this book and many other books and articles. This has helped us to tone down our own discipline-specific jargon in our writing. All organisations, including institutions of higher education, and discipline groups within and between them, use jargon and specific language, so we have listed key terms in the Glossary, each one in bold at first mention in the main text, to help you if you are not familiar with it.

At the beginning of each chapter, we provide a list of its main content, while within chapters we use Activities, Information Boxes, Reflection Points and Top Tips to help engage you, enhance your reading, bring ideas to life and help you to make effective choices. Of special note, we have collected advice and examples from current and recent doctoral researchers to ensure that we represent doctoral education from their perspectives as well as ours. These perspectives, some of which are also from supervisors and others involved in the doctoral process, such as librarians, are presented as the Voice of Experience. Each chapter ends with References and additional suggestions for Further Reading.

PART ONE

ENGAGING WITH THE PROCESS

1

WHAT IS THE POINT OF A DOCTORATE IN THE 21ST CENTURY?

In this chapter, we will consider how to:

- Understand the legacy of the doctorate
- Recognise what a doctorate means in the 21st century
- Grasp the implications of the contemporary doctorate for newer researchers
- Tailor your doctorate to meet specific needs, making the best of available opportunities

In this chapter, we hope that we can clarify both what a doctorate is, what its value can be in the near future and what attributes a doctoral researcher tends to develop rather quickly.

We will begin by outlining the recent history of the doctorate because that history will have some influence on your experience as a doctoral researcher whether you are new to the higher education system in which you are registered or are very familiar with it in general terms. This is because doctoral education worldwide has undergone radical changes in structure and function in recent times, at least at the policy level that impacts on the requirements placed on doctoral candidates. This caveat is included specifically because we want to make you aware of the variety of expectations of doctoral researchers held by both staff within your institution and external people such as examiners and prospective employers, each of whom may be, more or less conversant with the changes involved in doctoral programmes. With every development in education, there are 'early adopters' and 'reluctant engagers' and all possibilities in between. By reading this book, we hope you will become familiar with, and even expert in, the requirements of and possibilities within doctoral education now and in the future. Then you will be able to respond appropriately to those requirements, sometimes even guiding others about what is currently deemed appropriate.

Vestiges of the past

Historically, the purpose of the doctorate was to train people to become academics – future stewards of the discipline – through the process of a form of apprenticeship to an established academic. The evolution of the doctorate from an academic research credential to a process of researcher development to prepare researchers for a wider range of employment only began in earnest towards the end of the last century, some twenty years ago. Therefore, there are still many people employed in higher education posts who experienced that former function of the doctorate and, indeed, still perceive the doctoral process and purpose in that way for a variety of reasons. (For instance: they may believe it is best; they know of no other version; they are too busy with teaching and research to notice changes; they deliberately ignore new policy and procedures that may seem to threaten their professional identity.) We can have some empathy with those positions and have acknowledged elsewhere (Denicolo, 2016) that **widening participation** (sometimes seen as **massification** in higher education), the rise of **credentialism**, increased financial pressures and the requirement of research to make a significant contribution to the national economy and social wellbeing, present challenges to the apprenticeship model. However, our purpose here is to help you thrive in the doctoral world as it is now and is likely to be for some time in the future. The purpose of the doctorate nowadays has been elaborated to include preparing people for a wide world of work to which they will contribute a range of skills and attributes acquired or honed through the doctoral research process. We will elaborate on this next.

The doctorate in the 21st century

In this section, we draw on the UK Quality Assurance Agency's (QAA) 'Characteristics Statement – Doctoral Degree' published in 2015 and to which one of us has contributed. You will find in this document considerable information about the development of the doctorate with comparisons of purpose and structure between doctoral types and between disciplinary or national forms. In summary, though, the main message is that, despite variance in detail, all doctorates are based on original research conducted independently by an individual. We will go into more detail in later chapters about what is meant by the terms 'original' (particularly Chapters 4, 7 and 8) and 'independently' (particularly Chapters 5 and 6) but, for now, the key criterion is the process of conducting research, with all its skill and knowledge requirements. There is now also a requirement that researchers develop professional skills and attributes, building on those they bring to the task and developing new ones (Chapters 3 and 5 and then 9, 10 and 11 will elaborate on this). This is intended to recognise that all the professions researchers may subsequently engage in, within and outside of the academy, demand high-level skills of various kinds beyond being able to design and conduct a specific research project (see Denicolo and Reeves, 2014). In fact, only a small proportion of successful doctoral candidates will go on to a postdoctoral research post and/or have permanent or tenured academic positions. For more detailed information about (UK) doctoral career destinations, see the 'What Do Researchers Do' report on the **Vitae** website (www.vitae.ac.uk/). Further, any individual may engage in several different 'careers' over a lifetime, making skills that are generic and transferable very important. In Information Box 1.1, we present a section from the QAA document about what skills a successful doctoral graduate is expected to be able to contribute to their future work. These are characteristics that we hope to help you achieve by following the advice in this book and those documents and books we recommend.

INFORMATION BOX 1.1 CHARACTERISTICS OF DOCTORAL GRADUATES (QAA, 2015)

[Doctoral graduates] should all be able to:

- search for, discover, access, retrieve, sift, interpret, analyse, evaluate, manage, conserve and communicate an ever-increasing volume of knowledge from a range of sources;
- think critically about problems to produce innovative solutions and create new knowledge;

(Continued)

(Continued)

- plan, manage and deliver projects, selecting and justifying appropriate methodological processes while recognising, evaluating and minimising the risks involved and impact on the environment;
- understand funding and how it can be generated and managed as well as organise infrastructure and identify/locate resources;
- engage in professional practice, including ethical, legal, and health and safety aspects, bringing enthusiasm, perseverance and integrity to bear on their work activities;
- support, collaborate with and lead colleagues, using a range of communication, teaching and networking skills to influence practice and policy in diverse environments;
- appreciate the need to engage in research with impact and to be able to communicate it to diverse audiences including the public;
- build relationships with peers, senior colleagues, students and stakeholders with sensitivity to equality, diversity and cultural issues.

Further, doctoral researchers are increasingly being encouraged to develop their foreign language and enterprise skills and to cultivate business acumen.

During their research, all doctoral graduates will have developed additional specialist discipline knowledge while those who have studied a professional doctorate are likely to have been required to have specific professional experience that informs the topic of their research studies. They may well also have been required to engage in further study related to that professional field as part of their doctorate.

Finally, they must be able to prepare, plan and manage their own career development whilst knowing when and where to draw on support.

It is generally recognised that doctoral researchers begin the degree with a wide range of previous experience, personal attributes and acquired skills. Researchers will also have a varying range of opportunities to enhance current skills or learn new ones within their doctoral studies programmes. Thus, when they graduate, each will have a unique collection of attributes and skills developed to varying degrees. Therefore, the list in Box 1.1 is general for you to select which skills and attributes to focus on specifically over the course of your doctoral studies. Note that the first three bullet points emphasise that research still forms the core of a doctorate. At the same time, though, the intent to develop excellent researchers with a wide range of attributes and skills is at least as important as the purpose of simply producing written bodies of work describing the content of and process of the research. That written body of work, a **thesis** or **dissertation** depending on country of origin, is still a vital product and is the most readily examined (Chapter 8).

Whatever stage in the process you are currently at, do not be dismayed by the list, for much help is available to support your achieving these numerous skills. We all recognise, though, that undertaking research over several years can be a demanding task, one unlike your previous education, otherwise the title doctor would not be worth such kudos. Let us explore further what we mean by demanding and different to previous education.

Implications of the contemporary doctorate for newer researchers

For many new doctoral researchers, it is not simply the level of work required that comes as a surprise but also its nature. If we are to guide you to get the most from this degree, then we must start by being realistic and honest. When we meet new researchers for the first time we often ask for their understandings about the doctorate and are often concerned by descriptions such as the following:

> 'It is like a master's but much bigger;' 'It is called a doctor of philosophy but that is a historical name; not much philosophy now in doctorates;' 'My supervisor will tell me what to do and when, and I will get on with my bit of the big research project;' 'You have to write a thesis in complex language using multi-syllabic words to show your erudition!' 'It will involve loads of reading until my supervisor tells me to stop.'

Comments like those above indicate the need to consider what researching for a doctorate entails. There is, indeed, a large step-change between a master's degree and a doctorate, and, of course, a greater one if the transition is from an undergraduate degree. However, every doctorate involves some philosophical consideration of about the nature of knowledge and what are appropriate **paradigms** and ways of accessing it, while considering the **ethics** of the process. Further, one of the key skills that researchers should learn is to make the complex accessible and the specialist topic understandable to lay people. However, there are also other challenging features to contend with, such as:

- the increasing amount of independence required throughout the process;
- the continuing lack of certainty about the nature of the outcome;
- whether the research questions are relevant, sensible and unique;
- and whether the chosen research activities will answer them.

Indeed, prolonged uncertainty is a key feature of doctoral study, with many commentators suggesting that tolerance of uncertainty (finding it stimulating rather than dispiriting), along with stamina/perseverance and passion, are key attributes of good researchers. Angela Duckworth and colleagues (2007) incorporate these into their key attribute for long-term success: grit. They suggest that achievement of difficult goals (a doctorate must surely fit this description) entails not only talent but the sustained and focused application of that talent over time.

In the Denicolo and Reeves book (2014), although we had not then come across Duckworth's work, we compared levels of study with feats of swimming, likening undergraduate study to gaining awards in national competition and master's study to winning Olympic medals. In those cases, though huge effort is needed – and talent and stamina – the end of the race is visible; the lanes are clearly marked in a clean, clear and calm pool; your competitors are in view beside you in the water and supporters are close by, with cheers and warm towels at the ready. In contrast, the requirements of doctorate level study are more comparable to swimming the English Channel: the other shore is shrouded in mist; there are no lanes and many nasty or dangerous things are floating or sailing or swimming around you; you have little idea what the competition is up to; and you are alone in the choppy water albeit that your supervisor may be shouting encouragement and guidance from a dingy in the vicinity. Your personal supporters have little idea about what you are engaged in and keep asking if you are nearly finished yet! Although we cannot teach you to have grit in such circumstances we can nevertheless provide you with strategies to overcome some of the obstacles to success, or at least find your own way around them, building your confidence with each mini-success in the process.

You will find that a key feature of many of our recommendations in this book is careful planning. The first important plan relates to choosing the right kind of doctorate to meet your needs. If you have already made that choice, depending on the stage you have reached, then you may find it useful to go on to the next chapter, about making a good start, or Chapter 3 about developing your role as a researcher, or Chapter 5, which delves more deeply into making the best use of resources and opportunities that abound in higher education. If you have yet to make the decision about what kind of doctorate and mode of study would suit you, then the next section may be of help.

A doctorate to meet your needs

Selection

Two of us have much experience in training supervisors to select the best candidates with whom to work on a doctorate but we do take pains to remind them that selection is a two-way process; prospective doctoral researchers should have their own selection criteria that cover the kind of doctorate as well as the nature of the institution and calibre of the supervision that will suit them best. Supervisors have, in turn, assured us that they are impressed by prospective candidates who respond to questions and pose questions of their own that indicate some effort at researching the nature of the doctorate and the quality of research in their institution. Incidentally, they tend to support our findings from the development of Vitae's **Researcher Development Framework (RDF)**, of which more in Chapters 2 and 5 and Appendix II, that beyond having relevant subject credentials the most important attributes they seek in a doctoral candidate are a passion for the subject, linked to resilience and perseverance to sustain them through the complex journey to success.

One of the early decisions that you must make yourself is whether you will study in a full-time or part-time mode. This will depend on your personal circumstances, the stage in your career and the accessibility of opportunities to study in a specific mode, as well as for how long you think you might be able to sustain your enthusiasm and maintain the support of your family and friends (more about that in Chapter 6). Consider the question in Reflection Point 1.1.

REFLECTION POINT 1.1

DOES A DOCTORATE FIT INTO YOUR LIFE?

Everyone has a full-time life, with a variety of different commitments. To determine if doing a doctorate is right for you at this stage in your life, take a bit of time to reflect on where it will fit in with the rest of your daily and weekly activities for the number of years your programme will take. What are you willing to give up to make space for your doctorate? What will this mean for other aspects of your life?

If you are considering a full-time doctorate, you must think of this as a full-time job. For a part-time doctorate, you are still likely to need to dedicate at least 20 hours a week to your research. Can you commit this amount of time? Can you dedicate the necessary blocks of high-quality thinking time to doing research? Do you have the necessary support structures in place to help you achieve? If not, can you put them in place?

Of course, there are huge financial implications involved in either mode of study and institutions tend to check that candidates have enough funds (of their own, from a funding body or employer) to pay the fees for the whole programme and to provide adequate subsistence throughout the process. (Being based in a particularly 'high cost' area ourselves, we are sensitive to some of our own students' financial struggles so suggest that you might investigate closely the cost of living in a particular location before committing to a particular university there.) Full-time research affords the luxury of focusing largely, if not exclusively, on your topic (a situation that rarely repeats if one remains in academia), and whilst immersion in the project should be enjoyed (Chapters 10 and 11) the apparently abundant timeframe can lead to the mistaken thought that you have more time to do things than may be the case; so, you will need the skills of project and time management, evaluation and monitoring to the same extent as a part-time researcher. If you favour, or perforce must, study in part-time mode, you should consider how remote from your institution you can afford to be, balancing cost and convenience with what support the institution provides in such circumstances alongside other less tangible factors such as the lack of personal face-to-face contact with peers and maintaining motivation in isolation.

One particularly critical aspect that you must determine is the amount of time that you have available for study on a regular basis. Sadly, we have seen many researchers underestimating the time required, especially for part-time doctorates. This is not an enterprise that can be squeezed into bits of spare time, especially in the current economic climate when there is great pressure on supervisors and researchers for timely **submission** and **completion**. Returning to our swimming analogy, the more frequently you must get out of the water and the shorter the intervals spent swimming, the greater loss of momentum and orientation to the task experienced. It is important to establish a routine quickly and to allocate at least the same number of hours to a part-time doctorate as you would require for a half-time job. We say 'at least' because a lot of other 'life events' can occur over several years of adulthood that can divert your purpose. A perhaps unanticipated advantage of part-time research is that you will be managing differing tasks in a manner very close to the reality of a full-time academic position.

One special form of part-time doctoral study that brings certain advantages is that generally known as a professional or practice-based doctorate, which is generally a post-experience qualification, though sometimes required for entry into a profession as a licence to practice. Such doctorates usually contain a significant taught element related to its eponymous discipline (education: EdD; engineering: EngD; psychology: PsychD, are examples). This is in addition to professional or generic skills training and the important research project component, located within the theory and/or practice of the professional area. Some doctorates in the arts have a performance-based component so that the final assessment includes evaluation of a performance or created artefact. Another form of doctorate frequently undertaken in part-time mode, but earning the traditional more generic titles of PhD or DPhil, is a doctorate by publication. These doctorates are less common and have rules for entry specific to the awarding institution, many only accessible to academic staff or others who have a record of publication which can form the basis of a portfolio that will demonstrate an original contribution to knowledge. These doctorate types are examined in the same way as other doctorates (Chapter 8).

Once you are settled on which mode of study will be right for you, then you can begin to select potential institutions that may suit your purpose. Practicalities may heavily influence your choice, for instance an accessible location might be one of your own important criteria unless you have potential access to one of the globally rare distance-learning doctorates or are based in a remote campus. However, you should also evaluate the nature and amount of support provided by potential institutions. We have provided a basic checklist in Activity 1.1. You should tailor this to your own needs and circumstances, perhaps highlighting criteria that are particularly germane for you, adding any personal ones that we have not included.

ACTIVITY 1.1 CRITERIA FOR SELECTING A POTENTIAL INSTITUTION FOR YOUR DOCTORATE

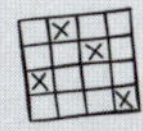

Using a web search, any available brochures and information you may glean at interview, tick the facilities, services and other support available for each institution, then evaluate which institution/s best fit your requirements.

(Continued)

(Continued)

Support/facilities	**Institution 1**	**Institution 2**	**Institution 3**	**Institution 4**	**Institution 5**
Supervision available in your proposed special research area					
Supervisor shows interest in your proposal					
Rapid and friendly (caring) administrative responses					
Critical mass of researchers in department/school					
Availability of kit, instruments, etc.					
Availability of study space/desk/IT equipment, well-stocked library					
Availability of funding for fees, etc.					
Availability of funding for conferences					
Contact provided with fellow researchers /buddy system					
Provision of regular seminar programme					
Wider support from a **Graduate School/Doctoral College**					
Professional skills training resources					
Dedicated career support					
Cross-disciplinary interactions					
Inter-institutional links					
Exposure to employment sector					
Reasonable accommodation/living costs in area					
Availability of childcare facilities or distance learning support					
Other (your own)					
Other					

Now, let us assume that you are successful and gain a place at one of your chosen institutions, to start your doctorate in a few months or so. How might you prepare for that adventure?

Preparation

Organising your personal circumstances

Undertaking a doctorate is a life-changing event that will impinge on all aspects of your private and public life; it is not just an intellectual effort. This latter, erroneous, assumption is sometimes compounded by an expectation that it can be separated entirely from other aspects of life. We suggest that it is more helpful to recognise how much your doctorate will consume your being, thinking, time and energy (even in part-time mode) and prepare yourself and significant others accordingly. It is vital that you have a network of people who are prepared to provide support, succour and sanity in the years to come. When planning your actual studies (see Chapter 3 about contingency plans for the unexpected), it is important to factor into your timetable space for family events, both those that are predictable and those that may surprise or shock – bear in mind that life happens while you are absorbed in your project. You may need, also, to prepare your loved ones for the rather more distracted version of you. (Two images spring to mind as one of us types: my child stood before me with hands spread across my book: 'Stop reading, Mummy, come back to us,' and a beach, sunglasses, sand castles and a pile of books!)

It is wise in the run-up to starting your studies to complete any major household projects, such as do-it-yourself or other large domestic projects. Indeed, you may need to negotiate some frequent lapses in attending to regular chores; while engaged with your doctorate, mowed lawns and tidy houses can fade into insignificance. Nevertheless, mindless tasks or chores often do have a way of freeing up thinking, solving problems and aiding complex thoughts, so do not dismiss them totally.

In all your excitement and pride about beginning a doctorate, you might be tempted to tell all and sundry. We recommend that you are very clear about how long the whole process takes and/or restrict the news to your nearest and dearest – only because of the frequency with which we have overheard remarks such as: 'I dread meeting the postman, who keeps asking if I am a doctor yet!'

Getting up to speed

We are assuming that, in preparation for your application or interview, you have looked up the specialist interests of your supervisors and the recent research conducted in your new department or school. If not, this is the time to do so in addition to finding out about the interests of other academics and researchers who inhabit that zone. You might also investigate other sources of support or expertise in the locality. See more about this in Top Tips 1.1.

TOP TIPS 1.1 CHOOSING THE RIGHT SUPERVISOR FOR YOU

1 Email potential supervisors and ask about opportunities:

- Even if they are not advertising doctoral projects, they may have availability.
- Ask about potential funding, being clear about whether this is a necessity or simply something nice to have.

2 Google potential supervisors:

- Look at social media to find out about experience, interests and qualifications.
- You will be working closely with this person over many years; it is good to have someone who shares some of your same values.

3 Read potential supervisors' papers:

- Consider whether the research you would like to do might be of interest to them.
- Check that their approaches would be interesting to learn more about.

4 Talk to potential supervisors ahead of time:

- See if you feel comfortable with them.
- Determine if your current research interests are aligned, both in topic choice and approach.

5 Visit potential universities if possible:

- Try to get a feel for the ambiance of the campus: how welcoming are the implicit messages.
- Check notice boards in the faculty that interests you for the tone of the messages displayed.
- Contemplate whether it is a place in which you could spend a good deal of time over the next few years.

6 Meet with their current doctoral researchers:

- Weigh up how contented they seem with the support they receive.
- Reflect on how supportive of each other they are.

7 Try to establish how long it takes their doctoral researchers to complete their degrees:

- Check if there are figures for the department, and for your potential supervisor. This can give you an idea of how long the programme is likely to last. Sometimes reality is different to advertised programme descriptions.
- Keep in mind some doctoral researchers may be part-time and therefore take longer.

8 Find out how many publications their doctoral researchers typically produce and, if possible, what their next career steps are:

- Co-authored papers with doctoral researchers are likely listed on each academic's profile page of the university website.
- Career data may be harder to find; however, LinkedIn may prove useful.

9 Investigate what collaborators they work with:

- You may be able to determine this from co-authored papers or from projects described on the internet.
- International or inter-sectoral collaborators may signal potential for you to work with these partners as well.

10 Be open with potential supervisors about what you want from your doctorate and what your expectations are of them.

You can ask your prospective supervisors for a list of recommended reading about the topic and about research methods so that you can begin to get a feel for the nature of language used and issues considered important, as well as noting significant journals in your area which you are likely to need to access.

You might also begin to compile your birthday present list of equipment that will help speed your progress (IT gadgets, marker pens and sticky notes for study and a slow-cooker for domestic support, perhaps). If you accomplish all this before your official start date, then go on to the next chapter, which will give you more ideas on gaining a great start to your doctorate.

References and further reading

Denicolo, P.M. (2016) 'International developments in the purpose and process of the doctorate: Consequences for supervision, examining and the employment of graduates', chapter 2 in M. Fouri-Malherbe, C. Aitchison, R. Albertyn and E. Blitzer (eds), *Postgraduate Supervision: Future Foci for the Knowledge Society*. Stellenbosch: African SunMedia. pp. 15–31.

Denicolo, P.M. and Becker, L. (2012) *Success in Research: Developing Research Proposals*. London: Sage.

Denicolo, P.M. and Reeves, J. (2014) *Success in Research: Developing Transferable Skills*. London: Sage.

Duckworth, A.L., Peterson, C., Matthews, M.D. and Kelly, D.R. (2007) 'Grit: Perseverance and passion for long-term goals', *Journal of Personality and Social Psychology*, 92 (6): 1087–101.

QAA (Quality Assurance Agency) (2015) *Characteristics Statement – Doctoral Degree*. Gloucester: QAA (http://www.qaa.ac.uk).

2

HOW CAN YOU MAKE A GOOD START?

In this chapter, we will consider how to:

- Prepare for new roles
- Research your supervisor and department/school
- Develop good habits and work routines
- Contact potential supporters
- Identify resource sources
- Read and begin writing
- Review your expectations
- Prepare a plan

The scientist and inventor Alexander Graham Bell is reported to have said, 'Before anything else, preparation is the key to success,' whilst the great teacher and philosopher Confucius taught that, 'success depends upon previous preparation, and without such preparation there is sure to be failure'. Although more than two thousand years separate Confucius from Bell, they both recognised the same vital principal, which is that good 'prep' (as chefs say), or preparation, would seem to be an essential ingredient for success in most things, and this is especially true of research. As with any venture, adventure, expedition or activity, such as making a cake, it helps, first, to lay out your equipment, resources, maps, mixing bowls or other much needed materials that will help to get you started and, as with all longer journeys (making a cake is miniscule compared with a research project), you can lay down the basic preparation for your research project in the first 100 days.

As a *professional researcher*, you should think of undertaking doctoral research more as being appointed to a new (and important) job, rather than being a 'student' who largely is instructed and directed by others.

We think language is very important in this respect because the terms you use to describe yourself and your work – because it is work – will influence your own and others' perception of your status and standing. You may receive a good deal of instruction and direction in the first year or so, as a student might, but the aim and goal is for you to emerge, as a well-honed professional person with a doctorate! So, you should think of yourself in professional terms. Even if your department/university does not refer to you in this way, you can rise above any limitations by beginning your journey in a professional frame of mind.

There has been a good deal of focus and debate about the first 100 days in a new role, much of it generated by presidents of the United States. Ostensibly, it began with President Franklin D. Roosevelt (FDR) in 1933, when he used his first three months in office to lay out the foundations of his 'New Deal' by getting an incredible volume of legislation passed into law. Since then, 'the first 100 days' have been an important period for newly elected American presidents. However, as David Greenberg (2009) pointed out in a *Wall Street Journal* article entitled 'The folly of the First Hundred Days', the first 100 days are an 'unreliable indicator of future performance' and, although first impressions count for something, the success or failure in the first 100 days is no indicator of what may follow. In the case of US presidents, as Greenberg noted, although some got off to a flying start (he cites Reagan and FDR as two of the most effective), most performed their overtly significant work later in the presidency. We agree that it is unfair to judge an individual, even a new president, by the actions of their first 100 days in a job since we can all make mistakes in eagerness to make a good impression. Nevertheless, this period of the first few months is important for initial establishment in all roles. The early stage of any role is the time to get most of the basic requirements out of the way and to use the time to lay down good foundations for the future. Employers would certainly expect a new manager to 'bed in' within three months. You need to use this time to get some of the basic issues out of the way and to make sure you can comfortably and confidently manage the remaining years. A researchers' first 100 days are only the start of a marathon, so you need to pace yourself. There are lots of views on the first 100 days on the internet and many publications on the subject; we list a few at the end of the chapter in the further reading.

Laying down the basics

There are three key areas that affect how well a researcher settles into their new role:

1. The people – who are the people you need to know, and care about, and how will you build relationships with them or for them?
2. The environment – what is it like, what are the cultures and traditions, what resources are available or need to be identified?
3. Aspects of the role itself – what is expected, what is the 'doctorate' about and how can you ensure you are prepared for it?

You will need to work on all three areas concurrently, although some may take precedence over others at key stages, but by the end of the 100 days, if you have addressed those questions well, you should be in a good position to begin your research project effectively. Make a start right now by engaging in Reflection Point 2.1

REFLECTION POINT 2.1

THE BASICS FOR A GOOD START

Reflect on what you would like to have achieved by the end of 100 days. Make the generic questions above specific to your context by, for example: challenging yourself to introduce yourself to named people in salient roles such as your subject librarian; asking about regular seminars, or expected conference attendance; checking with more experienced peers about local traditions related to the doctorate.

The people

You might be enthusiastic and eager to get stuck into the research, and that is, indeed, an excellent ambition; however, the sensible thing to do is to get to know your supervisors first. At least track them down in the first few days of enrolment (within a week of your arrival) and arrange an introductory meeting – s/he/they may do this first, but you should not be shy and wait around to be invited to say 'hello' – especially if you are new to the department or university. First impressions count for a lot, so signal that you are a professional and friendly person, willing to make contact and establish a working relationship (NB: it is not necessary to become best friends with your supervisor, because you are aiming to establish a professional relationship). Once you have made 'first contact' and introduced yourself, more formal and work-focused meetings or 'supervisions' as they might be called, will be set up. Your first formal supervision may not take place for a few weeks, depending on how busy your supervisors are and what induction events are available, but we would certainly expect that meeting to take place within the first four weeks – ideally sooner rather than later in that period.

It is important to repeat the point 'depending on how busy your supervisor is' because sometimes researchers are unaware of the volume and range of work that supervisors will be doing alongside supervising doctoral researchers, i.e. they may be teaching undergraduate and master's courses, doing administrative work, attending committee meetings, conducting their own research, attending conferences, managing a team or department, writing their own papers/books and putting together funding proposals, etc. Whilst almost all supervisors enjoy the time they spend with doctoral researchers, as a new researcher you will probably need to be more pro-active in managing this relationship than an undergraduate or master's student is expected to be in their relationship with a lecturer (see Chapter 6 on the relationship with your supervisors), which means you will also need to manage your own diary in respect of theirs. They may only be able to meet with you for an hour or two every couple of weeks or once a month (although weekly interaction is best in the early stage), so you will need to accept that you should work around their availability but still ensure that you do meet regularly.

Use this early relationship-building time with your supervisors to find out how they would like to work with you, what their expectations are (for example, whether they expect you to record or log your supervision meetings) and what kind of timetable (if any) they have in mind for your research. This can then be negotiated and incorporated into an overall work schedule or plan (see the final section below). Ideally, as a new researcher, you can warm up your research skills by approaching your supervisors' existing doctoral researchers, if any, to gain another insight into your supervisors' way of working – that is, specifically ask for views on the supervisors' strengths and any weaknesses that you may have to work around or manage if their style differs from yours.

Other people will also be crucial to your research success, so use the first 100 days to get to know other staff in the department and especially take time to get to know your peers in the department. Your peer researchers will be an important source of friendship and support, but also will be valuable later in your career. It is surprising how useful contacts from your doctoral research days can be as you progress through your careers at roughly the same pace (see Chapter 6 on networking).

If you are new to the university or local area, there may be other practical people-matters to take care of: you must register with a local medical practice and general practitioner (GP), you may want to register with a dentist and, if required, attend to any visa registrations/requirements. If you have family, especially if you are an international researcher, you will be juggling the demands of getting children registered and settled into local schools or nurseries while also ensuring your spouse is also adjusting to the new way of life. Often, as Stephanie Doyle et al. (2015) have pointed out, this aspect of postgraduate life gets overlooked by supervisors and universities. It is very important that you resist the pressure, from external sources or internal panic, to focus solely on getting on with the research. Use the first three months to focus as much on helping you, your spouse and/or children to settle into the new environment as on orienting yourself to your actual research project. This will prevent many later traumas but it is a tough balancing act, and one that part-time researchers will also be facing even if they live relatively locally. There are two ways in which both international and part-time researchers can help themselves with this transition:

1. Find out what kind of support your institution offers to international researchers and their families or how they support distance learners if you are part-time. Some have informal networks for international visitors, or societies/clubs for specific interests, or they may deploy spouses in more formal ways.
2. Track down and talk to people in a similar situation – these colleagues will be a vital source of information and insight, and will, likely, recognise the challenges you will be experiencing and can provide pertinent advice from their own experience, something your supervisors may not have had.

The whole point of the first 100 days is about building relationships and laying the foundations for your future networks. Use this time to find out about who you are working with and for, and enable those people to find out about you.

The environment

Your immediate 'place of work' will need the first attention so that you can settle in quickly and have a base from which to become more adventurous. Departmental secretaries/administrators are likely to be your best resource in this respect because they can guide you in a variety of areas; for instance, they will know where doctoral researchers usually work, if there is allocated desk space and how the allocation system works. They will also be familiar with other aspects of the system, such as what resources are available, who holds them and how to gain access to them. They will also, along with any research administrators, be able to give you insights into departmental customs and practices such as regular meetings or seminars, who usually attends them, who contributes to them, whether attendance is obligatory, superficially voluntary but expected, and so on. Such people will be pleased if you check with them about such social niceties as whether there is a shared obligation to contribute to funding coffee/tea/biscuits, a rota for bringing in milk or tidying the fridge; it will demonstrate your willingness to become part of the community.

Once you have found out about your immediate environment and colleagues, you can then begin to look to the broader environment and context in which you are working. This entails finding out what you need to know so that you can do the job brilliantly. Initially, you will need to find out what resources and information are there to help you and then begin to refine this to the needs of your specific project. You will need to build a picture of what this thing called 'doctoral research' is about in your specific context. Initially, your supervisors will be a great resource but do not underestimate the knowledge of librarians, researcher developers, careers advisors, postgraduate administrators and fellow researchers who will value being asked for information and advice. Indeed, the wise researcher learns very quickly to draw in the resources they need from a variety of sources. Do not expect your supervisor to know everything – part of being a professional researcher is being able to track down the expertise needed if it is not readily to hand. We cannot provide details of such things as availability of computer terminals, **inter-library loan** schemes, cost of or how much photocopying is free, and so on because these not only differ between institutions but between departments too, since they are budgetary items. Thus, do not assume that because a colleague in another department has certain privileges then you will too. However, it is essential that you get yourself set up with referencing software as soon as possible and you should aim, by the end of the 100 days, to know how to use it properly. Your institution may provide some software, but there is free software available. Using the search terms 'Comparison of reference management software' within Wikipedia (https://en.wikipedia.org) provides a summary of the different formats and what operating systems they require. It would be wise to check with peers and your supervisor which ones are regularly preferred in your discipline/geographical location. The advantage of cloud-based systems is that you can use them anywhere and anytime, after you have successfully completed your doctorate and perhaps gone to another institution or organisation.

Another area of difference is that some institutions may have formal contracts or agreements that researchers and their supervisors need to adhere to. These may specify contact hours, how supervisions are recorded, and what is available to the researcher and what is expected of them, such as lab duties or teaching/tutoring, as well. There is a UK national code of practice that includes a section on researchers, the Quality Code – Chapter B11, that researchers are advised to read to find out about the expectations surrounding research degrees. There is also a national statement, the Researcher Development Statement, that identifies areas of learning that all researchers in the UK are expected to cover (especially if they are funded by the research councils) and a fuller framework, the Vitae Researcher Development Framework, that all researchers should find useful as an overview of the researcher role and as an aid to professional development (see our companion book for more detail: *Success in Research: Developing Transferable Skills*, Denicolo and Reeves, 2014).

In Chapter 5, we consider other resources and opportunities that you should avail yourself of, either in your department, school or in a facility especially focused on the needs of postgraduates or doctoral researchers, such as Graduate Schools and Doctoral Colleges. Such entities are likely, as are departments/schools, to have some form of induction event at the beginning of the academic year or each term/semester during which facilities, activities and resources will be summarised and key people introduced.

Even if you have completed your undergraduate and/or master's studies at the same institution as the one in which you are undertaking your doctorate, do not underestimate how different the doctoral process is and what is available only to doctoral students and research staff. Our advice is, do not skip any induction events on offer or tours of library resources. You may think you know how to use the library already, but that may turn out to be a self-limiting assumption and cost you time later. There may be disciplinary resources you have access to as a postgraduate researcher (PGR) that are not generally shared with other students. Similarly, learning to use social media for research or identifying useful software available to researchers will set you up for the project ahead.

Special note for part-time and/or distance learners or those who start their registration on a non-traditional date: Planning ahead of your first registration date should, if possible, include taking an opportunity to attend the inductions available in your institution, even if they do not coincide with your actual start date, since they will be the source of much useful practical information and provide opportunities to meet significant people (supervisors, administrators, peer researchers). If this is impossible, then seek out all the documents that were provided at the last induction and a contact email for a peer attendee who might be willing to talk through with you (even via Skype) what s/he found out.

The role

Transitioning into the research process is a progression that should not be underestimated or ignored! One of the biggest problems facing new researchers is failing to reflect on their expectations – so we have provided

Activity 2.1. Until you have completed the whole process, it is difficult to appreciate just how different undertaking doctoral research is from all other roles in higher education, whilst it is widely acknowledged that it entails one of the more challenging of **pedagogies**, a point we discuss further in Chapter 10. Two questions (and our suggested answers) may help you to reflect on the difference:

1. Dealing with uncertainty: How will you manage the unknown? This is likely to be the first time that you are seeking not simply a new answer to a project question but, in the initial stages at least, a new question within the discipline. *Answer:* You must adopt a flexible attitude so that you can manage the changing environment, your changing expectations, the excitements, occasional disappointments and even fluctuating levels of motivation. It is inevitable that things go wrong or you encounter unexpected barriers to progress, but this can open new avenues for research and often leads to better ideas, so should not always be viewed negatively. (Experienced researchers do often forget to warn new recruits of the truth of the adage 'if anything can go wrong, it will' because they have become acclimatised to it.)
2. Dealing with immensity: How do you eat an elephant (or a comparably large vegetable)? *Answer:* One bite at a time! This is an old joke – but a truism when faced with a very large project that stretches over years. So, to avoid choking or being overwhelmed by the size of the thing, you need to methodically munch your way through it one mouthful at a time. This is where your ability to plan is vital; dividing up the tasks not simply to undertake them in a logical order but also to check that they all can be completed in time (Chapter 3).

ACTIVITY 2.1 EXPECTATIONS AND ANTICIPATIONS

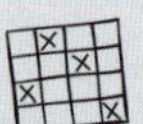

Take a blank sheet of paper and list your answers to the following questions (part-time researchers will need to adjust the time slots accordingly):

1. What do you expect will happen, what will you be doing in the beginning stage i.e., first year full-time/first and second years part-time?
2. What do you expect will happen, what will you be doing in the middle stages?
3. What do you expect will happen, what will you be doing in the final stage?
4. What do you expect from your supervisor?
5. What challenges (if any) do you anticipate?

Once you have constructed your list, compare it with the comments below provided by other researchers in their first few weeks at a university.

1 What do you expect will happen in the beginning stage?	Getting to know people – department and supervisor • Reading • Getting into field • Narrowing focus of research • Knowing the sources • Being guided about what is researchable • Chaos • Being kept on track • Gaining more insight into research • Keeping a research diary • Start writing something
2 What do you expect will happen in the middle stages?	• Gathering data, interviews, fieldwork, etc. • Going to conferences – giving papers • Writing chapters • Reading, reading, reading • Doing field/lab/archival research, etc. • This is the busy stage • May be difficulties with perseverance
3 What do you expect will happen in the final stage?	• Writing, writing, writing • Isolation • Headaches • Lack of sleep • Discipline • Dedication, commitment from myself • Look for a job
4 What do you expect from your supervisor?	• Accessibility (may expect to see them every day) • Guidance and support • Feedback • Guidance on structuring the research • Keeping me on track (telling me when to stop) • Help with time management • Help with financial advice • Help with careers • Available for personal support, family matters • In-depth knowledge of subject • Enlarge our horizons – help us to think creatively • Pushing us • Honesty • Professional quality evaluation
5 What problems (if any) do you anticipate?	• Funding • Data collection • Getting lost half-way in the process • Maintaining fitness • Exhaustion • Time management • Language • Originality in the research

(Continued)

(Continued)

We have conducted the same exercise with research supervisors! Now, consider the supervisors' views on these topics – notice how they differ from the researchers' views:

1 What do you expect will happen in the beginning stage?	• Expect literature addressed • Selected and learned methods/methodology • Ethical considerations and procedures engaged with • Found their way around university/department • Done a lot of reading • Got some pilot data (**STEMM**) • Theoretical framework development (**HASS**) • Begun training (research methods, transferable, professional)
2 What do you expect will happen in the middle stages?	• Presentations regularly made locally • Data collection and analysis well under way • Chapter drafting (HASS) • Publications (STEMM) • Conferences presentations • Possible formal assessment/review
3 What do you expect will happen in the final stage?	• Thesis writing • Publication • **Mock viva** • Viva • Corrections/amendments
4 What do you think researchers expect from you, as their supervisor?	• Availability (but nervous about how much) • Knowledge and expertise • Guidance on the thesis (perhaps on academic career) • **Critical feedback**
5 What problems (if any) do you anticipate?	• Distraction from main project task • Research 'not working' • Second year dip in enthusiasm/motivation • Getting lost in the literature/data • Isolation

When you compare the researchers' expectations and responses with the supervisors', it becomes clear that the supervisors are very much focused on the thesis and might even be described as 'thesis-driven'! Individual supervisors may not be interested in or knowledgeable about useful things for helping their researchers with their financial problems or even time management; some might, but you need to consider how you would deal with the situation if yours does not. Similarly, although you may see your supervisor regularly, you may not see them every day as some researchers have expected. Indeed, although you may only be expected to see your supervisor once every two or three weeks in the first few months, you may only meet monthly thereafter or even less regularly depending on your subject. This aspect of 'working as a researcher' differs sharply with working in most other kinds of environment, where you probably would see your line-manager most days, if not daily. Indeed, if you are in a lab you may see a **postdoctoral researcher** (**postdoc**) more often than your main supervisor. On the other hand, you may physically work beside your supervisor but not actually be 'supervised' in relation to your own project.

The issue here is how you will respond if your assumptions, expectations or personal needs are not met. Examining your own expectations and challenging them – asking if your views are realistic or ill-informed – is the first sensible step. Learning to find out about others' expectations and then adjusting to them if necessary, or negotiating a mutually agreeable alternative if possible, are part of the role process of any new professional.

Did you notice that the researchers left writing until a good way into the process, that is until years three or four? This is a major but common misunderstanding of the doctoral process – all three of your present authors and probably your supervisors agree that you should be writing ALL the time. You can find in Top Tips 2.1 many aspects of doctoral study that you can make a start on during your first few months. We will elaborate on these things next and in the following chapters.

TOP TIPS 2.1 STARTING YOUR DOCTORATE WELL (YOUR FIRST MONTH)

1 Get into the habit of working set hours:

- If you are full-time, that means full-time job hours.
- If you are part-time, work the hours you have agreed with your university and supervisor(s).
- Stick to these times even if you do not feel you have enough to do (see below for tips on what to do).

2 Plan your weekly reading:

- Pick a defined area to read about.
- Identify a doable amount of reading for the week.
- Put aside a few hours for reading every day.
- Do not try to read constantly for an entire day; this is too intense and your retention will be poor.
- Mix reading with other activities.

(Continued)

(Continued)

3 Write:

- It is not too early to start writing.
- Write notes about what your read, trying to put summaries into your own words.
- Write lists of words and concepts you do not understand.
- Write down your thoughts and ideas in a specific (private) notebook.

4 Start learning computer programs/technology/techniques:

- Even those in non-technical disciplines would be wise to learn how to use reference-managing software.
- There may also be analysis software you could start to learn.
- For those of you in lab-based disciplines, shadow more senior PhD students and postdocs to learn as many lab techniques as you can.
- (These skills you develop will be helpful later in your research life.)

5 Explore:

- Take time every week (every day, if you are full-time) to explore resources available to you within your department, your faculty and the larger university.
- If you are on a campus, take different walks and see what you can find.
- Take time to introduce yourself to administrators, support staff, technicians, fellow doctoral researchers, librarians, fellow researchers.
- If you are working at a distance, explore virtually. Find resources, and perhaps make phone or Skype appointments to establish contacts and support.

6 Build your relationship with your supervisor:

- Share with your supervisor your expectations.
- Plan meetings.
- Talk with them about what you are reading.
- Set some initial objectives.
- Ask questions.

7 Develop yourself:

- Identify training workshops that may be helpful to you and sign up.
- Identify seminar or lecture series and put those into your diary.

8 Enjoy:

- Plan time to reflect on what you are learning each day.
- Think about your subject and let your mind wander.
- Make time for those activities that help you feel energised.
- Do make sure you are getting enough sleep; your brain will be working hard and you will need to take care of it.

From those tips, you can recognise that, as much as you need to get into the habit of reading and regularly checking what is going on in your research area, you also need to get into the habit of writing and reviewing your work (Chapter 4). This achieves two things: first, it will improve your writing skills and proficiency, and, second, doing a doctorate is an iterative process, not a linear one, so developments in the procedures and in your thinking, can usefully be logged as a record.

One of the things that new researchers may not expect is how much of an emotional and motivational roller-coaster the process of researching for a doctorate can be. A doctorate is a long project full-time and even more so if you are part-time, and a lot of life can happen in that period – think about the ups and downs you may have enjoyed and endured over the past three years, and this will give you some insight into how you may need to manage the doctoral process over the forthcoming years. Knowing that there may be times of complete boredom, irritation and frustration as well as those of complete joy and a sense of real accomplishment, as there are in other parts of life, means you need to think as much about how you will manage the high points as well as the low ones. See what others from the world of research have said in Voice of Experience Box 2.1; perhaps none of the comments is an inspiring or glamorous one, but certainly they are realistic. Start as you mean to go on: use your first 100 days to find out what might be useful to know about the rhythms or life-cycle of the doctorate in your discipline, including key milestones, expectations and conventions – more advanced researchers can be a vital source of advice in this respect.

VOICE OF EXPERIENCE 2.1 DOING A DOCTORATE

A PhD is as much a test of character as it is about ideas! (*Postgraduate researcher*)

You get a doctorate because you can stick it out for three years. (*Postdoc and developer*)

You should treat a PhD like doing a job – you need to work consistently as you would in any 9-to-5 job. (*Supervisor*)

You get a PhD because you REALLY WANT one! (*Associate Dean of Research*)

To help you work your way through the doctorate (or eat the elephant) you need to develop good habits and work routines as quickly as possible. If you treat your doctorate as a job, establishing a standard working day, this can be highly beneficial. Ideally, this should be based on a 9am to 5pm routine (taking account of your own body clock rhythms, but recognising that this is also a preparation for your future working life so do not sink into an unsustainable 'lark or owl' pattern, working very early in the morning or late at night).

We do know the reality is that you will sometimes work longer than this when deadlines loom or working on data analysis, or data are difficult to obtain – however it is essential that you maintain a healthy work–life balance, which means having at least one day off a week. If you must work at weekends, limit it to a few hours. One of us began her weekdays with a walk with a friend, 8am to 8.30; then read the newspaper whilst having breakfast until 9.30 (because she counted keeping up with world events as useful background work); she stopped for lunch every day from 1pm to 1.30; worked until supper at 6pm and never worked in the evenings because of family commitments. Similarly, she only worked on Sunday mornings for a few hours, whilst the dinner was cooking. Part-time researchers will need to block out chunks of time for research and it is a good idea to put these into your work diary (which you will have set up in your first week, we hope). Part-time researchers more than any other researcher will know that you do not have to work all the time on your thesis, because for them that is not possible anyway, so that is a lesson full-time researchers should learn. Indeed, James Patterson kept a timesheet of his research and showed how important non-core PhD work was not only for his thesis but also to his wellbeing and career prospects – reminding us that doing a doctorate is not just about the research (see https://thesiswhisperer.com/2016/05/11/how-long-does-it-take-to-do-a-phd/).

Making the most of your first 100 days

To reiterate, the first 100 days should involve getting established in your new researcher role. Even if you have been at the institution for some time, you should still approach this as a new job in a new department and enthusiastically look at everything you may already be familiar with from a fresh perspective. You should think of yourself as a professional researcher and not a passive student.

By the end of 100 days (or three months), you should know who your supervisors are and how you will work with them; you should know the people who can help you with your work; have become familiar with the people in your department and be thinking about who you might like or need to know outside of your department or institution, too. You should be conversant with the university environment and what resources are available to you within it, and you should be beginning to take advantage of available opportunities, that is, accessing the training and development that you may need to help you conduct your research. None of the three key aspects (people, environment, role) are discrete or provide you with finite tasks: you will always be adding to your people contacts, which will eventually become your 'professional network'; you will always be expanding your resources and refining your plans and understanding of what being a researcher is about.

However, by the end of the first three months, you should have the basic foundations in place. Although the checklist in Activity 2.2 might seem to indicate that you could work on these three areas sequentially, that is one per month, instead you will need to work on all three concurrently.

Finally, you need to come up with an overall plan of what you intend to do. Essentially you are on a 'fixed term contract' and have a limited amount of time to work on a project with a specific deliverable (a thesis) at the end. So, it is best to plan this out and draw up phases, stages or work packages that ensure you can deliver the thesis on time. By your second or third supervision, you should be discussing your overall plan with your supervisors. This plan will evolve over time – but the important thing is that you have a sense of direction that you can build on, manage and control. With this, you will have made an excellent start.

ACTIVITY 2.2 YOUR FIRST 100 DAYS – PERSONAL CHECKLIST

When by	Activity		Done		Still need to do
Week 1	Identified and know who your main supervisor is and met her/him.				
Week 1	Found your way around campus and the local town, if you are new to the area.				
Week 1	Know where the main facilities and services are located, i.e. library, student union, post office. Opened bank account. Obtained your email and any student card for access to university facilities. Obtained parking permits if required.				
Week 1	Begun asking colleagues in department for tips on how to do a doctorate, what is involved in doing a doctorate, found other resources on the topic. (See Further Reading at end of each chapter of this book.)				
Week 1–2	Met fellow researchers and other department members.				

(Continued)

(Continued)

When by	Activity		Done		Still need to do
Week 1–3	Received an induction to university and/or department and programme. Know what the main sources of support are for doctoral researchers in your institution and have located them, i.e. a Graduate School or Doctoral College, and websites for information.				
Week 2–3	Familiarised yourself with the professional guidance, such as Researcher Development Statement (RDS) and Vitae Researcher Development Framework (RDF) in the UK.				
Week 3	Registered with a local General Practitioner (GP – medical doctor).				
Week 3–4	Negotiated and agreed the frequency of meetings with supervisor(s), how they will be recorded/logged, and agreed general rules for first year.				
Week 3–4	Become aware of external sources of support, i.e. Vitae, PhD comics, The Thesis Whisperer.				
Month 1	Identified and know who your second and third (if appropriate) supervisor is and met with them.				
Month 1	Settled spouse and children into new life, i.e. registered children with local school, identified the support networks or groups your institution (or local community) offered to spouses, especially if you are an international researcher and new to the area.				
Month 1 (Check national requirements and time limits)	Registered with police/border agency for visa requirements – if international researcher and applicable.				

When by	Activity		Done		Still need to do
Month 1	Found out about the doctoral process overall and the general requirements for doctoral research – i.e. read university policy and codes of practice, RCUK statement of expectations and QAA chapter B11 in UK (or found own national equivalents).				
Month 1–2	Conducted a training needs analysis (TNA), learning needs analysis (LNA) or development needs analysis (DNA), skills audit – and identified development and research needs – possibly using the Vitae Researcher Development Framework.				
Month 2	Met with supervisor(s) and negotiated expectations for first year and for research period in general – set some goals.				
Month 2	Started to identify literature for review.				
Month 2	Establishing a system for managing reference materials and information related to your research – i.e., identified appropriate referencing software and learnt how to use it! Have a system for cataloguing and reviewing your research materials/information/reading/data/artefacts and/or findings.				
Month 2	Understand ethical requirements for research and researcher integrity – considered your own professional standards alongside those of the discipline.				
Month 2–3	Drawn up general plan for whole period – i.e. put goals above in a Gantt Chart (or other personal progress tracking mechanism/software)				

(Continued)

(Continued)

When by	Activity		Done		Still need to do
	and set milestones, including professional development goals.				
Month 2–3	Begun to find out about the process for ethical approval – even if not applicable, you should understand the process (this is very useful to know for future reference).				
Month 2–3	Started making friends or contacts with people outside of your discipline and social circle – you are now beginning to build your professional network!				
Month 3	Identified and know who any additional members of the supervisory team are (but you may not have met them all at this stage).				
Month 3	Identified and know your discipline-specific library resources and librarian, and appropriate databases.				
Month 3	Know your way around lab (STEMM) and/or have established office hours. **Have working routine and plan in place for conducting (the remainder of) research!**				
Month 3	Have started professional development or generic skills training programme, including provision for your wellbeing.				
Month 3	Attended the beginning of research methods training and begun thinking about what research methods you could use and why in your research.				

When by	Activity		Done		Still need to do
Month 3	Begun thinking about the general focus for research if you have chosen the topic, as in HASS, *or*, begun thinking about how you can make the research topic your own if allocated a project in other STEMM-based subjects.				
Month 3	Starting to attend and contribute (by asking questions) to research/ disciplinary seminars and workshops.				
Month 3	Begun to write up research to date – i.e., *started to write thesis*!				

VOICE OF EXPERIENCE 2.2 ADVICE FOR FIRST-YEAR DOCTORAL RESEARCHERS FROM THOSE IN THEIR FINAL YEAR

'Try to read a wide range of literature, even the articles you think might not be that relevant to your research, because your ideas change along the way. Trust me, you need to know more than you think to make sure your project stays on track and to be confident answering questions.'

'Write things down! New ideas pop up all the time, so you should note them. They might be useful, they might not be, but at least you know you have them noted down in case you need them. Reading loads without writing means you must read everything again once you need to draft your chapters.'

'I think it is important to remember that everything you do in the first year is at draft stage, both in terms of words written on the page and ideas exchanged with supervisors.'

'Try to attend training courses, public lectures, or seminars, as this helps you learn how other people conduct and present their research. This is also a great way to make new friends from outside of your research group. Having friends on campus makes the PhD experience so much easier, and you also don't know who will prove that invaluable contact when you're trying to learn a new technique or skill.'

References and further reading 

Bloch, M. and Willmott, P. (2012) 'The first 100 days of a new CIO: Nine steps for wiring in success', Digital McKinsey, December. www.mckinsey.com/business-functions/digital-mckinsey/our-insights/the-first-100-days-of-a-new-cio-nine-steps-for-wiring-in-success.

Denicolo, P. and Reeves, J. (2014) *Success in Research: Developing Transferable Skills*. London: Sage.

Doyle, S., Loveridge, J. and Faamanatu-Eteuati, N. (2015) 'Counting family: Making the family of international students visible in higher education policy and practice', *Higher Education Policy*, 1–15.

Greenberg, D. (2009) 'The folly of the First Hundred Days', *Wall Street Journal*, 21 March.

O'Keeffe, N. (2011) *Your First 100 Days: How to Make Maximum Impact in Your New Leadership Role*. London: Financial Times/Prentice Hall.

Robinson, W. (2004) *Your First 90 Days in a New Job (How to Make an Impact)*. Raleigh: LULU.

3

HOW CAN YOU DEVELOP YOUR ROLE AS AN EVOLVING RESEARCHER?

In this chapter, we will consider how to:

- Become increasingly aware of how you are likely to change during the course of your doctorate
- Enhance your productivity throughout different stages
- Understand the dynamic nature of the supervisor–researcher relationship
- Maintain a healthy research–life balance
- Plan and prepare for the unexpected
- Develop your professional voice
- Maintain drive and enthusiasm throughout the entire doctorate

In Chapter 2 we discussed how you can best get your doctorate off to a good start. Assuming you have now made a good start, we want to look at how to ensure you maintain this momentum throughout all the various stages of your research journey. The doctorate is a long-term commitment. Depending on your programme, your mode of study and the university/funding regulations, a doctorate can take anywhere from three to ten years (though you will see that most universities now expect even a part-time doctorate to be completed in six to eight years). During this period, you will develop an incredible amount. Change is to be expected over any substantial period of adult life, however, the process of the doctorate drives an astonishing degree of personal and professional development (regardless of age), such that you truly will see yourself as a different person by the end of this degree. However, the prospect of change can be daunting. Nevertheless, for researchers who are pushing at the boundaries of knowledge and discovering the unknown, change must be embraced. It is through managing the dynamic process of the doctorate and capitalising on the unexpected that you can truly maximise the potential of your doctoral experience.

Most books on doctorates describe the doctoral journey in a rather linear way. A new doctoral researcher enters a programme and is, in general, dependent on their supervisor for advice and guidance. Then, as they are settling in, they become increasingly independent; the supervisor can gradually step back and the new researcher blossoms into a newly fledged independent researcher (indeed, this is one of the things supervisors enjoy the most in supervising doctorates). In theory, this does happen; however, the beautifully linear regression line that these books refer to is but a model that perhaps can be thought of as being nicely smoothed out across the millions of data points of real doctorates (Figure 3.1). For any individual researcher, the experience is much more variable over time, with periods of increasing confidence interspersed with dramatic dips (Figure 3.2).

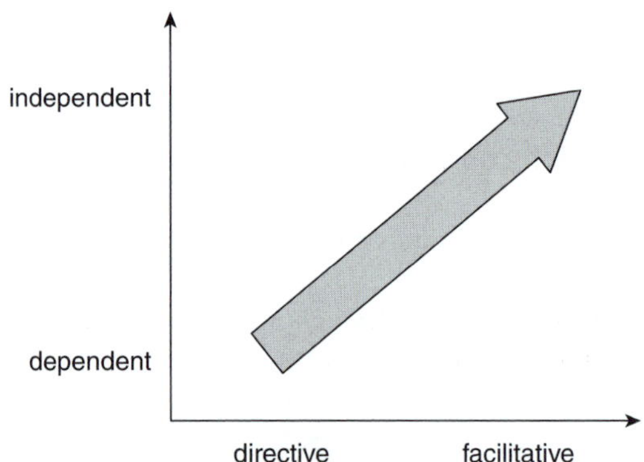

FIGURE 3.1 Model of the doctoral journey

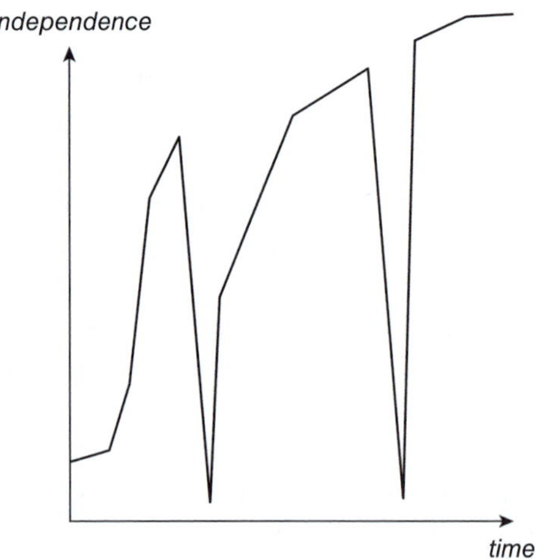

FIGURE 3.2 What the doctoral journey may be like for any given individual

As you can see from the figures, progressing in a doctorate can have its ups and downs. We are not showing you this to make you fearful, but to help you adjust your expectations, so that you can prepare for these drops in confidence. Key to managing this fluctuating research process is very good planning, which includes reflection and re-planning when challenges emerge and circumstances change. This will allow you to take advantage of times when everything is going well by prioritising important tasks, by planning both for success and for challenges, as well as by developing relationships that can adapt to these different conditions and, perhaps most importantly, by learning to relish the challenge, and rise to it.

Planning for success

Chapter 2 laid out some initial-stage planning exercises, making you aware of expectations and giving you an idea of important tasks to do at the beginning of your doctorate. Now we need to take this planning further, providing you with a basis to use in successfully navigating the various stages of your doctorate. Over the first few months, as you become more deeply engaged with the literature and theory of your field, and/or as you start to conduct pilot studies, your project will evolve. Throughout the beginning phases of your doctorate, you and your supervisor should work closely to crystallise an initial plan, with a clear end, and work to identify exactly how you will move the project forward. These initial plans are important as they will help you progress. However, it is important to know that, especially in the first year of the doctorate, but sometimes even later, this end goal as well as your approach to your research may change considerably. For instance, your whole research topic may change completely by the end. This is much more common than you might think. The most important thing here is to make sure you keep adjusting this end goal accordingly, so that you continue to know explicitly what you are working towards, and discuss these ideas with your supervisor. Some specific planning techniques may help you to shape your project, through the creation of milestones and deliverables. These can be used in combination with the formal review processes of your programme (discussed in detail in Chapter 7) to keep you on track.

Planning for the unexpected

One funny thing about research – it never goes to plan. Managing your novel research project is different to managing a project that has been done before somewhere else. You cannot know what will work or what the outcomes will be. Even the best-informed timelines may not hold true in practice, especially over several years of adult life when your circumstances, as well as those of the project, are less than predictable. This just means that you also must plan for challenges and unanticipated outcomes.

In any doctoral project plan, there should be sufficient wiggle room or contingency space. Time needs to be built in to reflect on progress and to adjust/change plans, while still allowing for timely completion of the doctorate. Importantly, you should remain aware of your plan and the timescales and quickly identify when something has happened that may require parts of your project to be re-evaluated. You are the person closest to the project and you will see problems or opportunities before anyone else. If you rely on your supervisor for this, you will lose a great deal of time. It may be helpful to do a SWOT analysis of your project to help build your awareness of your project's strengths, weaknesses, opportunities and threats. Free templates can be found on the Mindtools website (www.mindtools.com).

Building on your SWOT analysis, your next step could be to plan a general outline of tasks to do and when to do them to ensure that you complete on time. You will realise by now that this is going to have to be a flexible plan, one with time built in for changes of direction and so on. Indeed, at this stage, it may also include some alternative routes plotted in at certain critical points. For instance, you may not be certain yet about access for data collection so you may have a choice point before that collection stage that has thereafter a route A (in-depth data, one source) or route B (broader data, several sources). A Gantt Chart is a useful way of mapping this. Try to design your own in Activity 3.2.

ACTIVITY 3.1 PROJECT GANTT CHART

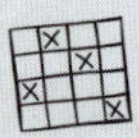

A simple form of a Gantt Chart can be completed on graph paper, using a spreadsheet or online (see www.gantt.com). It would have time logged across the top (perhaps in months across your projected registration period) and activities listed down the left side. These might include: **literature review**, design of project, implementation of project (collecting data), drafting chapters, analysis of data, interpretation of data, writing of final draft, for instance, and may include known fixed points like annual reviews. You might even find it useful to insert holiday times and special personal occasions to ensure that you recognise in your project planning that you have more to your life than the doctorate! You need to achieve a balance. Using colour to block out the spread of time required for each kind of activity will differentiate times of heavy demand and times when rest and/or creativity might predominate. You can find an example in Appendix I.

Prioritising for balance and long-term success

As you go through your doctorate, you will have a variety of different tasks and activities that you should try to balance within any given period as well as over weeks or months. A good plan helps you identify all the different activities that you will need to undertake and gives you an idea of deadlines you must meet to stay on track. However, it will then be up to you to manage your days and weeks, so that you keep to schedule. To maximise your productivity and maintain enthusiasm throughout, you should continually ensure that you are prioritising well, and creating a daily/weekly routine that not only keeps you on track with your research plans, but inspires you as well. As your project progresses and you evolve as a researcher, you must re-evaluate the way you are working to ensure this continues to be the case. Some warning signs that your routine may need adjusting are:

1. You feel like you are constantly rushing around to meet deadlines, working long hours, followed by periods of burnout and reduced productivity once a major deadline has been met.
2. You feel like every day is the same and the joy you once took in your research is waning. The repetitive nature of reading or writing or data collection is wearisome and may be leading to procrastination.
3. You are working hard, but feel like you are not moving your project forward.

Whenever you are feeling any of the above, or if you just generally feel like you could be getting more out of your days, re-examining your time management and your prioritisation can do wonders to turn the situation around. Every day, every week there are a variety of different tasks we do – sometimes, just a change of activity can be a real boost to one's energy and enthusiasm. Thinking about how you spend your time can help you be more productive or have time for more enjoyable tasks, recognising that all jobs have tedious aspects at some times. Try Activity 3.2.

ACTIVITY 3.2 LOGGING TIME ON TASKS

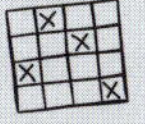

For one day (or perhaps several days), keep a strict record of what you spend your time on. How long does everything take you? Write down both work periods and non-work periods, including travel time, breaks, meals, checking email, etc. A table, headed Time, Activity, Duration, kept to hand for you to jot down information is simple to use each time you move from one pursuit to another. There is a plethora of time management apps available, some are free. It may be worth looking to see if something is helpful for you.

Activity 3.2 can help you gain a realistic idea of what you do, and you can identify any potential time bandits you may have. Time bandits are activities that take your time but do not help you move your doctorate forward. You may be quite surprised at how much time individual tasks take and how much precious time can be wasted on less important tasks like waiting for meetings, or answering emails. These are classic time bandits, and figuring out how to tackle them is a great first step to getting your routine back on track. Think creatively about how you can use bits of wasted time, perhaps by keeping a few papers on you always, so that you can catch up on your reading when you are stuck waiting for your supervisor to turn up for a meeting, or when the bus is late. You may feel that you cannot properly read under these circumstances, however, you will be surprised at how much time you save by skimming papers in advance of a big reading session. You certainly can identify if the paper is not as important as you thought it was … a great time saver. You could also try time management techniques, such as Pomadoro (http://cirillocompany.de/pages/pomodoro-technique), which are designed to help you work intensely and effectively for short bursts of time. For other time bandits, you may have to think how you are prioritising your daily and weekly activities. Perhaps it is time for a change?

Deciding what to spend your time on and what to say 'no' to, requires prioritisation. The priority grid is a tool in which you classify tasks/activities by their urgency and by their importance (Figure 3.3). Urgency is all about deadlines. The closer the deadline, the greater the urgency. Deadlines are either imposed by other people or are a result of your overall project plan and thus you often have little control over urgency. Importance is more relative because what is important for one person may not be for another. Therefore, when thinking about the importance of a task, it is necessary to define exactly what we mean by 'important'. Specifically, we need to clarify important to whom and for what. For our purposes, we suggest you use 'important to fulfilling the potential of your doctoral experience'. Therefore, when thinking about how important a task is, you must think about what you are wanting to get out of your doctorate and how important this task is to your achievement of this. Activity 3.3 shows how you can use the priority grid to re-evaluate the amount of time you spend on different tasks.

ACTIVITY 3.3 EVALUATING TIME ON TASKS

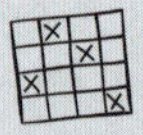

1 Using the priority grid (Figure 3.3), classify where you think the following tasks would lie within the grid: a departmental seminar presentation, checking a social media site, project planning, unexpected visitors to your office, writing a progress report for

your supervisor, networking, random phone calls, playing a new game app. Are they 'urgent', i.e. is there likely to be a deadline soon? Are they 'important' (remembering we are defining important as maximising your doctoral experience)?

2 Make a list of all the tasks you must complete this week, include all the different things you do within a day, including emails, surfing the web, etc. (Activity 3.2 may help you in completing this list realistically.) Determine which box these tasks sit in. In which box of the grid are you spending the most time?

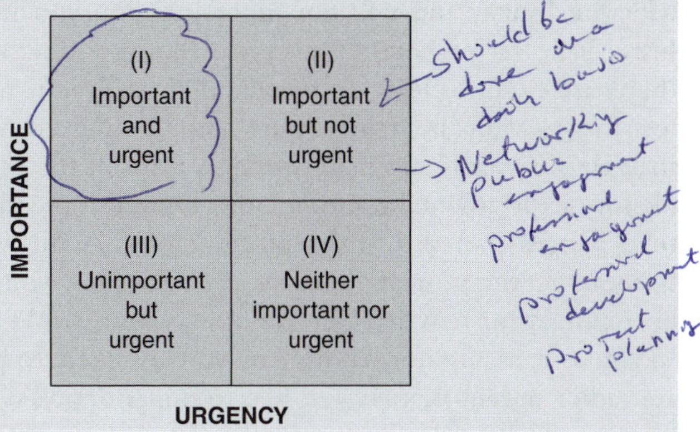

FIGURE 3.3 Priority grid

The priority grid can be used to maximise productivity and, importantly, quality by purposely prioritising tasks in Class I (urgent and important) or Class II (important but not urgent) over non-important tasks. When looking at the classes in terms of prioritisation, of course you should tackle important and urgent tasks first. These are your Class I tasks. Many people find that they spend a great deal of time on Class I activities, working from deadline to deadline and putting off other tasks until they become urgent. To some extent this is human nature. We find that urgency drives us forward and some people may even claim it makes them work 'better'. However, this pattern of working is also associated with a high degree of stress and burnout, with spurts of high productivity followed by definite dips. Therefore, moving forward with Class II activities, before there is any urgency attached, can maximise quality and reduce stress. This is especially important for the doctorate because so many activities that are important for maximising your doctorate experience are essentially Class II, including networking, public engagement, professional development, project planning, even reading and writing are often in the Class II box due to the long-term deadlines (see Chapter 9 for more about these tasks and their importance). Thinking about how you can establish a routine in which you are on top of all your Class I tasks but still able to chip away at your Class II is truly critical to getting the most out of your doctorate.

Class II is critical, but these tasks do often go against human nature, as we do tend to work to deadlines. Also, there are always quite a few Class II tasks to choose from, some we love and some we hate. Again, this is natural, but is likely to work against you here. You are likely to prioritise what you love, and put off what you hate until it becomes urgent (Class I). This is a recipe for disaster, because what you hate will take you longer and will put more stress on you if it becomes Class I. Just a little secret here .... everyone doing a doctorate has a part of it they hate ... or at least do not like. The degree is too all encompassing for this to not be true. Some people like to write, while others struggle for words and hate sitting in front of the computer. Some people love experimental research; others find it incredibly repetitive. Often, this changes over the course of a doctorate, with what you once loved becoming ever more tedious or perhaps what you thought you hated becoming your new passion. We did say you would change, did we not? In any case, as any normal human, you are likely to prioritise things that are either urgent or that you like to do, as opposed to those things that have no definite deadline and you do not enjoy. However, one of the most useful things we can tell you is that to get the most from this doctorate, you must attack that which is the hardest for you to do, that which you hate, that which challenges you, and prioritise it above all else. However, you can do it in bits and pieces; you do not have to eat the whole elephant/vegetable in one sitting, as we pointed out in Chapter 2. If you know that you hate statistics, start from your first day spending an hour or two a week at studying it. Take workshops. Talk to people who use statistics. Each week, move this forward. It does not have to take your whole week. Whatever it is you hate, do not think you can avoid it. Confront it, but do so in moderation, remembering how to eat an elephant. (Otherwise, it will end up in Class I and you will be doing this one thing you hate for a prolonged period.) You can then reward yourself by spending a couple of hours on a Class II activity that you love!

So, what about the other boxes?

Well, Class III is rather interesting. These tasks have urgency, there is a deadline. This makes them frequently confused with Class I tasks and often treated as such. However, when thinking about their importance, what you find is that they are more important to other people than they are for your doctorate. This means they are essentially 'favours' and should be treated as such. In other words, you could say 'no' and reduce your time on this class of tasks, increasing your time focusing on Class II. However, doing favours for others can be very good for relationship building and may have benefits of its own, so it may be that it is to your advantage to say 'yes' occasionally when you have a bit of space. The most important thing is to correctly classify it and ensure you are not spending too much time on things that are urgent and important for others, not for you. For more on when to say 'no' and how, see Chapter 5.

At first glance one could think that you should cut back on all unimportant, non-urgent tasks. However, Class IV tasks should not necessarily be eliminated without thought to make room for other activities. Balance is important. Not everything has to be about your doctorate and, in fact, having a work–life balance that makes you happy improves your productivity, so you could say that some tasks which at first look like Class IV, perhaps taking a walk with a good friend or going to a movie with your partner, may be Class II tasks in disguise, because they refresh you so that you are better able to be creative and productive. The key to Class IV is to not waste it. Make sure the time on these tasks does indeed have a positive impact on you. Balance is important: work hard on the things you enjoy as well as those that must be done.

What does all this mean for creating an optimal doctoral research routine? One key message: variety is good. A good doctoral routine usually involves doing a range of different activities throughout any given week. The balance may change due to the stage of your doctorate and the availability of resources, but a healthy balance between tasks such as reading, writing, data collection, analysis/interpretation of data and professional development tends to be beneficial for keeping your doctorate on track and keeping it interesting. Prioritise your deadlines, but make time for Class II, chipping away at what you struggle with, then treating yourself with those Class II tasks you love. It is important to establish a routine that not only keeps you working, but builds in challenge and personal professional development to ensure you are continually driving your project forward. Importantly, remember to make time for yourself. It may seem like Class IV, but this is Class II. You are your most important resource in your research Dream Team, so you must make time to renew and refresh.

Your research Dream Team

As your project evolves and you grow in independence, your relationships with key people in your life will also change and develop, none more so than with your supervisor. The expectations that you discussed with your supervisor in your first 100 days (Chapter 2) will change. In general, supervisors will expect you to increasingly take the lead on your project and may step back increasingly as you progress in your doctorate. We have seen that, sometimes, doctoral researchers misinterpret this as the supervisor no longer being interested in their research or even in them personally. Our wide experience of working with academics confirms to us that this is seldom the case. When supervisors step back, they are doing so because they feel you are now able to be more independent. It is a compliment, even if it is an unsaid one. Supervisors look forward to seeing you become independent. However, as these expectations are indeed largely tacit, it is a good idea to revisit them and re-establish mutual understanding with your supervisors periodically throughout the doctorate.

If you are feeling that your supervisor is not providing something you need, or that they are not appreciating your new-found independence, this is a signal that a talk about expectations will be helpful. Supervisors are aware that you will be changing and developing, so should be very open to discussing and renegotiating your relationship to ensure it continues to work well for all parties. This is something that will be key for you to take a lead on, as the supervisor cannot read your mind to understand exactly how to meet your changing needs, especially as your pattern of development is more likely to be along the lines of Figure 3.2, not Figure 3.1.

Figure 3.4 is based on Gurr's 'Alignment Model' of the student–supervisory relationship (Gurr, 2001). Gurr explored how doctoral researcher behaviour and different supervisory approaches interact, emphasising how this complex dynamic could lead to different outcomes. Looking at Figure 3.4, can you see where you and your supervisor sit in this model?

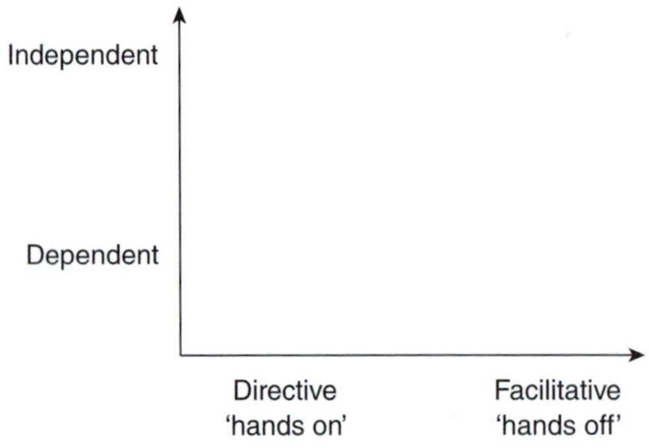

FIGURE 3.4 Gurr's 'Alignment Model'

REFLECTION POINT 3.1

DEGREES OF INDEPENDENCE

At this stage in your doctorate, what do you feel comfortable and confident to take forward with little supervisory input, other than feedback on the result? What do you feel you need more guidance with? What would you like to become more independent in doing, but feel you need a bit more time to get there?

Figure 3.5 may help you reflect on the behaviours you are displaying and how they reflect your degree of independence within different aspects of your project. Are you confident enough to ask questions about something? Are you confident enough to challenge an idea or approach?

The above reflection can be the basis for your discussion with your supervisor. It may be that your supervisors have different ideas than you do about what you should be leading on or what you are ready to do. If this is the case, do not be disappointed. People often have different opinions and your supervisors may well know something you do not. Listen to what they say (see Chapter 6 on dealing with feedback). Then talk to them about how you can both get what you need out of the relationship. You want a win–win outcome ideally, not a compromise that means each loses something. Since you are all on the same team, working together to produce amazing research and a successful doctorate, it should be possible to figure out how to best meet everyone's needs. Indeed, it may be that given the changing nature of the doctorate, your

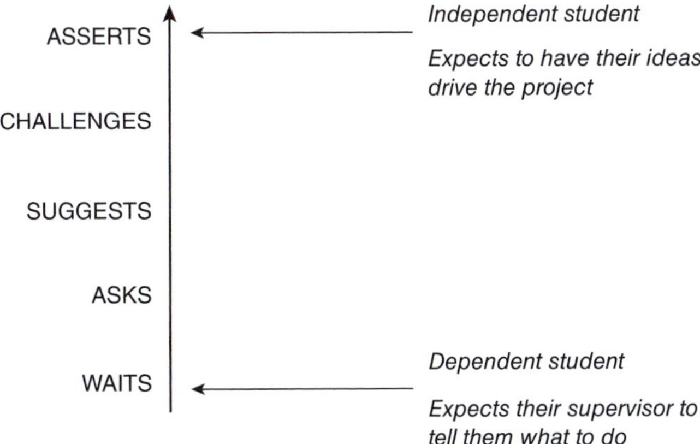

FIGURE 3.5 Capturing a range of doctoral student behaviour

supervisors (or you) just need to be confident that you can be more independent on a specific aspect of the doctorate. In this case, perhaps some short trials with increased supervisor feedback, for a specified length of time, will help you move forward in confidence and independence, giving both you and your supervisors peace of mind. All the time, it is important that you are pushing yourself to become an independent researcher, yet also being open and honest with your supervisors about when you still need support. This will help them understand exactly how they can guide you as you develop over the years. Ideally, this should be a relationship built on mutual trust.

It is also important that you feel able to seek their help when one of the Figure 3.2 dips occurs. These happen suddenly and are largely unpredictable, so be prepared to ask for help when you need it as a responsible thing to do. It is perfectly fine to try to find solutions on your own, or to go to a supervisor with ideas, or even for a supervisor to suggest that you spend some time trying to figure it out, but you do not want to be stuck in an unproductive phase for too long (two or three weeks is long enough). One important thing to learn, though, is that it is quite likely your supervisors may not have a ready 'right' answer for you. This is novel research and no one may know how best to proceed or what the outcome of different choices will be. However, your supervisors will have done novel research before, so they should be able to support you and give direction and guidance about how to get your project moving again and when it may be smart to give up on a certain avenue and try something a bit different. Finding a solution together, rather than hiding from your supervisor, is a good professional habit to cultivate.

Supervisors are not the only members of your research Dream Team, as we will explore further in Chapter 6. One thing we have observed is that, sometimes, people look around and think that everyone else knows exactly what to do and is succeeding, and that they are the only one struggling. However, in our experience, once we get a group of doctoral researchers together, even from a wide range of different disciplines, they often face very similar challenges. The doctorate is tough; it pushes you in ways you cannot imagine before you undertake it. Your peers will be dealing with these same challenges. It can be a great research resource to build up a positive peer group for reciprocal support. We have seen doctoral researchers who come into a workshop or event we are delivering, feeling down about themselves and their doctorate, becoming transformed after having an opportunity to talk openly with peers, realising that what they are experiencing is normal and others are feeling the same. In general, people can deal with complex problems, if they know they are not alone and that others also find these tasks challenging. We provide at the end of this chapter a reference to Mercer's (2017) article about how researchers can help each other. So, find a peer or peer group to get support from and, importantly, to celebrate each other's successes with!

It is important for your wellbeing to be able to put the research aside occasionally to enjoy those other activities that have always made up your life. We have seen people become so embroiled in their research that they lose touch with friends and give up on all other pursuits. Remember to prioritise things that give you joy, and nurture relationships that are positive and supportive outside of your research work. Your happiness will drive your productivity and spark creativity. You do not have time to neglect this.

Try out our task in Reflection Point 3.2 before we turn to another aspect of transformation during the doctorate – developing your own voice as a research professional.

REFLECTION POINT 3.2

RESEARCH DREAM TEAM

Think about who makes up your research Dream Team. Do you have a variety of support people? Are you prioritising bits of time to evolve and maintain these relationships? This is a definite Class II task!

Developing your professional voice

Doctoral degrees are transition points and where new personal and professional identities are forged. Until now, your academic studies have defined you as a student but, while you are still technically studying or learning, as hopefully you will continue to do in some form for the rest of your life, you are now a researcher with increasing responsibilities. When you introduce yourself as a doctoral researcher in a public forum, people will respect your achievement and have expectations of you as a professional person. Your views will carry some weight. Therefore, in public situations and in writing, it is important that you present yourself and your research in a skilled and authoritative way. To do this effectively, you must first work to develop your unique view point on your research field and learn to craft strong arguments to support your stance. Activities 3.4 and 3.5 are designed to help you start doing just this.

ACTIVITY 3.4 FINDING YOUR STANCE

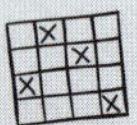

This activity concerns your developing independent research stance. This is guided by the previous work in your field, but should reflect your own critical evaluation of the relevant literature. This activity will take about an hour, but should be done using literature you need to read anyway.

When reading research literature:

1 Prior to reading an important piece of research in your field, think about what you want to get out of this article or chapter (if you are reading a book, it is easier to break it down into chapters for this exercise).
2 Write down some specific questions (at least three, but probably no more than five) that you want answered. Particularly note 'why' or 'so what' questions. Some general examples may be: 'Why have they chosen this approach or theoretical framework?' or 'What do they think are the implications of their findings or outcomes?'
3 Whilst reading, take notes by answering these questions in your own words.
4 For each question you have answered, ask yourself whether you agree with the author's reasoning. Then write a couple sentences explaining 'why' you agree or disagree. Again, use your own words and your own justification.
5 When you are done, answer one more question: 'What does this paper contribute to my thoughts on my own research?'

Note: The emphasis here is not on writing style, it is on getting ideas out; do not be too critical about your writing. Concentrate on formulating and honing your ideas.

ACTIVITY 3.5 DEVELOPING YOUR VIEW WITHIN RESEARCH DEBATES

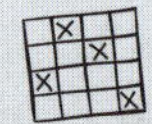

This activity should be done over a period of a week, dedicating a bit of time daily to reading and summarising, and a couple of hours on the final day. This activity is designed to help you understand differences of opinion within your field and establish your own personal view, along with a justified argument to support it. This is a great exercise to do when you are making key research decisions, such as those concerning methodological or theoretical choices.

1 Decide on a theme, choosing one that is divisive or controversial, for your reading this week. Examples may be: exploring different schools of thought, different choices of approach, or different forms of interpretation. If you do not know of any, your supervisor may be able to help.

2. On Day 1, collect papers that represent both sides of this controversy. Ideally, keep as much else the same as possible, that is, similar topics but different approaches. You will need a total of four to eight papers, representing each side as equally as possible. Again, your supervisor may be able to suggest a couple of good ones.
3. For the next three days, read a couple of papers a day, taking notes about specific arguments, findings and interpretations.
4. On day four, compare and contrast the different summaries, looking back over papers as necessary to clarify details. Start to think about what you agree with and what you disagree with.
5. On day five, sit down and write the answer to the following questions: What are the strengths and weaknesses of each side? Do you, personally, feel that the case is stronger for one side or the other, and why? Or perhaps you agree fully with neither (again, why?). Taking all of this together, how does this view influence how you will move your doctoral research forward?

Note: Again, the writing style is not the point of this exercise, so work more on developing the ideas than eloquence of wording (at least for now). We would suggest that you move forward from here and discuss the outcomes of this exercise with your supervisor. To do this, you might want to create a tidier draft of your justification.

As you develop your understanding of your professional stance, based on your understanding of the literature, you will grow in confidence and start to be able to assert your ideas and justify these with academic argument. In the next chapter, we will provide guidance on how to do that in written form, while in Chapter 5 we will direct you to opportunities and resources that will help you to feel confident in your new professional persona.

References and further reading 

Åkerlind, G.S. (2008) 'Growing and developing as a university researcher', *Higher Education,* 55 (2): 241–54.

Gurr, G.M. (2001) 'Negotiating the "rackety bridge" – a dynamic model for aligning research student needs and supervisor style', *Higher Education Research and Development*, 20: 81–92.

Medical Research Council (UK) (n.d.) 'Explore career and funding options: Interactive career framework'. www.mrc.ac.uk/skills-careers/interactive-career-framework/ (accessed 19 April 2017).

Mercer, R. (2017) 'By students, for students', *Nature,* 541: 125–6. doi:10.1038/nj7635-125a January 2017.

Research Councils UK (n.d.) 'Becoming a researcher and developing a research career'. www.rcuk.ac.uk/skills/develop (accessed 19 April 2017). (Provides an overall view of the UK career structure and has links to further information.)

PART TWO

SUCCESS IS IN THE DETAIL

4

WHAT MAKES A GOOD RESEARCH STORY?*

In this chapter, we will consider how to:

- Understand the role of writing in the research process
- Write for your readership
- Visualise your thesis before you write it
- Acknowledge the personal aspect of the story-telling process
- Write a convincing story

Understanding the role of writing in the research process

Producing a thesis takes time, and a common mistake made by researchers is to underestimate just how much time is needed to write one. Here, we highlight the dynamic and often intensely personal process involved in drafting a doctoral thesis. Whether you are a scientist, an engineer or a poet, the process of thesis writing will involve you in developing skills that are akin to artistry, for example, visualising your thesis before you write, story-telling, crafting chapters and then polishing them until they are honed. Here, we explore this dynamic process that will enable you not simply to complete your thesis, but to complete it well, with some enjoyment.

By the time you are at the final thesis-compiling stage of your doctoral research, you need to be well-practised in the research writing process.

---

* With thanks to Alison Yeung Yam Wah for her contribution to this chapter.

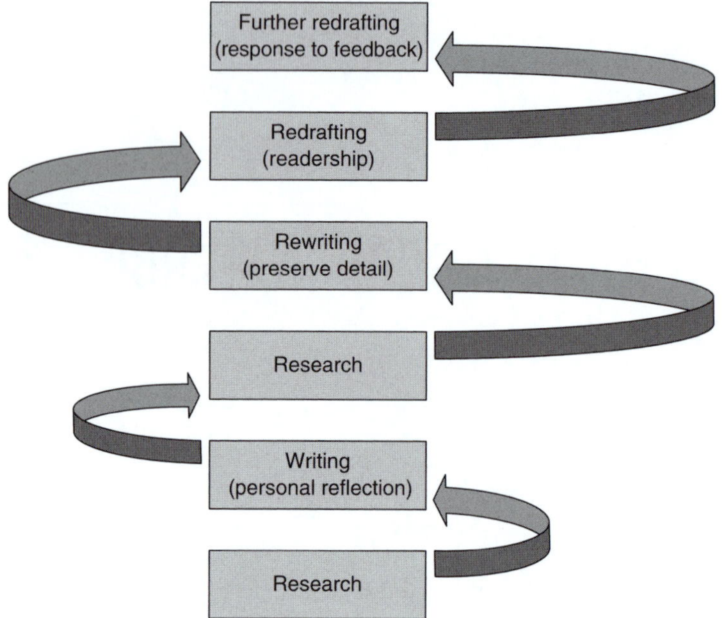

FIGURE 4.1 The research writing process
© Alison Yeung Yam Wah

This process, as outlined in Figure 4.1, is very dynamic and can be demanding at times, especially when you get feedback from your supervisor on something you have written. You may well be surprised at how intensely personal or emotional the process can be, as well as how time-consuming it is. Rest assured though, that time spent developing your writing skills through this process is time spent well because it is largely through the dynamics of this process that you clarify your research ideas and communicate them clearly and convincingly to an external readership. The sooner you start to practise and develop your writing skills, the more polished your skills will be by the time you construct the final version of your thesis. So, when should you start to acquire those skills? The answer is probably the moment you have something to say about your research, which could be as soon as you start to think about a potential topic.

Initial researching and writing for personal reflection

There are all sorts of ways you can start to hone your writing skills in the early stages of research, for example when you begin to review the literature. This is an ideal opportunity to use writing as a tool for developing critical reflection. One of the key differences between doctoral writing and master's level writing is the level of critique you need to demonstrate when reviewing the literature. At doctoral level, you are expected to communicate *your position* in relation to the literature. You are not simply comparing and contrasting studies on a topic; you are looking for the gap in the field that your study will address. This can be a tricky process early on for all kinds of reasons: you might not have a clear sense of your study; you might be researching a body of literature that is new to you; or you might think you know what you want to study and then discover in your reviewing that the topic has already been covered. Whatever the ambiguities you face at this stage, you can start to develop your critical ability in relation to the literature by writing down questions to direct your reading – we suggest some of these in Activity 4.1.

ACTIVITY 4.1 QUESTIONS TO DIRECT YOUR READING

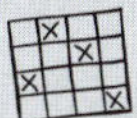

Keep the following questions in mind while reading and make notes of your answers to inform your thinking about future arguments about your choice of project and what it discovers in relation to previous literature:

- Is this title of possible value to my study? If so, why do I think so?
- What is the author of this paper attempting to persuade me of, and am I persuaded? If not, why not?
- Which part of this paper is of most interest to me and why that part?

Each question relates the chosen article to you/your research. By relating questions to your own research, you start to engage in doctoral-level critical reflection; in other words, you start to reflect on the literature *from your own position*.

These questions are tools for personal reflection, and you will find that you need to do this a lot as you go through your research journey. During the writing process, there will be many rounds of writing that are not for anyone but *you*. This is largely because of the way writing allows you to reflect on thoughts you have in your mind. Writing is a great way to fully formulate a thought. The adage, 'you don't know what you know until you write it down', holds particularly true in the doctoral writing process. Reflective writing allows you to bring your research-related ideas and thoughts to the surface. So, your writing focus at the beginning of your research may well be largely description or personal reflection, which will probably be read by you alone.

You will find that writing for personal reflection does not stop at the early stage of research; with every piece of writing that you produce throughout your doctoral journey, the initial draft (or drafts) will be for your eyes only. This also applies to even the most seasoned academic – the first draft of any document is the vehicle for personal reflection. That means that you do not need to worry about coherence and sound grammar at that stage – just get your thoughts down on the page and do not worry too much about how logical they are. A good research story will have been redrafted many times and will follow the process shown in Figure 4.1; it starts with the simple, and not necessarily logical, downloading of the author's thoughts.

Redrafting: turning the research journey into the research story

Your next round(s) of drafting may well still be for your personal reflection and for expressing your thoughts more deeply and fully. Part of this redrafting will also include writing to preserve detail. Here, we are referring to details of your research that might include reasons for the decisions you have made; changes of direction in your research caused by unforeseen problems, such as too few respondents for your study sample or unavailability of required instruments or equipment or access to documents; or perhaps world events that delayed your field trip and had knock-on consequences for your project. At this stage of writing, you are logging these details for your own reference as an aide-memoire. By keeping this record of your rationale for decisions taken along the way, you make it easier to turn your research journey into a convincing and coherent research story for the reader, which we explore in the next paragraphs, and for your examiners, to convince them that you can deal with the vicissitudes that impact on all research (Chapters 7 and 8). Once you are satisfied that you have explored your thoughts and decisions as deeply as you want to and have started to link them in a more coherent way, you are probably ready to redraft for a reader other than you.

So, why is it necessary to produce another draft with the reader in mind? In a good research story, the author has successfully translated their research *journey*, conducted in time and space, into a research *story*, conveyed through reasoned discourse. Translating the journey into a convincing story is not easy. As a *journey*, there have probably been many twists and turns in your research, some of which have been helpful, others of which have been very much the opposite. That journey, because doctoral research must be innovative, can be like a mystery tour at times; however, when writing your research *story* for someone who has not been on the journey with you,

you must replace the mysterious elements of the journey with a structured story based on logical arguments and discussions that convey robust study results, convincing findings, innovation and contribution to the field. If you can do this well, then you will have written a good research story.

One way to help you master the skill of turning your research journey into a research story is to draw upon the expertise of your support network. As we highlight later in Chapter 6, developing relationships, not just with your supervisors, but with fellow doctoral researchers and colleagues, is a crucial aspect of doctoral research. You will find that having a strong network of peers who can provide 'critical feedback' on your writing will help you to hone your skills far more effectively than if you work alone. You will get invaluable feedback on the clarity of your writing and on how well you have converted your research journey into a research story by calling upon your fellow doctoral researchers; they can be a very useful first port of call for a redraft before it goes to your supervisor.

The role of writing, then, is important not just for clarifying your research ideas, but also for translating your research *journey* into a good research *story*. Just as the research journey is a process, so the translating of the journey into a story is also a process, which you go through by researching, then reflecting on the research by writing, followed by round after round of redrafting, usually interspersed with more research. Rest assured though, as shown in Figure 4.1, this process is an upward spiral, not just an endless cycle.

Visualising your thesis before you write it

A key feature of a good research story is its coherence and flow, and fundamental to that is a coherent structure. We often find that researchers do not spend enough time thinking about the structure of their thesis before they start to write. If you think that your structure is an essay plan and jot down a rough outline with a few chapter titles or prompts, you are not taking the time to reflect on the document that you are about to produce. For a good story, you need to create a structure that helps you to weave the various threads of argument together into a cohesive, lucid and rational discussion of a complex piece of research. Think of your thesis as a work of art, full of carefully crafted arguments, woven seamlessly together into an integrated document, and you perhaps begin to see the level of artistry that you, as the writer, need.

In the next section, we will suggest a way of creating a structure (which we call the 'macro framework') that allows you to visualise how you will introduce and weave together all your complex arguments in a convincing way. By visualising your story, you begin to engage with your thesis before you start to write the substance of it; just as a sculptor creates a drawn framework to visualise the finished piece before starting chipping it for real, so you, the researcher, can create a framework that helps to direct and shape the writing of your final thesis. It can also help you to manage your writing, so that it is a fulfilling and intensely creative process. In these respects, you are working as an artist. Of course, there are many theses that have been written based on rough jottings akin to essay plans, and we do not dispute that you may well be able to tell a reasonable research story with such a plan; however, this chapter is not concerned with how to produce a reasonable research story; we want to help you to produce a quality thesis, and to have a fulfilling experience in the process.

Creating a macro framework

Before you start to create your macro framework (see Top Tips 4.1), remember that whatever you decide at this stage can, and probably will, change. As Rowena Murray (2017) notes, you should not expect this initial structure outline to be your final one. Sometimes, we get writing blocks because we think that the moment we start writing, we have committed ourselves to the ideas we put down. *Remember that anything can be deleted at any stage. Computers can hold many drafts – each clearly labelled, with the date or version number.* This will help you to avoid developing a writing block.

TOP TIPS 4.1 CREATING A MACRO FRAMEWORK

1. Ask yourself some fundamental questions about your research project. Possible questions include: What is my thesis about? Why, in a nutshell, is this thesis project important? Why have I used the method that I did to complete the project? What is my most important finding/argument, and what makes it the most important? What impact does my project have on the field? What could others do to build on my research?
2. When constructing a plan, use verbs as well as nouns. Murray (2017) recommends the value of using verb forms in a thesis structure because they help you get a clear sense of the purpose of each chapter or section. If you simply put the name of each chapter and/or section, you are likely to have a plan full of nouns (for example, *Introduction – background, gap, aims, thesis structure*). This does not help you to engage with the structure or to develop a feel for your unwritten document. However, asking yourself what you need to *do* in each section or

chapter forces you to think in verb forms, which will help you to start to engage much more actively with the document. For example, in your chapter entitled *Introduction*, what do you need to *do*? You will probably *set* the background context, *summarise* the key debates in the field to *identify* the gap. You will also perhaps need to *state* the main aim of your research and *justify* that aim. Finally, you will probably need to *outline* the structure of the thesis. Using verb forms helps to bring the thesis to life.

3 Allow your structure to change once you start to write paragraphs. There is a process involved within the structuring itself; the structure you create to frame your writing is very likely to change once you start the writing itself. In other words, writing leads you to make changes to the original structure. Allow this to happen; this is reflection and clarification working through the writing process. This perpetual dynamic between the overall structure of a piece of writing and the paragraph writing brings the writing process very much to life, and provides the pulse for the thesis; the overall structure both informs and is informed by the detailed writing of paragraphs.

4 Remember to save each structure draft and number it. Orna and Stevens (2009) emphasise the importance of saving each draft with a draft number. By the time you reach draft 7 of your structure, you might suddenly realise that draft 1 was the best all along! So, do not delete the drafts but store them carefully.

5 Towards the end of the process, finalise the drafts of the *Introduction* and *Conclusions* together. This will help to ensure that what you claim to set out to do matches what you finally achieve, making the story tight and allowing you to tie up any loose ends.

Acknowledging the personal aspect of the writing process

As we have emphasised previously, the writing process is both dynamic and deeply personal. This is largely related to the level and depth of reflection that you need to engage in to produce a piece of writing which conveys original research that also clearly has relevance to the academic field and possibly beyond. If you have already started your doctoral study, you are probably finding that you seem to be living and breathing research; it can become all-consuming at times, exciting and invigorating at others, and overwhelming on occasion. There will be times when you feel stuck, unable to see precisely what it is that you are doing or what you want to say. These are times when you may develop writing blocks. If you do experience these, rest assured that you are certainly not alone. Even the most established academic will have times when they just do not know what to write. Knowing some of the common causes of these blocks, as outlined in Table 4.1, can help you to find strategies to overcome them when they do occur.

TABLE 4.1 Common causes of writer's block and useful strategies for overcoming it

Common causes	Useful strategies
Fatigue from too many writing binges	• Develop the habit of writing a little every day, rather than a lot occasionally • Do some *free writing* (Activity 4.1)
Time pressure	• Start the drafting process well ahead of the deadline. If this is not possible, create a detailed but realistic timeline with clear writing targets throughout, up to submission
Uncertainty about what you want to say	• Use free writing to access your less conscious thoughts
Fear of supervisor feedback	• Detach your emotions from the words on the page and regard supervisor feedback as comments about the words, not about you
Loss of motivation	• Reward yourself after writing periods • Do some free writing to unlock fresh ideas • Choose a section from your macro framework that does not need too much brain power and focus on that for a while
Getting lost in your writing	• Draw up a clear macro framework as a road map for your writing • Use free writing to change focus • Do something physical that needs very little brain power

Free writing

In Table 4. 1, free writing appears in many of the strategy boxes. Gillie Bolton (2010) acknowledges the value of this type of non-critical writing as a way of getting your thoughts to flow. Follow the guidelines in Activity 4.2 to gain experience of free writing and its advantage.

ACTIVITY 4.2 SOME GUIDELINES FOR FREE WRITING

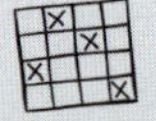

Follow the guidelines here and do some free writing. Once you have done it, read over what you have written. Do you think this exercise could help you if you encountered writer's block? Perhaps write a short reflective piece on your experience of, and feelings about, the exercise:

1 Set yourself a specific number of minutes (e.g., five minutes, perhaps using an egg-timer) that you will write in without stopping.
2 Use a pen or pencil rather than a computer keyboard to do this type of writing – during the five minutes, your hand must keep moving, even if the pen/pencil is not producing words (for example, it might simply start to scribble). This is not so easy to do on a keyboard.

3. Do not correct grammar, spelling or punctuation as you write – you do not even need to write in full sentences if you do not want to.
4. Do not stop the hand to think.
5. Allow your mind to direct any thoughts to the writing hand; they do not have to be structured thoughts or thoughts related to your research; you can write ANYTHING.
6. Know that only you will read this piece of writing.

So, what is the value of free writing? Most doctoral researchers are used to having to write tightly reasoned, and well-referenced, pieces of writing. In free writing, you allow your mind to escape the psychological controls that formal academic writing tends to impose. It can be enormously therapeutic to give your mind free rein to think and state whatever it wishes; it is a little like running through a field for no purpose other than to enjoy the run. Free writing is also useful for unlocking thoughts that you have not been able to access in normal writing. Sometimes, our most creative ideas lie hidden under more structured thinking or under emotions that impede our creativity. We recommend that you have a go at free writing; if nothing else, it will show you just how many words you can write in a very short space of time.

Writing a convincing story

An important aspect of writing a convincing research story is understanding what your examiners and supervisors are expecting from your thesis. Essentially, your examiners will be looking for a thesis that is coherent, robust, clear and critically analytical. They will also want to see that the study is innovative and makes a clear contribution to the field. The study must be rooted in the literature and provide a platform for future studies. Theses often fail to meet these expectations, as shown in Table 4.2, which lists issues frequently raised by examiners of doctoral theses relating to specific chapters. These are presented in order of critical importance by thesis section (the final chapters and literature review are extremely important) and within section (it is a lesser sin to omit your selection criteria in the literature review than to write a descriptive rather than critical review). As you will find in Chapter 8, presentational issues are likely after the final examination to require 'minor' corrections or amendments, whereas major corrections or required substantial re-submissions or fails are usually based on the problems found in the final chapters, literature reviews or research questions/hypotheses.

TABLE 4.2 Common thesis problems

Chapter(s)	Issue
Final chapters	• No clear and detailed indication of the contribution made to knowledge/practice • Lack of depth to discussion and conclusions • Cursory back reference to the literature to indicate what has been supported, exemplified, refuted, etc.
Literature reviews	• Descriptive rather than critical literature review • Search system and procedure not described in enough detail • Selection criteria for references unclear
Research questions/ hypotheses	• Not clearly or sufficiently focused • Lack of transparent, well-articulated link between previous literature and research questions/hypotheses • Little indication of ownership of research
Results	• Not clearly presented – lack of or poorly presented summaries/ tables/graphs, etc. • No clear differentiation between Results and Discussion/ Conclusion
Design, Methods, Procedures	• Inadequate/muddled rationales for approach, design and methods • Lack of evidence to support selection of approach, design, methods, participant/subject or instruments • Long-winded descriptions when tables or diagrams would be clearer
Presentation	• Account not taken, or unjustified assumptions made about, readers' knowledge: jargon, acronyms and topic details not clearly explained • Main thread of argument from Introduction to Conclusion/ Discussion difficult to follow or not apparent • Lack of guidance to the reader using signposts, links and cross references

Many of the issues listed in Table 4.2 relate to lack of clarity, which often results from failure to write in a coherent way. So, next, we consider some useful techniques for telling a coherent research story.

Coherence

As outlined earlier in this chapter, the first stage in creating a coherent document, whether it is your thesis, a research manuscript or a short literature review paper, is to create a clear macro framework. We have already discussed this (see Top Tips 4.1), and so we will not discuss this any further; just remember that other aspects of coherence are based on a strong macro framework.

For your thesis to be convincing for your readership, which will be your supervisors and examiners in the first instance, your research story needs to flow. The challenge for you here is how to create flow for a story that is complex, consisting of many elements and possibly numerous arguments and sub-arguments. Once you have your macro framework clear, your focus will switch to creating flow in the detailed writing of chapter, sections, paragraphs and sentences.

First, remember that we are focusing on flow for the reader. This means that you need to ensure that the thesis is as easy to read as a complex piece of research can be. The key structures for conveying your arguments and discussion are paragraphs, so use them skillfully. We suggest that you copy out the top tips that you find most useful from those in Top Tips 4.2 to keep beside you when you are writing.

TOP TIPS 4.2 PRODUCING A COHERENT THESIS

1. Use topic sentences to help you to structure your paragraph. A topic sentence conveys the essence of the point you wish to make in a paragraph. It should be early in the paragraph (often the first or possibly second sentence in). Below is an example of a paragraph with a clear topic sentence.

   EXAMPLE

   The results of this research may contribute to the resolution of two significant issues facing sub-Saharan Africa. The first issue, discussed in depth in Chapter 2, is the need for less expensive irrigation systems in sub-Saharan regions. As argued in 2.2.1, current irrigation systems are costly to implement due to the nature of the materials used, many of which must be imported. As the materials used in the irrigation system trialed in this study are readily available in the region, costs would be substantially reduced. The second issue, discussed in Chapter 3, is the need for less complex systems that can be easily used by local smallholders with minimal training. The simplicity of the trialed system is likely to encourage more local smallholders to use the system.
2. Consider repeating key terms from one topic sentence to another to help the reader follow your discussion.

   EXAMPLE

   The results of this research may contribute to the resolution of two significant issues facing sub-Saharan Africa. The first issue …

   Resolution of these issues is vital for continued development of the region for a variety of reasons. These include …
3. Use signposting in your thesis. This includes major signposting, linking words and phrases and cross referencing, as shown in Table 4.3.

(Continued)

(Continued)

TABLE 4.3 Signposting, linking words and cross-referencing

Type of signposting	Where used	Example
Major signposting	Often found at beginning and end of chapters to remind reader of what has been discussed before or to explain what will be discussed and why	*In the previous chapter, the issue of xxx was examined. This was necessary to highlight the importance of xxx. In this chapter, the focus shifts to xxx in order to xxx.*
Linking words/ phrases	Used in paragraphs to demonstrate the connection between one sentence and the next or one argument and another	*Despite/however/ nevertheless* *In addition/furthermore/also* *Particularly/specifically* *Simultaneously/at the same time as*
Cross-referencing	Used when discussion of a point is interrupted or resumed	*As discussed in Section 3.1 ...* *(For more detailed discussion, see Section 4.2.1)*

Reviewing literature

For your supervisor and your examiners to be convinced by your research story, you will need to satisfy their expectation for critical engagement. So how does a good research story convey your ability to analyse issues critically? The most obvious place for critical engagement is the literature review. There are various types of literature review: **systematic review**, **narrative synthesis** or a more standard **narrative review**. In this chapter, we will focus on the standard narrative review because this is perhaps the most frequently written type of review for doctoral theses in general. We will briefly introduce the other two types of review mentioned above, and will direct you to useful resources if you would like to find out more about them.

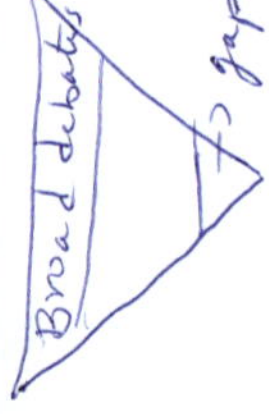

In many ways, the narrative review is a strategic document; in it, not only do you need to demonstrate thorough understanding of the literature relevant to your study and the key debates in the field, as well as significant researchers/authors in the field, but you also need to guide the reader from the broad debates to the specific gap that you address in your research. The way that you structure your review is key to guiding the reader efficiently and effectively. Find out more about reviewing the literature in Top Tips 4.3.

TOP TIPS 4.3 REVIEWING THE LITERATURE

1. Reviewing the literature is how professional researchers (like you) remain on top of their subject and it also alleviates one of the major doctoral fears, which is that someone will publish the essence of your thesis before you finish. (This is a widespread myth among doctoral researchers and leads to a lot of unfounded and unnecessary anxiety; it is unnecessary because, if you have kept up with the new literature published in your area, have attended conferences and simply trawled the internet regularly, you will know who the key contributors are in your field, and you will also know what they are likely to publish – so, you should be ahead of them or at least be up to date with their work.)
2. Your supervisor will give you some suggestions about where to begin your initial search and there are usually key texts in the discipline or subject area. Start by identifying the key texts, the key journals and online repositories. (This is a good excuse to get to know other people in your department, peers, colleagues and librarian by asking for 'suggested reading or literature'. One of us went to the library and pulled all the books off the shelf that had titles that looked vaguely relevant to her topic. She then spent a happy afternoon going through the Contents pages and **abstracts** of the mountain of books on the table to see if they were still vaguely useful – she put about 80% of the books back on the shelf – knowing she could always come back for them later.)
3. Do not underestimate the value of other people's knowledge and their bibliographies! Do not be afraid to ask people for their advice. Academic authors are often happy to be recognised and to provide more information about their work. However, if you suspect that a big name in your field is unlikely to reply, use the bibliographies in their publications instead. Another common starting point is by doing internet searches of key words in online repositories; indeed, this is proving one of the best ways of beginning a literature review.
4. Compile a list of all the items your searches identify and then decide which ones you should read first, perhaps because you know the work is important to the field, because it is a canonical text, because the author is a major contributor to the area, or simply because the title sounds interesting and you might just like to read it. (This is how most literature reviews begin – but they never end because there is always something with an interesting title to read! After a while, you will find that literature repeats itself and that everyone cites the papers you have read, so now you can widen your literature search and interests.)
5. Finally, make sure you put all your references into a reference management system from the outset, whether that is a software package your institution provides, a free online service like Mendeley, or a hard-copy index you maintain yourself on cards or computer. Although most software packages are compatible with each other and with most operating systems, it is wise to select one with an appropriate **citation style** that is currently used by your departmental colleagues so that you can readily share information and conform to the requirements of discipline journals.

Saunders and Lewis (2011) highlight the value of thinking of your literature review as a thematic funnel which starts broad and guides the reader in a progressively focused way to your study aims and objectives. Figure 4.2 shows how we think your funnel might look.

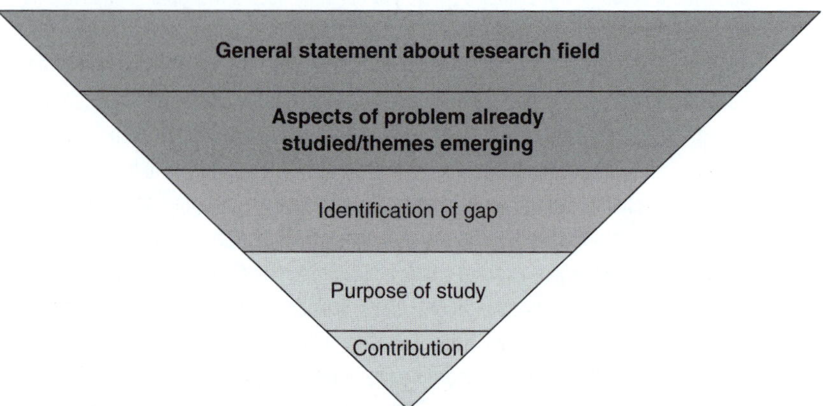

FIGURE.4.2 Creating a funnel structure for your literature review

As Saunders and Lewis (ibid.) suggest, one way to structure your review is to present the literature thematically. Identifying themes emerging from the literature allows you to engage one study with another in your chapter, and will maximise your opportunity for critical engagement with the literature.

Another type of narrative review is a narrative synthesis. This type is sometimes found in health sciences and is often used when a systematic procedure for conducting the review is necessary to minimise the risk of **researcher bias** in the review. This type of approach is often useful when you are conducting more qualitative research in a field where quantitative methods predominate. A good source of information about this type of review is Hannes and Lockwood's (2012) book *Synthesizing Qualitative Research: Choosing the Right Approach*, which we include in the Further Reading at the end of this chapter.

Systematic reviews, which tend to be found in specific disciplines, especially medical sciences, psychology and business management, are often an entire research project in themselves. The purpose of such reviews is to provide a summary of all the literature relating to a very precise research question between a fixed set of dates. These reviews are different from standard literature reviews and should not be confused with them. Such summaries are of tremendous value to professionals and practitioners who do not have time to trawl what can be hundreds of articles on a topic, but who need to be conversant with the current knowledge. One of the most important features of systematic reviews is their transparency. This means that the review should be very explicit in the procedure that was undertaken, such as search terms and databases used and **inclusion criteria** and **exclusion criteria** for the search. There are normally strict protocols to follow to reduce the risk of bias in the review process and therefore potential distortion of findings. A useful resource to find out more about systematic reviews is the Cochrane Library, a reference for which you will find at the end of the chapter.

Whichever method you choose to review the literature, critical analysis is key. Of course, the literature review is not the only place to demonstrate this; it needs to be demonstrated throughout your thesis, as shown in Table 4.4.

TABLE 4.4 Facets of critical thinking in a doctoral thesis

Chapter	Critical thinking conveyed through
Literature review	• Thematic rather than chronological structure of review • Selection of strongest and most appropriate references used in review • Use of references to defend author's argument • Clear line of argument leading from literature to research questions
Methods/Design/ Procedures	• Rationale clearly discussed • Use of appropriate evidence to justify choice of research approach/ design/methods/procedure
Discussion/ Conclusion	• Discussion of possible alternative explanation of results • Linking of study findings back to literature review to demonstrate contribution to field • Acknowledgement of study limitations + justification • Evaluation of how research will impact on theory/economy/social life and welfare, etc.
Thesis as a whole	• Authorial voice throughout entire thesis

Clarity

A good research story conveys clarity throughout, and this is essentially achieved through the redrafting process. Clarity relates to the honing – the sharpening and polishing – of the thesis document. Intrinsic to clarity is coherence, which we have already considered, and conciseness, which we explore now.

Conciseness

To tell your research story as concisely as possible, be prepared for the rounds of redrafting we mentioned earlier in this chapter. Conciseness refers to the most economical way of telling your research story in a way that is meaningful for the reader. In the early draft stages, as we are clarifying our ideas, we will probably think in a less than sharp way; perhaps we think around the topic. The purpose of the redrafting process is first to sharpen the thinking and then to sharpen the way we articulate the thought. The editing process is how you sharpen, or hone, your writing. Top Tips 4.4 offers a few ideas to help you edit your thesis more effectively.

TOP TIPS 4.4 EDITING TO ACHIEVE A CONCISE STORY

1. Never start to edit your work as soon as you have finished writing; take a break and distance yourself from your words so that you are more detached from your writing when you do edit it.
2. Do not edit your work too early. Remember the danger of focusing on grammar and paragraphing too early, which might lead to writer's block.
3. When you are in the final drafting stages, have various editing rounds, each with a specific focus. For example:

   Editing round 1: Generally, does the chapter say what I want it to say and do my arguments develop coherently?
   Editing round 2: Do my paragraphs have a clear focus, and are they clearly linked?
   Editing round 3: Do I have a consistent academic writing style throughout the chapter, and are there any proofreading errors?

Some cautionary notes

We all recognise that researchers' lives seem to be a complex mix of reading, discussion, listening, seeking, relishing, challenging the ideas of others as well as our own. Within that process it is often hard to disentangle the source of good ideas or ways of expressing them, and yet we must be always alert to the ethical requirement to acknowledge our sources of evidence or support for our ideas. We refer you to David Gray's (2018) book *Doing Research in the Real World*, which includes sections on the ethical aspects of different data collection procedures, and to John Gibbins' (2018) chapter that provides an overview of research ethics. Both are listed in the Further Reading. Here, we recommend that for peace of mind about your research integrity you create a log of new ideas and their sources so that when you are writing, you can assiduously reference the original authors' works. For UK readers, it is well worth reading 'The Concordat to Support Research Integrity', published by Universities UK (www.universitiesuk.ac.uk). This will avoid any sense that you are engaging in plagiarism, a very serious issue in research. For those of you who might use quotations from eminent authors to support, exemplify or provide evidence for your assertions (but never to replace your own words), do remember to log the page numbers of potential inclusions in your thesis or articles so that readers can check the relevance and import of the source.

For researchers' views on references and quotations, which may serve as caveats, see Voice of Experience Boxes 4.1 and 4.2.

VOICE OF EXPERIENCE 4.1 CUTTING OUT AUTHORS

I was so proud of my huge amount of reading that I had done for my thesis – there were hundreds of tomes on my list – that I felt despair for a while when my supervisor insisted that I weed out my reference list to considerably reduce it. I had to select only the most salient author to refer to in the text and then only include those references in my final bibliography. It felt like tearing up months of work but I must admit that it was useful when my examiners asked me why I had selected which authors to include – it gave me a chance to show off my analytic skills. (*A recent successful history researcher*)

VOICE OF EXPERIENCE 4.2 MISSING PAGE NUMBERS

Whenever anyone asks to see my thesis I feel a guilty twinge and hope that they don't notice that I have omitted the page numbers for two of my favourite quotations that I used to clarify a point I made in my Methodology chapter. As I was putting the final thesis together I spent days in a panic trying to track those page numbers down and in the end crossed my fingers that the examiners wouldn't notice. They didn't but after many years I still feel guilty and insist that my own doctoral researchers always log the full references for quotations … and I check those in theses I examine! (*One of your authors*)

VOICE OF EXPERIENCE 4.3 WHAT'S YOUR THESIS?

One of the things I struggled with, certainly in the early stages, was when people would ask what was my thesis and not just how my thesis was going. Worse still, they'd ask about the thesis in my thesis and to be honest, I had no idea what this meant until I got to the stage when I had too many 'theses' (arguments) for my thesis! By the middle of the third year, I had enough research and substantial chapters to submit at least two theses! It was then that I realised I had a choice of what story to tell. I spent a couple of weeks pacing around the house before deciding what was the juiciest question to answer and which bits would make the most interesting narrative. That meant cutting out whole chapters and reducing much of the second year's work to a paragraph! (*One of your authors*.)

Knowing when and how to stop perfecting your thesis

One of the greatest challenges you may well face when writing and editing your thesis, when you reach the stage of putting it together, is knowing when and how to stop. Figure 4.1 at the start of this chapter demonstrates that redrafting could go on endlessly; be warned, it will if you do not make a conscious decision to end it! Knowing when and how to stop is largely down to your frame of mind. This applies as much to individual chapters as it does to the whole thesis. In the early stages of writing, you will probably be rather perfectionist, wanting a thoroughly polished and convincing account of your research that truly reflects you as a researcher. Remember, though, that the process of thesis writing is about converting your research *journey* into a research *story*. As this transformation unfolds through the writing process, you need also to start to detach from your research project, so that you can begin to let individual chapters and then, finally, the thesis itself go. This detachment is difficult for many of us; nevertheless, detach you must if you are to finish your thesis. This is a fine balance to achieve because you must be careful not to detach too early in the redrafting process; if you do, you will lose your motivation to finish the thesis!

Once you are reasonably happy that you have converted your personal research journey into a convincing, coherent, concise and clear research story, you can then start to ask yourself if you have done enough to get your doctorate. To help you make that decision, have a look at the guidance we provide in Chapter 8 (particularly the advisory notes in Box 8.1) on examiners' expectations of theses. Asking yourself whether you have done enough marks a shift away from that perfectionist mentality that could stop you from finishing. Our advice, then, on knowing how to stop, is this: in the later rounds of redrafting, let go of the perfectionism that has successfully brought you this far, pluck up the courage to tell yourself that it is *only* a thesis you are writing, not a life's work, check with the guidance in Chapter 8 and ask if you have done enough to get your doctorate. If the answer is 'yes', and your supervisors agree, then that is when you stop.

So, by now, you are probably appreciating the time and energy needed to produce a good research story. Yes, it does demand energy, but if you start drafting the story early, the process can also be energising and extremely rewarding. Just as the labour of the artist is rewarded by a beautiful work of art, so your labours can be rewarded by a beautifully articulated research story.

References and further reading 

Bolton, G. (2010) *Reflective Practice: Writing and Professional Development.* London: Sage.

Cochrane Library http://uk.cochrane.org

Gibbins, J. (2008) 'Research ethics', chapter 11 in G. Hall and J. Longman (eds), *The Postgraduate's Companion.* London: Sage.

Gray, D.E. (2018) *Doing Research in the Real World*, 4th edn. London: Sage

Hannes, K. and Lockwood, C. (2012) *Synthesizing Qualitative Research: Choosing the Right Approach.* Oxford: Wiley–Blackwell.

Hart, C. (2008) 'Searching and reviewing the literature and information skills', chapter 10 in G. Hall and J. Longman (eds), *The Postgraduate's Companion.* London: Sage.

Murray, R. (2017) *How to Write a Thesis*, 4th edn. London: Open University/McGraw–Hill.

Orna, E. and Stevens, G. (2009) *Managing Information for Research*, 2nd edn. Maidenhead: Open University Press.

Saunders, M.N.K. and Lewis, P. (2011) *Research in Business Management.* Harlow: Pearson.

Wallace, M. and Wray, A. (2006) *Critical Reading and Writing for Postgraduates.* London: Sage.

5

WHAT ARE THE POTENTIAL RESOURCES AND OPPORTUNITIES AND HOW CAN THEY BEST BE UTILISED?

In this chapter, we will consider what potential resources and opportunities you may have available and how to get the most out of them, particularly how to:

- Identify your needs
- Locate potential resources and opportunities
- Establish networks for the future
- Learn when to say 'yes'
- Develop techniques for saying 'no'.

What do you need?

Before you can identify and utilise resources, you must determine what you need and prioritise these needs. This can be harder than you may initially think because the path and direction of the project is excitingly dynamic. While you may have some understanding of your research project and your individual strengths and weaknesses when you start your doctorate, you are unlikely to understand right at the beginning all the resources you will need or the variety and level of skills necessary to succeed during and beyond your doctorate. Likewise, although your supervisor will know some specific resources to help support you and may also have some ideas about training to help develop your skills, they are unlikely to know everything you will need throughout the course of your doctorate. Therefore, it is important that you and your supervisor develop a relationship that allows you to work together to identify your needs as they emerge. Importantly, at doctoral level you will be expected to take the lead in identifying resources and opportunities as well as your skill development needs; indeed, this is one of the major differences between being a student and being a professional researcher. Your supervisor is there to support and guide you in this process, but not to tell you what to do and arrange everything for you. This chapter is designed to help you feel confident in taking ownership of your own professional development.

Training needs analysis (TNA)

The fundamental and most critical resource in the success of your project is YOU! The preceding chapters will have alerted you that the following will all determine the nature of your doctoral experience: how you manage your time; how you organise your work; how you build relationships and manage different people positively; how you react to criticism and respond to feedback; how adept you are at communicating your ideas; how you handle reading, writing, evaluating and thinking critically; and how you control and accomplish tasks, especially over a long timeframe.

You will already have established certain working habits and acquired a range of skills and abilities, the question is: are they appropriate for the doctoral research process? It is easy to underestimate the significance of this and fail to appreciate how vital such questions are to your future success; however, it is worth reflecting on what you already bring to the project, where might you need to improve, what you need know about yourself, and what else you might need to acquire. Start by celebrating through Reflection Point 5.1 the skills and attributes you already have.

REFLECTION POINT 5.1

CELEBRATING EXISTING SKILLS

First, set aside modesty. Nobody reaches the stage of being accepted to study for a doctorate without having accumulated a considerable number of skills and attributes, both academic and professional/personal. Take some time to think through all the skills you have learnt from your studying thus far, like organising your work and making notes. Then, recall all of those that you learnt through any previous employment, part- or full-time, paid or voluntary, like dealing with the public, and those skills and attributes you picked up to survive, like cooking, self-care, picking yourself up after being faced with disappointment. If you make a list of these, you will find that it is quite extensive.

A high level of self-awareness and self-knowledge is central to professional success; undertaking a doctorate is not purely about getting on with the research, although this is seldom discussed in academe. Some supervisors may volunteer a discussion about expectations with you, and a few may initiate a discussion about your skill level, but you may have to broach the topic yourself; fortunately, many institutions and doctoral programmes now have independent tools or surveys that will help you analyse your own skill level, which you can then discuss with your supervisor. If you are unsure if there are tools available, it is worth checking your institutional website or asking within your department if some pro forma 'needs analysis' tool exists. These are commonly called 'training needs analysis' (TNA), or 'development needs analysis' (DNA), 'learning needs analysis' (LNA), 'academic needs analysis' (ANA), or a 'skills audit tool'. Try your Graduate School, Doctoral College or Researcher Development Team for details. If you do not have any local resource, or if you would just like to try a different TNA, see Activity 5.1.

As mentioned in the 'first 100 days' checklist in Chapter 2, a training needs analysis (TNA) is a task to undertake early on in your doctorate. However, as professional development is an essential, ongoing component of the doctorate; you should plan to undertake a TNA at regular or key points throughout your programme, perhaps coinciding with formal review stages (Chapter 7). So, what is a TNA and how do you go about doing one?

To determine your training needs, it is important, first, to have a clear idea of the skills required of a researcher. The Vitae Researcher Development framework (RDF) (see Appendix II for a summary diagram of the main attributes required of researchers) was compiled through research into what the research profession considered essential for a successful researcher career. The research informing the RDF drew out the important knowledge, skills, qualities, behaviours and attitudes of successful researchers through interviewing over a hundred, mostly senior, researchers with years of experience. The original data set comprised 'over 1,000 characteristics and their variants', thus indicating the rich range of attributes required for research that you, as a researcher, could potentially acquire. These characteristics were distilled into four main domains, twelve sub-domains and sixty-three descriptors. Importantly, there are also five developmental phases included in the full RDF package so that you can see how these skills develop over time from novice to world-leading researcher. For the full version of the Researcher Development Framework, see the Vitae website (www.vitae.ac.uk/).

The phased progression is of key importance, because the skills necessary to perform as a researcher continue to develop throughout one's career, building on the skills set that you bring with you at the beginning of your research. Each researcher will have a unique, complex profile of attributes and skills, some still in an early phase of development and some more refined and advanced. Do not assume that a world-leading professor will be excellent at everything; they may, for instance, be less confident than you in the use of digital media and perhaps not as familiar with project management tools or budget management as someone coming to doctoral research from business or industry. It is this continued professional development, which you may already be familiar with if you are a mature researcher, that you must start to take ownership of as a doctoral researcher, and continue to manage for the rest of your working life. As mentioned in Chapter 2, it is worth taking the time to fully familiarise yourself with this framework. Whilst you are not expected to improve on all sixty-three descriptors, indeed Vitae suggest selecting only three to five per annum to work on, you should consider all four domains and the twelve sub-domains to achieve a balanced portfolio. (We will discuss this further in the final chapter.) If you think a sub-domain, say D3 Engagement and Impact, is not appropriate for you at your current career stage then you must be able to explain why that is the case, rather than simply dismiss it because you are not interested. Think about that as you undertake Activity 5.1.

ACTIVITY 5.1 USING THE VITAE RESEARCHER DEVELOPMENT FRAMEWORK TO IDENTIFY TRAINING NEEDS

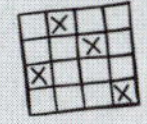

When using the RDF for needs analysis, the behavioural descriptors within the phases are particularly helpful. A thorough assessment of your training needs takes time and you may want to focus on one domain at a time or specific skill areas from different domains, moving on to different areas later. You may like to come back to this later but at least look at the attributes displayed in the summary version of Appendix II to ask yourself some of the following important questions in Steps 1 and 2, then consider the advice in Step 3.

Step 1: Skill/attribute evaluation (shortened to simply 'skill' in what follows)

1 How confident am I in this skill area?
2 Am I as skilled as I would like to be in an area?
3 Compared to the phase descriptors, what phase do I perceive my skill level to be equal to?

(Continued)

(Continued)

4. What experience do I have?
5. What proof or evidence do I have that confirms my skill at this level?
6. What past feedback have I received about this skill?
7. Do I have experience of using this skill at doctoral level?
8. What are the differences in expectations of this skill at doctoral level compared to other contexts?
    a. If you do not know the answer to this question, it is worth discussing with a supervisor, a more experienced peer and/or another trusted person with experience of a research degree.
    b. Note that many skills are often qualitatively different at doctoral level, for example writing and communicating in a scholarly way is quite an art and significantly different from report or essay writing – see Chapter 4.

Step 2: Prioritisation

1. How urgently do I need to use this skill?
2. How important is this skill for my success within the context of this doctorate? Within the context of my long-term career plans?
   Using what you learned about prioritisation in Chapter 3, prioritise urgent and important skill development first, but also make sure that you make time for important, but non-urgent, development. This will ensure that you are ready to do what you need to in the future.

Step 3: Discussion with your supervisors

1. Take the results of both Steps 1 and 2 to your supervisor(s) and discuss them during a formal tutorial meeting.
2. Be open to suggestions and feedback from your supervisor(s). As they are more familiar with the doctoral process, they may be able to give insight into your skill level and help with prioritisation.
3. Do not be discouraged about the need to undergo professional development. A doctorate is an education process and you are not expected right at the start to have the skill level of someone who has completed a doctorate.
4. The next step is to identify resources and opportunities to help you achieve your development goals.

Locating resources

One of the major differences between other educational degrees and the doctorate is the individuality of the work you will be doing and, therefore, the increased resourcefulness you will need to identify and access resources and opportunities. It is highly unlikely that everything you will need will be handed to you by your supervisor. This is not because your supervisor does not want to help you. It may simply be because they are unable to anticipate everything you will need and often may not themselves know where the resources you need can be located. Indeed, one of the things supervisors enjoy is learning from the doctoral students they supervise, such as when you bring new papers or literature or new connections to their attention. However, in the early stages your supervisor should have some good suggestions for key resources, or they may suggest another colleague to approach, so it is always worth asking. What is very likely later is that you must identify resources yourself. This can be a daunting prospect, but we would suggest you see this in a positive way: learning to be resourceful and taking the initiative to go out and find what you need is a critical skill for an independent researcher. See Activity 5.2 to begin this process.

ACTIVITY 5.2 RESOURCE-GATHERING EXERCISE

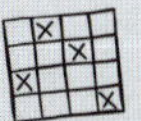

Here, we have started a list of the common resources for you to elaborate to suit your own case.

Resources	**Tick if you need this resource**	**Who, what, where or in what format do you need these resources?**
Work space /office		
Equipment		
Software		
Consumables		
Literature		
Data		
Courses – research methods		
Courses – professional skills		
Events to attend		
People to contact		
Other resources		

Certainly, you should take the time in your first few weeks to explore all the resources available within your department. Get to know your local administrative team. Talk to other doctoral researchers, learning both about them and what they do as well as resources they have found valuable. It is good to keep a note of what you uncover, because even if you do not need these resources immediately, they may well be very useful someday. If you are in a technical discipline, do make sure you learn who has specific expertise in the variety of techniques used within your department and in using the various types of equipment. People who hold this knowledge range from academics to postdocs, technicians and other doctoral researchers. All are very good resources in themselves. It is also helpful to uncover what types of training and courses are available to you. Many departments will allow doctoral researchers to sit in on, or audit, undergraduate or master's level courses if you feel you need a refresher, or if the topic of your doctorate requires disciplinary knowledge that was not covered in your previous taught programme. (This is frequently the case with multi- or cross-disciplinary projects.) The key thing is to establish good working practices and approaches quickly, so that once you have the basic information/resources in place, then it becomes a matter of keeping them up to date, refreshed or topped up for the remainder of the doctorate, building up a network of people (Chapter 6) to whom you can turn for further advice. It is a wise idea to reconsider your resource needs in advance of each staged formal review (Chapter 7).

Departmental knowledge is important; however, you should not expect all your resources to be provided for you by your department; you must look to the wider university and beyond as well. Universities are complex institutions and can be hard to navigate, even though you may have had recent experience with them in your previous degrees. The areas of the university that have resources for researchers are often different to those that focus on students on taught courses. Even the familiar library may hold hidden resource gems that you never knew existed. Again, it is often good to go resource hunting before you are in desperate need of them, so, in your first year, you might find it useful to set bits of time aside to do some exploring. Take an hour or so to go and talk to a librarian – it is not all about books: they will know about digital repositories and online resources available to you, as you will read in Voice of Experience Box 5.1. Have a look around different departments that may have some areas of overlap with your project (in theory, method or application) for equipment or literature that might be borrowed or hired. Chat to other doctoral researchers from these different departments, learn about what they do and what resources they are aware of. Most departments are happy to have doctoral researchers from other areas come along to their seminar series or sit in on courses. However, it is polite to introduce yourself and ask permission.

VOICE OF EXPERIENCE 5.1 A LIBRARIAN'S PERSPECTIVE ON RESEARCHER RESOURCES

Every researcher will need to use library resources, even if you are primarily accessing these virtually. Contextualising your research within the wider body of knowledge is something that every researcher needs to think about, and the library offers an ideal starting-off point to discover the literature and research that is already out there.

Libraries are evolving at a tremendous pace; in libraries, you will find that most of the holdings are not on the shelves and measured in metres but held on servers measured in terabytes, accessed via your library's subscriptions and electronic platforms. 'Discoverability' is the watchword of libraries nowadays. Your library will usually have a 'discovery platform', which is how you search for what is on the shelves as well as accessible online. Using the great resources that the library provides you with ensures that you are using the best quality information available to researchers around the world.

Through your own institution's library, you can also access print resources from other libraries through reciprocal access agreements, as well as using services such as inter-library loans to request material from other libraries. Remember that libraries may also have special collections or archives full of primary material in your area to explore.

The library may also be able to help you towards the end of your research degree, by developing your skills in data management or making your work more visible through institutional repositories.

All the information that we provide you with is great, but the best resources you can access in the library are the people – librarians can help you navigate the shelves and the weblinks, as well as help you get the most out of the plethora of online services. Spend a bit of time with your librarian to be certain of finding out how to access straight away key resources you need, how to get hold of that elusive paper cheaply and how to manage your ever-growing list of references from the start. Librarians are expert on finding, handling and navigating information and making it work for you.

(Catherine Stephen, Library Client Services and Academic Engagement Manager)

If there is a central or faculty Doctoral College/Graduate School/Researcher Development Programme, it is worth exploring the variety of resources and opportunities on offer. These are gold mines for resources as they are designed specifically to support researchers. Having a conversation with the staff within these departments is a great idea; that way you can get a good idea of the breadth of resource available, from internal and external training courses to equipment-sharing or loan facilities. Other key resource areas include central departments that support student finance, wellbeing and social activities (including the Students Union). These may seem to be set up for taught students, however, they often support doctoral researchers too, and may even have special provision for you. This is worth considering. Remember, all universities are organised slightly differently so, if you are new to your institution, do not assume everything will be in the same place it was at your previous university. When in doubt, ask someone.

Do also look outside of the university. As a doctoral researcher, you are not just part of a university community, you are becoming part of your disciplinary community. Most disciplines have professional societies/organisations that have student memberships at an extremely discounted rate. You should become a member as the newsletters and emails will keep you up to date on conferences, publications and training opportunities. If you are an interdisciplinary researcher, you may want to sign up to more than one professional society if there is not one that fits your whole research area completely.

It is also worth looking around at other universities. Many universities are happy to have doctoral researchers use various resources, such as libraries and archives, and even attend some training courses. This is especially true if your university has a special partnership with these other institutions. If there is something you need that you cannot find where you are, you may well find it at another institution. Also, get to know the researchers in your field, search their names on the internet, look at their pictures, and make a note of the various approaches each favours. It is common for researchers who work within the same discipline to discuss their research interests, share publications if you are unable to obtain them through your library, or even learn techniques from each other. However, it is a courtesy to ask your supervisors prior to approaching an academic from another institution; they are likely to know the person's temperament and advise you on how or if contacting them is a good idea. If there is some resource you need, it is likely it is out there somewhere, so never sit still wishing you had access to something – make it happen! Usually, academics and fellow researchers are flattered to be approached; you could start by asking for 'suggested literature' from contacts as suggested in the previous chapter, which is a great way of doing several things at once: expanding your network, getting yourself known, improving your literature review and bibliography. From that network, you might find yourself a mentor.

Mentoring

Your supervisor(s) and your peers in your department are amazingly important resources, but mentors can be key to thriving throughout your doctoral journey, while they are certainly essential for future career success. A mentor is someone you can talk to freely about a variety of issues and who you trust to give you sound, supportive advice. This is a resource more valuable than gold, and vital for academic careers. There is no limit to the number of mentors a person can have, either at any one time for a single issue, such as for obtaining advice on how to write a specific proposal within their special area of expertise, or over a lifetime for general advice about professional development. Therefore, a good mentor is always someone to be on the lookout for, especially when you are undertaking something as life-changing as a doctorate. Many universities have a range of mentoring programmes, so this may be a great place to start looking for a mentor. When offered such an opportunity, you should not turn it down. The worst that could happen is that you have an interesting conversation with a new person but do not continue the relationship for very long. However, you may just find someone who will deeply enhance your life.

Nevertheless, you do not need an official mentoring programme to find a mentor. Each of the three authors has had a great many mentors standing beside them through their life-journeys. When you find someone you admire, or who has skills or attributes you would like to develop yourself, or can help you navigate a situation, or who just makes you feel more powerful when you are around them, nurture this relationship. A good mentor is a key resource and can help and guide you through the highs and the lows of your research career. They can be sounding boards for your ideas and provide insights into the arcane workings of organisations. It is the independence and experience of the mentor that is most valuable, so they do not even need to be in your discipline area or department to mentor you. First, you will need to reflect on why you want a mentor and what your priorities are that they could help with. They will expect you to clarify your expectations of them so that they can be clear about the commitment and their suitability. They will be suitable: if they have similar values to yours so that you respect them; if they are willing to develop the partnership with you so that you earn each other's trust; if they have the expertise and experience to provide the advice you need and/or the skills you want to develop yourself; if they are available and have the time to give you; if they are not linked to you in any assessment or evaluation capacity. Top Tips 5.1 summarises things to do and to bear in mind while finding a suitable mentor. This is followed by Voice of Experience Box 5.2, which provides one mentee's perspective.

OP TIPS 5.1 FINDING THE RIGHT MENTOR FOR YOU

1. Check out university- or organisation-supported mentoring schemes, but know you can also find mentors yourself.
2. Think about what you want to work on developing, and seek out a person who is successful in this area:
   - For example, if you want to start publishing, identify someone who has experience in publishing. Perhaps even someone who would be open to co-publishing with you.
3. Your supervisor may become a mentor, but they may not. There is no right or wrong with either situation.
4. Look for people you admire, for a variety of reasons, personally or professionally. Mentors do not have to be at the top of their profession to provide guidance:
   - It can be quite helpful to have a mentor who has just recently overcome a challenge like the one you are currently facing.
   - A more senior PhD student or postdoctoral fellow can be an incredibly helpful mentor to an incoming PhD student.
5. You may explicitly ask someone to be your mentor, or they may naturally become a mentor though your interactions.
6. Being mentored is about learning from someone, not becoming them, so be open to mentors who are quite different to you. They can help you see the world in new ways.
7. Every life has room for a variety of mentors, each one contributing uniquely to your development.

VOICE OF EXPERIENCE 5.2 A FORMAL ACADEMIC MENTORING EXPERIENCE

I chose to have a mentor when I started a leadership course at my university. Leadership is not something I naturally aspire to or am comfortable with but, as it is increasingly needed for academic and non-academic roles, I felt a mentor would help guide me. The leadership course was geared towards women and my mentor had spent many years in a leadership role in departments run mostly by men.

Her experiences as an academic in higher education are common in that she has suffered sexism and now looks upon these anecdotes and stories with humour. We met about four times over the period that I attended the course and she engaged with what I was learning. She would set 'homework' for me. For example, she asked me to bring to one of our meetings pictures of leaders whom I admired and encouraged me to make a list of attributes they had that I aspired to. These meetings were often more helpful than the activities on the course itself and certainly cemented for me some of the more abstract themes about leadership.

One aspect I struggled with was my sense of my own position within my role. I felt that I had no business giving advice to senior managers or academics on my views on my subject and its relation to the university strategy and I would usually avoid strategic discussions. I would barely say a word at committee meetings. It was through mentoring that I began to look at my role differently and realised that when asked for an opinion it was honestly meant and that I was an expert in my field.

Through discussions we reflected upon how I handled certain situations and, through goal-setting and gentle nudges, my mentor pushed me out of my comfort zone and I began to reappraise my career development with new insights. I gained an enormous amount of confidence that has led me to trial new initiatives that I perhaps would not previously have tried without first discussing it with a mentor. Opportunities that I may have ignored were encouraged. I now advocate the benefits of mentoring to my students as, if the match is successful, it can greatly improve outlook on personal and career development.

(Dr Laura Christie, Royal Holloway, University of London)

It is also an amazing experience to act as a mentor for others. We have overseen mentoring programmes throughout the years and one striking observation is that the feedback from mentors is as positive as the feedback from the mentees. Mentors often remark on how the experience of being a mentor has helped them appreciate their own personal development, enhanced their skills and led to a greater feeling of wellbeing. Therefore, opportunities to be a mentor yourself with junior colleagues or undergraduates, can be valuable experiences, and will be a useful addition to your portfolio and eventually in your CV (Chapter 11).

A sea of opportunities: When to say 'yes'

Throughout your doctorate, you will have an array of different opportunities to participate in seminars, projects, conferences, events and activities, some directly relating to your research and some more peripheral. How do you know what opportunities are available? How should you choose what to get involved with? When should you be participating in different activities? These are good questions, and perhaps not entirely straightforward to answer as each individual person and research project is different. However, we have some words of advice that can help you navigate opportunities and get the most out of them while you are doing your doctorate.

Firstly, it is important to think of your own development. In the training needs analysis above, we talked about identifying what skills you want to work on developing. Once you have an idea of this, then you can think about which kind of opportunities will help you develop these skills.

An obvious example might help: every researcher needs to develop effective presentation skills in the context of academic research. Despite your background and prior experience of presenting to different audiences (fellow students, a class you teach, a group you manage and so on), it is likely that presenting your own research to an academic audience will be a new venture. Therefore, opportunities to develop this skill should be grasped with enthusiasm, even if tinged with initial trepidation. We suggest that to avoid procrastination, you choose a relatively safe and friendly venue, such as a departmental seminar or university doctoral researcher event, as a good first step. Hesitating too long only builds up anxiety so we would advise giving a presentation early, once you have a general research plan, but before you are too far into the actual research. This will not only build up your presentation skills but will also hone your ability to pose an argument while providing you with feedback that can help shape your research project. Our researchers have found that their first presentations also provided them contact with 'interested others', who then became a supportive peer group or a mentor. Perhaps the best time to present is a bit before you feel comfortable in doing so.

Considering the skills and attributes that you need to develop as part of your doctoral project is important but should not confine the activities that you engage in; we would urge you not to be too closed-minded. Some activities will develop skills you will need for the future beyond the doctorate. Often, these skills may not easily be developed in the context of your everyday research; you must bravely grasp good opportunities as and when they arise. Leadership skills may be one example. Not many doctorates provide the opportunity to practise leading others during the research process but you may well be presented with the opportunity to develop leadership skills through other activities. Perhaps your department needs someone to organise a seminar series, or maybe your professional society offers doctoral researchers a chance to organise a conference, or you could hear of an opportunity to lead a public engagement activity in a local school. Alternatively, you could stop being simply alert to opportunities by being pro-active: organise a seminar series, arrange a public engagement event or suggest that your peers manage a conference on a topical theme for your department. Such activities will also require 'negotiating' skills as you will want the endorsement and support of your supervisor at least.

Whether taken as they arise or deliberately manufactured, these fantastic opportunities will expand your skills, enhance your portfolio/CV and provide you with concrete examples for future interviews.

Of course, we must insert the caveat that you must be able to balance these extra commitments with your research. However, many people find that these extra activities make them more productive, not less, giving an added zest to life. We can always find time to take up serendipitous offers – a celebratory night out, a visit from a dear friend, free tickets to a show. So, time can expand to accommodate the things we want to do, as well as the things we suddenly must do that are less pleasant – visiting the dentist with an aching tooth is an innocuous example.

Experienced researchers often talk about the importance to discovery and innovation of serendipity; frequently, people treat this as just luck and chance. However, a great deal of serendipity that happens in the research context is not as much down to chance as you might initially think:

> I am a great believer in luck, and I find the harder I work, the more I have of it. (Thomas Jefferson)

ACTIVITY 5.3 CREATING 'LUCKY' OPPORTUNITIES

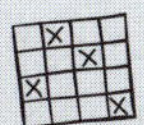

Reflect on your life to date, considering where luck/chance/serendipity played a role in helping you to achieve the position you are in now. Working as a doctoral researcher in a university is a privileged position, with opportunities both shouting from the roof tops and hiding behind corners. Researchers who discuss their research with a wide variety of people are more likely to find a connection or a collaborator that will help shape their research into something unforeseen. (We return to the benefits of this for research impact in Chapter 9.) Therefore, we suggest setting aside a bit of time within your doctorate to do something a bit outside of your normal routine. Something that takes you away from the people within your discipline, perhaps outside of academia altogether. Put yourself in situations in which 'serendipity' can happen. (See Voice of Experience 10.1.)

Another reason to take on opportunities may be as a favour to others, perhaps your supervisor or a peer. This is a valid reason to do something, and often does develop skills and build your CV along the way. Furthermore, if you do favours for others, they are more likely to help you out when you need a favour in the future – and this is how you build your network (Chapter 6). All of this is very positive. However, it is also important to be careful not to over-extend yourself so that you are spending large amounts of time doing things for other people that have little benefit to your own doctoral research or to your own skill development (see Chapter 3, Prioritising). To be able to balance your resources effectively, including your own time and energy, you need to develop the skills of knowing when and how to say 'no'.

The power of 'no'

Although it is good to participate in a wide range of activities throughout the course of your doctorate, there are times when you should decline certain invitations or requests. When should you say 'no'? First, and most importantly, are you struggling to keep up with what you must do for your doctorate? If you are at a busy point in your doctorate or you are caught up in a flow of moving your research forward, your research must be prioritised and other activities should be politely declined. Saying 'no' can sometimes be a challenge, however, learning this skill will help you now and for your entire working career.

It can help to remember that saying 'no' is a healthy, mature response when saying 'yes' would put your other commitments at risk of being fulfilled; saying 'no' honours the other obligations. This includes saying 'no' to yourself when tempted to procrastinate, but saying 'no' to others needs some special consideration.

Politely saying 'no' to others

It is of key importance to try to understand the perspective of the person asking for something. In this way, you can say 'no' in a more empathetic way. Determine how important/urgent it is to the person, and how important it is that you are the one to do it (Chapter 3). Determine if there is any flexibility in the time schedule. It may be that you cannot say 'yes' now, but perhaps you could do it a bit later? Take time to communicate your decision well, making sure they understand the reason why you are saying 'no'. This can help to ensure you do not miss out on future opportunities, because people assume that you will automatically turn them down. It also helps you maintain good working relationships and networks.

Good working relationships are key, as you will discover in the next chapter. During your doctorate, you will need favours, or to make requests for support from others, and these good working relationships are built on reciprocity. This can make saying 'no' especially difficult when the person you must say 'no' to is your supervisor. Before you say 'no' to your supervisor, you should be very clear about whether what you are declining is fundamentally important to your doctorate. It is best to have a very open and mature discussion with your supervisor about this. Ask if this is critical to your project, ask if it must be done now or could be done at a different time. If your supervisor insists that this is something you must do, or at least strongly advises you should do, then you probably should consider changing your mind. Perhaps you could say 'no' to something else. A good strategy would be to sit down with your supervisor and share with them all your commitments and timetables and ask them to help you with some re-prioritisation. It may be that by seeing exactly what you must do, your supervisor will agree with you that you are unable to undertake this additional task, or they may help you offload something else. The bottom line is that you can only do so much in each period. This does mean that you will likely have to turn down some opportunities or requests at some point. The key is to work with those around you to ensure that everyone understands you are doing your fair share and are working consistently. We imagine you will be pleasantly surprised at how understanding most people can be about this. After all, we have all been there. Below, one of us has included her story of the first time she said 'no' to her supervisor.

VOICE OF EXPERIENCE 5.3 SAYING 'NO' TO MY SUPERVISOR

I remember the first time I said 'no' to my supervisor. I am, by nature, a 'yes' person. Sometimes, it jumps out before I even realise what has happened. Usually, this has served me well, and meant that I have pushed myself to do things outside of my comfort zone and benefited from doing so. However, it can sometimes be a problem, like this example in the middle of my doctorate.

It was a frantic week. I had several things going, the biggest being a conference presentation that needed to be completed soon. The real problem was that my experiments were just not going well, so I had to run another whole series to get the data I needed for the presentation. I had a young baby at home, so only a limited time during the day that I could do these experiments. I was frazzled, and running frantically between my office and lab.

Then, in walks my supervisor with a paper in his hand. He plops it on my desk and says, 'This is a really interesting one. It would be quite good for your development if you were to review it. One of the reviewers we assigned to it has informed us he will be unable to undertake this now. I do need the review back before you go to conference, however.' (Just a note of context, my supervisor was an editor of a journal, and this

(Continued)

(Continued)

situation was not unusual. 'For the benefit of my development,' I had been asked to review papers for his journal on several occasions previously.)

What happened next was rather unfortunate ... my 'yes' reflex kicked in. Out the word popped before I had any chance to censor myself. And off walked my supervisor, with a satisfied look on his face. I looked down at the paper. It was huge, and the title signalled that it was only peripherally related to my research. This would take ages to properly review!

What was I going to do? I knew I had to tell him I couldn't do it. However, I felt awful as I had just committed myself. And it would be good for my development; I had learnt a huge amount from acting as a peer reviewer in the past, both about the subject and about how to write for publication. But I just did not have the time, so I pulled myself up, went to his office, taking a deep breath as I entered.

Then it all came out: I told him how busy I was, how the experiments weren't working and I hadn't been able to even start the analysis yet, much less get the presentation together. How I was so sorry for saying I would do it, and I knew it would be good to do, but I just didn't think I could right now. I don't think I stopped for a breath for a good 10 minutes while everything came tumbling out. My supervisor looked at me and smiled and said, 'Oh, sounds like you are quite busy right now. I'll get someone else to do it.'

He picked up the paper and walked back down the hall, peeking into office windows to see who else he could visit with a developmental opportunity. He didn't care at all if I did it or not, he just wanted someone to do it (besides himself, of course). He fully expected that I would say 'no' if I were unable to fit in the extra work. It was only me who thought I had to say 'yes' all the time.

(Bioscience Researcher)

Establishing good working relationships involves many skills, especially when you are in a novel situation such as embarking on doctoral study. We have dedicated the next chapter to exploring some of the particularly challenging but fulfilling aspects of relationship development in this context.

References and further reading 

'How to get a mentor', Tedx Talk from Ellen Ensher. www.youtube.com/watch?v=87qjIZRkkio

Snyder, M. (2014) *The Art of Self-Confidence: How to Be Assertive in Any Situation*. CreateSpace Independent Publishing Platform.

University of Warwick, 'Identify your development needs'. www2.warwick.ac.uk.

6

HOW CAN RELATIONSHIPS BE DEVELOPED TO ENABLE CONSTRUCTIVE FEEDBACK AND SUPPORT?

In this chapter, we will consider how to:

- Establish yourself in the academic community
- Develop awareness and sensitivity
- Work well with your supervisors
- Use criticism effectively
- Build other supportive relationships
- Deal with less supportive situations
- Manage your emotions to good effect
- Become an authority with authority
- Recognise how modes of study and discipline interact with these issues

This chapter will build on the advice we gave in Chapter 2, which encouraged you to start building good habits and relationships during your first 100 days as a doctoral researcher. We will refer to specific points as they become relevant to this part of our guidance on how to make the most of the opportunities provided by contact with other people during your doctoral studies.

The myth of the lone researcher

We urge you not to translate the need to demonstrate independence as a researcher as a need to be isolated, nor to associate successful interaction with people as purely social skills. Undoubtedly, there are many aspects of doctoral study that involve the researcher taking sole responsibility, making autonomous decisions and becoming an independent researcher. We alluded to this in our first chapter when we compared the feat of completing a doctorate to swimming the English Channel, or another marine equivalent. You will also find literature reports on the loneliness experienced by some, nevertheless successful, doctoral candidates. However, although making a personal, unique contribution to knowledge is a requirement of the assessment system (Chapter 8), we want to emphasise that you need not be alone throughout the process. Indeed, you can find an enormous amount of guidance and support, personal as well as intellectual, from a range of communities related to the doctoral process. We contend that building networks within these communities as you go through your programme will stand you in good stead for your future work and life beyond the doctorate.

It is normal that individuals differ in the degree of support and contact they think they require from members of immediate and/or more remote communities. For instance, a mature doctoral candidate who has returned to academia after a period of work may already have nurtured a strong network of colleagues and friends who can provide personal support. However, that network might not be familiar with the nuances, tribulations and celebrations related to intense research, nor may those involved be prepared to be neglected when the passion for the research project outweighs the need to be sociable. Alternatively, another doctoral researcher may have chosen that academic pathway specifically because they prefer solo intellectual activity to social engagement. In both cases, the doctoral researcher should not distance themselves (or worse still hide) from their supervisor, nor should they avoid interaction with others in academia. As we noted previously, the contemporary doctorate requires that researchers can communicate well with their supervisor(s), fellow researchers, with actual and potential funders and with the population at large to disseminate and justify their research. There are many aspects of research that require us to engage in valuable interaction with a variety of communities within and outside of academia. For instance, **peer review** is a two-way process that requires understanding of the intent of criticism, so that it is both given and received well. In Chapter 7, we will consider the special case of criticism within assessment procedures, but here we want to take a broader view, recognising that, to become a fully accepted member of an academic community, able to grow from feedback and provide cogent advice to others, we each need to nurture relationships. To do so means recognising and understanding the perspectives, values, tenets and beliefs of other participants in the task. In other words, we need to learn about and work with diverse people and within and between 'cultures'.

Developing sensitivity to cultures and diversity

One of the great joys for your authors of working within academe is the opportunity it provides us to meet and work with people from all over the world with expertise in different disciplines. It is great fun to learn of different ways of life and pedagogy; it is stimulating to encounter different perspectives; it is challenging to have our views and beliefs tested by anomalies and contradictory evidence. All of this is part of our daily life in universities, indeed we suggest that this rich range of diversity is one of the key resources within higher education institutions, so that it is important you learn to manage and respond positively to this asset during your doctorate. The first step on that pathway is recognition that you, too, will be bringing to the situation sets of assumptions that are likely in part to match with those of people important to your doctorate and may in part be at odds with them. Think about the similarities and contradictions in expectations between newer researchers and supervisors presented in Chapter 2. There are differences between researchers and teachers and researcher–teachers, and differences (from doctoral to professorial level) between disciplines in terms of how they do things, what they value as significant, and how they communicate such things. This all serves to make higher education a multi-layered and varied working environment, perhaps more diverse than you have been used to. Some of the more obvious differences derive from our individual upbringing and personal context; this may reveal itself as the customs/habits and values (including religious, political, social, sexual and personal values) that we all bring with us and help us identify who we are. This form of cultural background interacts with the professional and disciplinary customs/habits and values, or professional cultures, making daily life and research work both interesting and challenging. We explore these aspects of culture in this chapter, exemplifying how they interact to influence perceptions.

You may already have some fundamental perceptions in common with your supervisors, possibly based on disciplinary approaches to knowledge (**epistemology**) and what constitutes reality (**ontology**). However, even within discipline and certainly between disciplines, such perceptions can differ radically, so it is important to explore such topics both with your supervisors and within your department as early as possible. This can be a source of great intellectual stimulation and possibly a seismic shift in the way you view the world, especially if you are involved in inter- or multi-disciplinary research or have supervisors from HE and industry/commerce. (You can find out more about what these highlighted words imply in terms of approach to research projects in Crotty's *The Foundations of Social Research*, 2003, or any book that deals with research philosophies or paradigms.) The differences between disciplines in worldviews and approaches to intellectual tasks are cleverly distinguished in Becher's (1989) book about academic tribes and territories. These books can be found in the Further Reading for this chapter, while we provide some specific points of discipline variance in the concluding section. Before you read further, consider your natural questioning inclination in Reflection Point 6.1.

REFLECTION POINT 6.1

QUESTIONS THAT COME TO MIND

What kind of intuitive questions come to your mind when faced with a challenge in your discipline? Once you read the literature on different research approaches, you will find that questions such as 'How are these things related, does one cause another?' along with 'How often, how big, how many?' tend to fall into one paradigm, while questions such as 'What is going on here' leading to 'Why? In what way?' tend to be asked in another. These are not exclusive within any one project, but a preponderance of one group of questions does suggest a certain paradigmatic stance.

Less commonly recognised differences in approach can also be sources of challenges, from bemusement to consternation. For instance, the forms of address used between doctoral researchers and academic staff members differ between countries and universities, making initial encounters range from comfortable to very awkward or embarrassing. For example, in the UK, academics and researchers tend to be on 'first name terms', with respect for status displayed in more indirect ways. In other countries, professors and doctors are addressed using their titles, with some of them using formal titles for researchers in response, for example Ms or Mr Surname. It is worth doing some informal research to find out what is the practice in the location in which you are studying. If, as a visitor to the UK, you find the informal first name form difficult to get used to, then most of us would be gratified if you prefaced our first name with our title (Prof. or Dr First-name). Establishing the preferred mode of address, in talk or writing, in new situations is part of a range of communication skills that form the basis of effective working life whether in universities or other organisations.

In fact, it is worth giving early attention to finding out what is considered polite, what causes discomfort or is offensive to others in that culture or cultures in which your doctoral studies take place. This may be a university in a different country, working across disciplines within a university, departmental culture (or ways of doing things), conducting fieldwork in a different community or country, or perhaps working in an employment organisation outside an educational setting. All of these provide opportunities to develop your **cultural sensitivity**, widen your horizons and prepare you for work beyond your degree, an issue that we will explore further in Chapter 12. Suffice it to say here that we are all members of a variety of cultures (family, workplace, national and so on), each of which shares attitudes, beliefs, values and traditions that provide a frame of reference, but also generate stereotypes of other groups and can lead to prejudice, at worst, or unconscious bias.

Most universities across the world put great pride in instilling respect for all members of their communities, and one way of demonstrating respect is to try to learn the etiquette of the groups you join. Universities generally provide formal diversity training, at least to staff members, and have harassment procedures to protect all community members who may feel discriminated against because of their ethnicity, culture, gender, age, disability, sexual orientation, socioeconomic status or faith. However, you can be pro-active in developing your awareness and sensitivity. We provide suggestions in Activity 6.1.

ACTIVITY 6.1 DEVELOPING YOUR CULTURAL AWARENESS AND SENSITIVITY

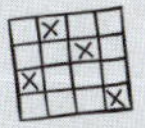

Below we suggest steps you can take to ensure that you settle comfortably into a new environment. Note, this exercise will be valuable to you whether you are undertaking your doctorate in your home country or have travelled great distances for this opportunity. While working through the activity, you might like to tick off the customs you are sure about from the final list and make a special effort to find out about the others, remembering that none of the variations is right or wrong, only different:

- *Heighten your awareness*: Read about non-verbal communication and cultural anomalies (as a start, see Appendix III, and books by Desmond Morris, 2002, and Kate Fox, 2004, which we have included in the Further Reading). Listen carefully and watch out for culturally influenced behaviours – your own and that of colleagues and friends.
- *Acknowledge your fears*: Recognise and face your own fears of acting inappropriately toward members of different cultures, ethnicities, gender, ages, abilities, sexual orientations, socioeconomic status or faiths.
- *Identify and appreciate differences*: Be attentive to the differences between yourself and those from other cultures and cherish their distinctiveness. Be curious and interested in others – everyone has a tale to tell and welcomes that being valued.

(Continued)

(Continued)

- *Recognise differences within groups*: While recognising differences between yourself and others, distinguish the often enormous differences within any given cultural grouping. Diversity within groups can be as wide as that between groups. Value people's individuality.
- *Realise that words are only symbols and mean different things to different individual people and within different groups*: Be especially attentive to differences in meaning attributed to words that are specific terminology used by professional groups, as well as in everyday life (for example, 'interview' means different things to an employer than to a researcher), or are academic jargon (for instance, different meanings of 'feedback'), or are dialect words or are used differently by different generations ('sick' as a positive description and 'peak' meaning horrible, bemuses some older people).
- *Be custom conscious*: Become aware of and considerate about the rules and customs of others. If you are unsure, simply and politely ask. Some specific examples to be alert to are:

  - Greetings and farewells – should you shake hands, bow, kiss or hug?
  - Titles (modes of address) – to use or not to use? – See earlier discussion.
  - Gender differences – should you treat everyone the same or are there conventions to observe?
  - Present giving – is it expected and accepted or considered a bribe and unprofessional?
  - Money – will you be expected to pay for others, be paid for by others or each pay their share?
  - Celebrations and holidays – do you know those of your colleagues and are you respectful of them?
  - Personal grooming and dress codes – what is considered appropriate for work and what for leisure activity?
  - Topics of conversation – what is acceptable and what is taboo?
  - Yes and no – are people comfortable with and expect a definite response or do they demur and avoid any confrontation?
  - Possessions and privacy – what to share or not to share, touch or not touch? Is a closed door a firm barrier or simply a draught excluder?
  - Time-keeping – is punctuality considered very or not important; when and by how much, if at all, is it acceptable to be late?
  - Humour, wit and silliness – what topics and styles are laughed at and by whom and in which contexts?

Given the diversity of people working in universities, it would not be unusual to find that your supervisors differ from you and each other in many cultural respects – and these are important people to develop a comfortable rapport with very early in your doctoral career.

Working with your supervisors

A point we want to emphasise here is that supervisors are human beings, with human virtues and flaws. They, like us, will have expectations, assumptions, prejudices and unconscious biases. They will also have a large number of academic roles to contend with, in addition to doctoral supervision, such as undergraduate teaching and marking, administration and management duties, publication and funding-seeking activities and, of course, their own research. Thus, we recommend that you negotiate carefully with them how you can best work together. Indeed, being able to appreciate the position of others is one of the key attributes when developing sensitivity to others; as the old saying has it, we can never know another person until we have walked a mile in their shoes. While recognising that supervisors may be more 'thesis-completion than professional development' focused, they are, nevertheless, extremely influential people for your near and even distant future. They may or may not eventually become your best friends but they should be a source of considerable guidance, at least in the early stages of your project, and are likely to become collaborative authors, gateways to networks and providers of references later. In Information Box 6.1 we outline the core duties of a supervisor to give you a feel for how much they can help you. You can see how you can reciprocate in Information Box 6.2. You should also find on your university's website the specific role responsibilities of supervisors and researchers required by your own unique institution.

INFORMATION BOX 6.1 CORE RESPONSIBILITIES OF A DOCTORAL SUPERVISOR

Supervisors should:

- Use their expertise in the field to make sure that the selected research topic can be developed and completed to required standards with the resources available.
- Recommend, encourage and regularly review appropriate training programmes in research methods, professional skills and doctoral study.
- Advise on appropriate completion dates for each stage of the research project and thesis development.
- Provide feedback on the progress of skill development, research and thesis-writing.
- Regularly monitor progress and make sure that formal monitoring procedures (Chapter 7) are adhered to.

(Continued)

(Continued)

- Guide and advise on: literature sources, literature critique and review, the project plan, the choice of appropriate research approach, methods and analysis techniques, ethical issues and health and safety procedures.
- Encourage and support dissemination activities over the course of the project (seminars, conferences, written articles and reviews, public engagement activities).
- Coach and provide practice for the final examination process (Chapter 8).

INFORMATION BOX 6.2 CORE RESPONSIBILITIES OF A DOCTORAL RESEARCHER

A doctoral researcher should:

- Work with supervisors to identify, select and review appropriate literature to refine the research topic.
- Set aside adequate time and energy to complete the project.
- Behave professionally, ensuring that contractual obligations and regulations are adhered to and recognise that they are accountable to employers, funders, professional bodies and society in general.
- Attend research and professional skills training and improve competences by submitting written work for feedback and presenting work in seminars or similar.
- Seek necessary approvals (ethics, access) before commencing the project.
- Regularly meet with and correspond with supervisors, providing progress reports and seeking feedback on plans and progress.
- Keep to agreed targets and prepare records of progress for formal and informal assessment.
- Implement the research according to safe working practices and legal requirements such as data protection and confidentiality.
- Gradually take responsibility for the project and its communication to interested parties.
- Disseminate, in appropriate form for both specialist and lay people, accurate information about methods employed and results, so that judgements can be made about applicability and relevance.

Both supervisors and researchers have multiple responsibilities and obligations to each other. The process will run more smoothly, if you all work hard and are accessible to each other. There is emphasis also on the provision of responses in various forms and on the taking of initiatives. Let us explore some of those aspects further.

Accessibility and hard work

Accessibility is more than simply being present in your department or online. It is about ensuring that your supervisor knows where you are and how you can be contacted. It is also a two-way process, but even if your supervisor does not keep you informed, you should inform them as this is a good professional custom/habit to acquire. Both researchers and their supervisors are entitled to free time, vacations and private time, but they also both have responsibilities to each other. Part of that responsibility is to make sure that they are available when needed, so negotiation is required about frequency, duration and nature of contact and communications. That negotiation should be revisited regularly because communication needs – support or reassurance for both parties – is determined by a complex interaction between the stage of the project, university requirements and your developing independence. Fortunately, we are now able to both write and talk to people electronically, so proximity, being 'at your office desk', is no longer critical (though lab work might be). However, this plethora of communication modes can also raise unrealistic expectations about frequency and immediacy of responses. It is wise to include in your negotiations some ground rules about emails, for instance when and how often you should 'check in' with your supervisor, especially when either of you are off-site or abroad, how swiftly you can each expect a response and how to indicate politely the degree of urgency required for a reply.

Regular communication is often the only way your supervisors can be assured that you are indeed working hard and in the right way. The latter is an important issue because we are aware that sometimes researchers, not wanting to 'bother' their supervisors or wanting to impress them, 'work hard' on their own, but may go off track. It would greatly help your supervisors if you send them in advance of a meeting material (drafts, lists of questions, outlines of a line of argument and so on) that will form its main focus. This will allow them to think about it, to produce a more useful response. In contrast, presenting your supervisors, after several weeks of silence, with a long list of books you have read can elicit a disappointing response. Though you may have ensured that the reading list is appropriate to your topic or potential **research methodology**, simply reading them is not what is required at this level, nor is providing a lengthy description of the content of each tome or research article. Remember the section in Chapter 4 on critical engagement. We cannot stress too much the need to constantly evaluate what you read (see Activity 3.5) and what you say, giving reasons for each choice you make throughout the progress of your project and evidence to support your contentions. You should be aware of the number of revisions and re-drafts of written material that come between first ideas and presentation in a thesis or for publication. To effectively manage this process, clear communication about expectations between yourself and your supervisor regarding timeframes for drafts and feedback will be critical.

Further, you will have noticed the different forms that writing can take – for yourself to begin to articulate your thoughts, drafts to share ideas with your supervisors and drafts of chapters or papers for a wider audience. This written material is evidence to your supervisor of your hard work, while also providing them with opportunities to guide your writing and your research practice. It will make that guidance more fruitful if you clearly indicate the status and intent of submitted material (the draft stage), so that their comments are relevant and their time not wasted. Therefore, you should be proactive in communicating with your supervisor about the type of feedback you currently require, for instance big-picture feedback on your ideas and overall justification, or more detailed feedback on the grammar, structure and tightness of the written argument. A plea from a supervisor: once you have submitted work for feedback, resist working on it until after you get it back – it can be disheartening for supervisors to spend time commenting on scripts and then be told, 'Ah, but I have changed it in the meantime and here is an updated version!' While waiting, do carry on with a different chapter or different task, so that you are continually productive.

Make a point of agreeing a reasonable return date so that no one feels misunderstood or taken for granted. If your work is not returned on the agreed date, give it a day or so and then politely remind your supervisors that you are anxious to learn their views on your work. Do not assume any negative reason for the delay; it is likely that they have either been extremely busy or have forgotten it because of distractions – the human element! A good way to politely keep all parties to deadlines, is to tie agreed dates to meetings. For example, schedule a supervisory meeting a few days or a week after your supervisor has agreed to return your work. This makes a hard deadline for you both, because if feedback is not provided by the meeting date, there will be nothing to talk about. It is also good policy to discuss in advance what forms of response are most helpful for all parties – for instance, preferences for written notes and/or numbered comments on hard-copy script or Comments and/or Track Changes on electronic versions.

Create a new custom (work habit) by adopting a structured and planned approach to supervision, perhaps by sending and agreeing an agenda or discussion points in advance. Crucially, you should always make a record of the key points and agreed actions or next steps that were discussed during the supervision. Some institutions may provide pro forma or have a formal log-keeping system; at a minimum, an email summarising the key points for your supervisor to agree by a return confirmation email, will ensure that both of you have understood each other's words and intentions.

Responses and initiative

Like accessibility, being responsive is a reciprocal activity. Written work and comments on it provide evidence and reassurance to everyone concerned. Although we all find criticisms of our creative products uncomfortable, they are very much to be deliberately sought out during your doctoral studies as this is how to improve and learn. Indeed, it is essentially contradictory to, on the one hand, want guidance from your supervisor but on the other hand, hope that there will be few comments on your written work. Without being given the opportunity to read, digest, ponder and critique your thoughts, plans about and responses to research activities, how can supervisors guide you? The more you share your ideas, respond to requests for chapter drafts or seminar/conference presentations or joint article writing, the greater your volume of guidance. Further, rather than only *responding* to hints or requests for written material or presentations, you could volunteer them, suggest opportunities for feedback, put yourself forward for review. Such examples of initiative-taking confirm to supervisors that their critical feedback is respected and is helping you along the path towards research autonomy. It also helps you receive the feedback you need, when you need it.

Remember that, in time, you should take responsibility for the results of your project, including the data obtained and conclusions drawn. There may, as your expertise and confidence develop, be occasions when you disagree with suggestions and feedback. It is important that you address these by putting forward your arguments and evidence for this different perspective, listening to responses and then deciding whether to revise your view or stick to your interpretation. In the long run this is going to be your thesis to defend, so be sure that you believe in it.

Responding to critical feedback

People like us, who write or present professionally, seldom, if ever, create a perfectly organised, logical, grammatical, cogent, accessible and attractive piece of work at first attempt. Therefore, we establish networks of trusted colleagues willing to give honest but supportive comment on our drafts until we are satisfied that our public at large will not only understand, but become engaged and hopefully inspired by our crafted and honed work. Your main sources of feedback are your supervisors, so when you receive your first, tentative drafts back, try to be glad rather than despairing if they are covered with corrections and comments. These will help you to 'craft and hone' your work and present it in the quite particular fashion required in a thesis. Remember that even after assiduous proof-reading (which you should always do), the most experienced of us sometimes indulge in over-long sentences or fail to make points clearly because they seem obvious to us.

Because supervisors will be seeking to improve your writing and lines of argument, you may need sometimes to request more positive feedback, such as which parts are written in the required style, to help you understand the expected standard. Do not be shy if this kind of feedback would help you. Also, seek out a range of potential informants in addition to your supervisors. Integrating this greater variety of feedback will help your individual writing style develop and mature.

Building up sources of support

Although supervisors may well be happy to provide a quick 'you are on the right track' (or not) kind of response when specifically requested, occasionally researchers might want some informal feedback on their work before showing it to supervisors. Feedback from people from outside your discipline focus, but familiar with doctoral requirements, also helps ensure that you explain ideas clearly to non-specialist readers. However, proof-reading and/or feedback provision are arduous tasks so you need to cultivate potential volunteers well in advance and consider how you could reciprocate. Peer support networks may already exist that you can tap into to find compatible colleagues with whom to share jubilation and frustrations, eventually building a bond suitable for reciprocal proof-reading. If not, then we urge you to take the initiative.

Invest in some coffee and buns and invite others in your department or faculty to an inaugural 'Doctoral Mutual Support Group' (or 'Scaredy Cats Club' as one of the authors did), choosing an appropriate title for your locality and needs. It will help to have a focus, such as a debate about a controversial research method, practice of a useful analysis technique or simply an exchange of research passions and problems. It need not be a very formal group; an ad hoc group that meets when inspired by a member's need or interest, at times and locations to suit those for whom it has relevance, often works well. Later, more experienced people might be invited to share their wisdom: postdocs, for example, might be persuaded to talk to your group or simply to you personally about your interests and challenges. Such a group can form the core of your network, remaining as active resources in a wide range of ways (as referees, co-authors, collaborative researchers, examiners for their own students, sources of wider contacts and so on) in later years.

It would be sensible to seek advice from your supervisors about which conferences to attend and when, so that you start with one that is supportive and encouraging of doctoral researchers – perhaps with a doctoral conference running before or in parallel with a main event, saving the more prestigious conference for nearer your completion to help you hone your arguments and deal with critical lines of questioning. Even then, we would advise attending such conferences alongside your supervisor. Most conferences are venues for meeting your favourite authors/researchers, providing opportunities to review the style and professional persona of potential examiners as well as making new network contacts.

TOP TIPS 6.1 MAKING THE MOST OF CONFERENCES

1 Set specific goals ahead of time: ideally, include at least one personal development goal, one knowledge-building goal and one networking goal. For example:

- Goal (1) Present paper. Goal (2) Learn about ________ technique. Goal (3) Make three new connections who use ________ approach.

2 If you are presenting, practise, practise, practise ahead of time:

- The more confident you feel, the better you will do.

3 Read abstracts and, if available, delegate lists ahead of time.
4 Identify key presentations and delegates that interest you:

- Read recent research papers by the presenters or delegates of interest.

5 Draw up a plan of what presentations/sessions you want to attend:

- Try to find ways to be in the same place at the same time as the people you are most interested in.

6 Do not skip the conference dinner!
- This is a great opportunity to make interesting contacts.
- Try to get a seat next to someone you want to add to your network.

(Continued)

(Continued)

7 Talk to people at the poster sessions:

- Poster sessions are perfect for meeting the researchers who have done the data collection, usually fellow doctoral researchers or sometimes postdoctoral fellows.
- Ask them to walk you through their poster.
- Ask questions.

8 Take your business cards and do not be shy to give them out:

- If you don't have any, get them made (inexpensive and swift delivery online).

9 In networking situations, listen more than you talk:

- Ask questions about people's research. Researchers love to talk about their own work.
- Smile and be friendly.
- Be enthusiastic about your research. You never know who may end up being the reviewer for your next paper or examiner for your doctorate.

10 Follow up the conference by emailing any people you talked with:

- A simple, 'It was lovely to chat with you at the ___ conference. Could you send me a copy of your paper we discussed?' would suffice.
- Sending people a LinkedIn request is also a good way to keep in touch.

Of course, passive conference or seminar attendance does not extend networks. What is required is listening and responding to others' presentations, approaching them at break times and showing interest in their work, hoping they reciprocate. Afterwards, you can follow up people who asked you questions during your presentation (especially if you did not have an answer at the time but said that the question was interesting so you would give it further thought!) as well as those whose presentations interested you. Be brave in making these kinds of contacts, including writing to authors of work that relates to yours and helps or intrigues you; you are likely to be surprised and gratified about how most academics and researchers are delighted to have their work appreciated. While you should avoid any potential examiners becoming friends or even substantial contributors to your project, you can interest them in it, and you may find others who can become good sources of feedback and fruitful debate. If you would like to establish such a relationship with another academic, be diplomatic by checking with your supervisors that they are comfortable with such an arrangement – in case they are sensitive to their expertise, support and feedback appearing to be rejected or superseded.

In case you, too, are sensitive or introverted, try not to reject these suggestions out of hand because it is impossible to over-value the benefits of professional networks. Sometimes, it helps to first make connections with the doctoral researchers of a famous academic, instead of approaching the professor directly. Especially in science disciplines, poster sessions are a fantastic opportunity to do this. These sessions present a perfect opportunity to meet and discuss research, usually with fellow newer researchers, without worrying about how you are going to start a conversation, since the poster content is the trigger.

Another way to extend your networks is through more formal, perhaps less daunting, activities such as volunteering to sit on a Staff Student Committee, representing your peers in a Postgraduate Student Union post or attending workshops and presentations outside your university. For instance, in the UK, the **Society for Research into Higher Education (SRHE)** provides workshops for the professional development of doctoral researchers and their Postgraduate Interest Network welcomes doctoral researchers to their programme of debates on a range of topics relevant to their research (www.srhe.ac.uk/events/). Similarly, the **UK Council for Graduate Education** (**UKCGE**: www.ukcge.ac.uk/) provides workshops and conferences in which researchers are very welcome participants. Other countries have similar organisations that gather together annually or bi-annually at international events, so opportunities abound to extend your networks and challenge your assumptions.

Dealing with disagreements and tensions

Most academics would confess to tending to be opinionated, so it is to be expected that differences of opinion will arise in academic work. Indeed, many will also confess to enjoying a good argument – in the sense that it provides opportunities to check your evidence and hone your propositions. As such, passionate debate or conflicts of opinion can be a positive benefit if they encourage sharper justifications of positions, raise awareness to the needs and values of others, stimulate creativity and promote change for the better. Nevertheless, they can be intimidating for newer researchers or for international researchers unused to such prevailing academic cultural customs, especially if they discover that different members of the supervisory team have diverging opinions on some significant issues (almost inevitable in academe). While in the past, we have urged supervisors to try to resolve their differences away from their doctoral researchers, there is a growing body of opinion and some evidence that discovering these differences, and hearing supervisors debate them, can be advantageous to researchers, alerting them to the tentative nature of 'truth' and requiring them to decide and defend their own viewpoints. If you find yourself in this position, remember that what is being challenged is only a viewpoint, not the person, and the purpose should be to clarify issues and seek mutually compatible solutions. This requires negotiation. Top Tips 6.2 provides some suggestions for how you might engage in such negotiation to achieve a positive outcome.

TOP TIPS 6.2 NEGOTIATING TO RESOLVE DIFFERENCES

Useful steps are:

1. Identify the problem, its main factors and further information required before the next step. (Take as much time as you need to do this; sometimes a little further information can resolve an impasse.)
2. Explore who is affected by the problem and how, and who might provide an informed sounding board. (This kind of problem may have arisen before and, indeed, have special procedures for resolution.)
3. Ensure that everyone's input is valued and each person has a voice. (A real solution cannot be achieved if parties feel that their opinion was not appropriately considered.) Sometimes it is helpful to have a neutral facilitator.
4. Brainstorm potential solutions, producing as wide a range of perspectives and ideas as possible. (Sometimes, apparently ridiculous ideas can have a spark of creativity that leads to resolution, or can provide a basis for opposing parties to agree on something to start with, if only that some ideas are preposterous.)
5. Consider how each potential solution will impact and by how much on key parties. (It may cause less angst to agree to differ on some points.)
6. Collate the best suggestions. (Again, the parties have an opportunity to agree on what might be viable.)
7. Work towards a consensus choice of outcome. (Each party can evaluate the pros, cons and what they can concede most readily, continuing to feel part of the give-and-take process.)
8. Make sure that the final decision is noted and ratified by all.

As for other relationships, it is possible, on rare occasions, for there to be an unresolvable incompatibility between supervisor and researcher. All universities have procedures to deal with that. Our advice, should you find yourself in that situation, is to find out what those procedures are. However, first find another member of staff, perhaps the departmental director of research, if not your other supervisor, to arbitrate a meeting between you and the supervisor you are having difficulty with. Often, you will find that the problem lies in conflicts between unarticulated expectations that each has of the other which can be resolved. If the problem is more serious, at least you will have behaved professionally by trying to resolve it, rather than ignoring it or taking inappropriately drastic steps. You will find such things emotionally draining though, and may feel as vulnerable, so get some support and allow time for a healing process.

Managing your emotions

Even without the serious issue of supervision incompatibility, you can expect doctoral study to proceed through a series of emotional ups and downs. Hopefully you began your studies with great enthusiasm. Furthermore, you will encounter moments of great joy and pride when your hard work pays off and you see your ideas coming to life. However, research as a process has intrinsic frustrations, large and small: the library not having the journal/book you need; the great idea being already studied by someone else; the equipment failing; the data collection process being slow and tedious; experiments 'going wrong'; promised participants not turning up; results being contradictory – OK, enough! Hence, in Chapter 1, we, and the Vitae Researcher Development Framework (Chapter 5), suggested that key attributes required of a researcher besides passion, are resilience and perseverance (Chapter 11). There might also be occasions when you feel inadequate as well as demotivated when several frustrating events occur in unison (often during the second year of full-time study). Take heart from the notion that we know this is common and that those who persevere usually pass the doctorate, even though their research may not proceed as expected. Moreover, having overcome their difficulties and drawn on resources, they discover themselves intellectually stronger. Those resources include supervisors (who generally prefer to be alerted to any low morale or stressed periods, no matter what their cause, so that they are afforded the opportunity to help) and the network of peers, supporters and critical friends we have urged you to establish.

However, you may simply need to get away from research activities temporarily to refresh your brain. One of us, having amassed much data, could see no significant patterns in it. It took three weeks of spring cleaning the house and garden, sinking into bed each night physically exhausted, for the patterns and significance to suddenly emerge unbidden. We cannot guarantee that it will work for you but suggest that sometimes a bout of physical activity helps the brain to work quietly, unstressed by pressure. If you plan such a break, remember to let your supervisor know so they recognise that you are confidence-building rather than giving up.

We have noted that researchers often remember the times when things have not worked out or the critical feedback that they have received disproportionately to the more positive events and successes. One way to enhance your experience as a researcher is to actively work to balance this out. Create a successes folder (physically or virtually) and fill it with your accomplishments. Things you may like to include: first literature review completed on time; first conference abstract accepted; supervisor said 'good idea'; audience member complemented your presentation; etc. There will be hundreds of little successes and a few major ones along the way. Keeping note of them can help you keep positive, despite problems on the way to success.

Becoming an authority

In the final stages of your doctorate it is likely that you will know more about your research topic than your supervisors because, in the end, you should be the expert on it, an emerging authority who can write and speak authoritatively (with credibility) about it. The way to build up your confidence about this is to subject yourself deliberately to increasing challenges, presenting your written work and your oral arguments first to those who will provide relatively gentle feedback (friends and family who think you are very clever), gradually increasing the testing nature of the encounters as we suggested in relation to conference presentations. It takes practice to garner information and evidence and present it in an informed, structured and clear way both in written work (Chapter 4) and in person in debates. This build-up process will be particularly helpful if your doctorate, as most do, culminates in a viva voce of some kind (Chapter 8). The award of the doctorate signifies to others that you indeed are an authority on your topic, and learned about related areas of your subject, even if you have become so humbled by the process that it is hard to believe it yourself.

Special points for part-time and distance doctoral researchers

All the advice we have provided here is relevant, but you should recognise the extra effort required to access the nuances of a culture and build up relations when you are seldom able to meet people face to face. An occasional campus visit can establish links with peers and staff to facilitate later correspondence by email, Skype or other electronic means. If that is not possible, try to put a face to your name by including in correspondence a small photograph while also building up a webpage or, for example, a LinkedIn profile so that people can have further glimpses into the person behind a signature. It is essential, also, that you build and maintain an online professional profile for people to keep up with you and for you to follow others in your area. Your supervisors will be able to engage with you more personally if you ensure that they know your timetable, your plans for working on your degree and how and when you can be contacted. Even if you have 'got behind' with your studies, if your other work or family must take precedence for a while, keep your supervisor informed and negotiate new contact and delivery times (project planning will be vital – see Chapter 3 and Appendix I). They will recognise that it takes special attention and energy to constantly swap cultures, not simply between study and home like other researchers but also between work and study and home.

Such a diverse personal programme can also be challenging for your family, friends and work colleagues to adapt to. It will serve you well in the long run to plan a study timetable and alert those people to it as well as your supervisor. It will save you time and frustration explaining to your friends that just because you are at home does not mean you are now at leisure! Some part-time or distance students find it useful to find a 'hidden place' to study, be it the local library or a garden shed. However, take care not to become too isolated. Critical feedback that feels constructive when accompanied by a supervisor's smile can be perceived as quite devastating when received coldly in writing after a long day at work.

Special points related to different disciplines

Frequently, in the sciences and engineering (STEMM), researchers work as part of a team with a senior academic, often in a lab or equivalent shared space whereas in other disciplines research is more independent, contact with academics being less frequent. However, scientists and engineers should not consider frequent lab-based contact with their supervisors as equivalent to supervision sessions focused on the development of the doctoral project. In those disciplines, although you are likely to be working on a project originally designed by your supervisors due to the constraints of experimental work and equipment, make certain that you have special discussion time with them on your aspect of the project, and how your doctoral studies are evolving.

If you are a social scientist or studying in the arts and humanities (HASS), then you are more likely to have the advantage of working on an issue with personal salience, through a process designed by you. However, that may well mean that data/information collection occurs at a much later stage during your registration. Thus, interpret your progress accordingly and do not panic if you hear that your STEMM peers are accumulating data when you are still refining your research questions.

These differences are another reason to communicate well with your immediate peers so that, although all doctorates differ, you can get a sense of the parameters for studying a doctorate in your discipline. Making collegiate links more widely across disciplines, gaining understanding of the different practices and constraints, will prepare you for the world of employment in which the pace of different processes is necessarily different (Chapter 12). You will also appreciate the patience and understanding required in cross- or multi-disciplinary research.

References and further reading 

Becher, T. (1989) *Academic Tribes and Territories: Intellectual Enquiry and the Cultures of Disciplines.* Buckingham: SRHE and Open University Press.

Crotty, M. (2003) *The Foundations of Social Research.* London: Sage.

Fox, K. (2004) *Watching the English: The Hidden Rules of English Behaviour.* London: Hodder & Stoughton.

Hall, G. and Longman, J. (eds) (2008) *The Postgraduate's Companion.* London: Sage. See chapter 8, 'The supervision process and nature of research degrees', by P. Denicolo and L. Becker, and chapter 9, 'Managing the research process and the supervisory relationship', by L. Becker and P. Denicolo.

Morris, D. (2002) *People Watching: The Desmond Morris Guide to Body Language.* London: Vintage.

7

HOW CAN YOU PREPARE FOR SUCCESSFUL FORMAL REVIEWS DURING THE DOCTORATE?

In this chapter, we will consider how to:

- Take more control of your doctorate's formal review processes, ensuring that you get the feedback you need
- Understand how various stages of the doctorate may be assessed
- Become familiar with what you need to do to meet expectations at these stages

Assessment of progress

To understand how to make a process or procedure work for you, you must first understand the purpose of it, and the intended benefits.

Progress reviews: Why have them?

What is the purpose of formal reviews within the doctoral process? From a university point of view, it is to ensure that a doctorate is on track for timely completion. Much of this university perspective is due to increasing pressure to make sure that doctorates are completed within a given period (Chapter 1). In days gone by, when there were fewer doctoral candidates, research could go on for years. Today, the review process helps to encourage early identification of problems and reflection on whether the current lines of enquiry are going to plan. It also requires the creation of specific objectives that will help track progress towards them.

The university perspective may feel quite far removed from you as an individual doctoral researcher; the likely timeframe for your doctorate should be a salient consideration for you as well. Even at its most enjoyable, a doctoral degree is not something you should be doing forever nor are you likely to be able to afford to be a perennial doctoral researcher.

Furthermore, in working with thousands of doctoral researchers over the years, we find that concern about progress comes up frequently, with questions along the lines of: 'Am I doing enough?' 'Am I doing the right thing?'; 'Am I on track?' This is because the unique and individual nature of the doctorate makes it hard for a newer researcher to judge their own progress. In taught courses, you have learning objectives linked to assignments and assessments and these tell you how well you are doing. In doctoral research, there can be a void of three to four years (or the part-time equivalent) to produce that nebulous (and perhaps daunting) entity: new knowledge. Certainly, there will be points within the process when you will feel you cannot remember where you began and have no idea where you will end up. It is not uncommon to have this 'lost at sea' feeling, to continue the metaphor from Chapter 1, especially so in the middle stages of the research process. Therefore, the review process can provide a structure of support as well as forced moments of consideration and evaluation of your progress. Further, it is only by reviewing or reflecting on what we have done that we can recognise the value within it.

Each institution has its own rules about the frequency and timing of formal reviews; in the UK, these are frequently set at annual intervals, usually just before the end of each year of registration so that, if some re-orientation or catching up is required, it will not be so great as to be impossible to incorporate into the process. Even in the worst case scenarios, researchers will generally be given an opportunity to improve their situation, but most often the formal review has a more positive and constructive purpose. One of the key aims of these review points is to prevent you from reaching the end of several years' work, only to be told in the viva to go back to the beginning and start again. The review process is, then, a formal recognition by the institution of its obligations towards researchers. Formal reviews act as a point to re-orient yourself and reflect on where you have been, to establish if you are on track, to consider any ethical issues (which you may have overlooked or not been aware of) and decide whether you should carry on in the current direction or perhaps need to adjust the navigation a bit. However, this process only works if you engage fully and honestly with it. A good review should feature reflective practice, realistic project planning, as well as a professional development focus. You should leave the process with clear ideas about what to do next or soon.

Reflective practice: A balance between the American and British versions

As a writing team, the authors are international, with American, British and European perspectives represented. We greatly value these cultural difference as all have their strengths and weaknesses, which we can share with you. We note that when it comes to approaching reviews, the American and British can be quite different. Americans tend to play to their strengths and have learnt to be fabulous at listing accomplishments and putting a general positive spin on things. On the other hand, the British seem to be extremely capable when it comes to dissecting every problem, wrong turn and laying out exactly what has come in the way of progress during any given period. However, a good review is balanced, featuring equally accomplishments and challenges, with reflection on what they mean in the context of the research and for the progress of your project. Therefore, no matter what your nationality, it helps to adopt both approaches described above … resisting extremes (a challenge we know!). To help you with this, we have suggested a series of questions to consider in Reflection Point 7.1.

REFLECTION POINT 7.1

QUESTIONS TO ASK YOURSELF TO REVIEW THE SUCCESS OF YOUR PROJECT

- What has worked well? (During this week/month/quarter or year?)
  - Why did it work well?
  - What skills have you brought to bear or developed to make these things work?
- What are you most proud of?
  - Why are you particularly proud of this accomplishment?
  - What did you do? What skills did you use?
- What has not worked as well as planned?
  - Why has it not worked? Or was delayed?
  - What did you do to try to make it work?
  - What might you need to do to rescue the situation?
  - Do you need to further develop your own skills and knowledge to make this work or do you think it just is not the way forward?
- What does this mean for your research?
  - Does it have theoretical implications?
  - Does it have implications for your overall research plan?
  - What is your next step and why?

Moving forward

The real key to a successful review is that it should be forward-looking. It is important to reflect on the past in order to learn from your experiences. However, even more critical is that after a review meeting, you have a very clear sense of where your research is going. You must have a plan both for your research project and for your own development, with objectives that you plan to accomplish within specific timelines. This helps you and everyone else know whether you are on track or not. When you look at your accomplishments and your challenges, you should be able to see how well your progress maps on to your expected research plan. Therefore, in every formal review, you should create specific objectives that help you reach an ultimate research goal.

Note that we did specifically mention a 'plan for your own development' as well and it is worth emphasising that any review (even a personal one) should not be all about the research; you need to have the professional skills-set, qualities and attitude, as well as the actual knowledge, to carry out the project. Your development is something that sometimes gets neglected. Usually this is not intentional. Often, it can be just because you and your supervisors get so excited about the research that all parties forget everything else. However, your professional and career development are critical to your success both during your doctorate and beyond, so it is important for you and your supervisors to take the time to prioritise and plan this as well, irrespective of what you may hope to do after you have successfully completed.

Mid-stage examinations: Understanding expectations and preparing for success

Different countries and different doctoral programmes have quite varied approaches to mid-stage assessments/examinations. For example, in the United States there are often qualifying examinations, which consist of formal tests of one's breadth and depth of knowledge of the chosen field, whereas in the UK and other countries the transfer/upgrade/confirmation examination focuses more specifically on an individual's research project. This demonstrates the variability of the structure and content of these processes which makes it quite hard to discuss details in a book that aims to be helpful and relevant to doctoral researchers globally. However, there are specific skills and expectations of researchers at this level that are universal. Furthermore, there are some strategies that all researchers can use that should help them prepare to impress their examiners, despite the differences in format and nomenclature. We are using here the terms 'mid-stage assessment' or 'examination' to encapsulate all the formal activities applied at selected intervals that are used to evaluate project progress and skill development during doctoral study of any kind in any university or country.

A critical skill

Certainly, one skill area that is universally important to develop to a high level over the course of a doctorate is critical thinking, especially in relation to evaluation of research literature and others' and own research. This is a skill that, although important at other levels of education, is quantitatively and qualitatively different in nature at this level. Critical thought is truly central to achieving a doctorate. Therefore, much of the first year or so of doctoral study is designed to help hone this skill. Furthermore, most (if not all) mid-stage assessments require researchers to demonstrate critical analysis, most commonly through writing and/or discussing the strengths and weaknesses of different research studies/approaches/methods/findings (Chapter 4). We provide an opportunity to practise this skill in Activity 7.2.

Common mistakes made in reviewing the literature or evaluating research methods are describing, instead of critiquing, or focusing solely on finding fault, instead of on providing a balanced academic evaluation. Whether you are answering questions for a qualifying examination or writing a document/report/proposal/chapters for your mid-stage assessment, your examiners will be wanting more than just a description of past research done in your field. Of course, you should know the **seminal research**, but you also need to know why it was seminal and be able to place in within the story of the discipline and context. What were its strengths? In what ways did this specific research move the field forward? What are its weaknesses? All research has weaknesses, even if it is published in the most prestigious journal in the field, but good researchers note the limitations of their research and can suggest ways to improve replications of it; remember that when writing your final thesis chapters. Importantly, although 'critical' can mean find fault with, the academic usage of the term 'critical evaluation' is more balanced. This is something that even seasoned academics forget! Thus, when deciding what your research focus will be and how it will be explored, consider all the current research in the field and draw conclusions based on evaluation of multiple works that use different theoretical perspectives or approaches/methods.

ACTIVITY 7.1 LEARNING TO BE CRITICAL

Find a group of research papers (between four and eight), all investigating a selected topic/phenomenon (these could be papers that you are already familiar with):

1 Do they all come to the same or similar conclusions? If not, which one(s) do you think has a stronger argument? What evidence is used to support their case and how strong is that evidence?
2 Are some of them more rigorous in approach than others? What checks and balances in the procedures were used to improve rigour?
3 Are there aspects of the studies that you think could have been done better or differently? What would be your argument to justify such changes?
4 How well were the various contentions presented? How could they support the position more effectively?
5 Looking at the whole collection, what is your overall opinion of this area and what evidence would you use to support that view?

Arguing your case

Another area that is important for this mid-stage assessment, and for the final viva, is your ability to construct an argument and justify the various decisions you have made (or are making) as you design and conduct your research. This justification draws from your critique and extends to logical decision making. A strong argument proposes something and then weaves the research literature together to demonstrate a coherent and systematic approach with evidence to support it. At doctoral level, the depth of this justification is often underestimated at first. So much so that at times, supervisor feedback can be quite monosyllabic, with one word appearing repeatedly: 'Why?; Why?' or even just '?' Although this may feel frustrating, what supervisors are trying to do is deepen the argument. At doctoral level, you must not just answer the first why, but dig down several levels of justification. It is this type of thought and argument construction that examiners want to see emerging and then growing in progressive mid-stage reviews, so that it will be competently demonstrated in the thesis and final viva, if the latter is included as a final assessment (see the next chapter). Activity 7.2 provides an opportunity to practise a technique for digging deeper.

ACTIVITY 7.2 THE 5 WHYS 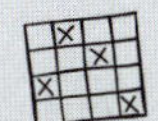

Begin by asking the question 'Why' of a subject and try to come up with TWO answers. You could begin with your research topic: 'I am studying X … Why? Because of A and B.' Repeat, asking 'why' of each subsequent answer, still finding two responses to the question each time, and make a note of your new answers, following the pattern in Figure 7.1. By five **iterations**, usually something interesting happens – that is, some lines of enquiry appear more fruitful than others, revealing both the nature of the problem and, often, the solution.

Originally designed by Sakichi Toyoda for the Toyota Motor Corporation and used to identify root cause problems with processes, the 5 Whys is a useful tool for researchers – especially when projects become stuck.

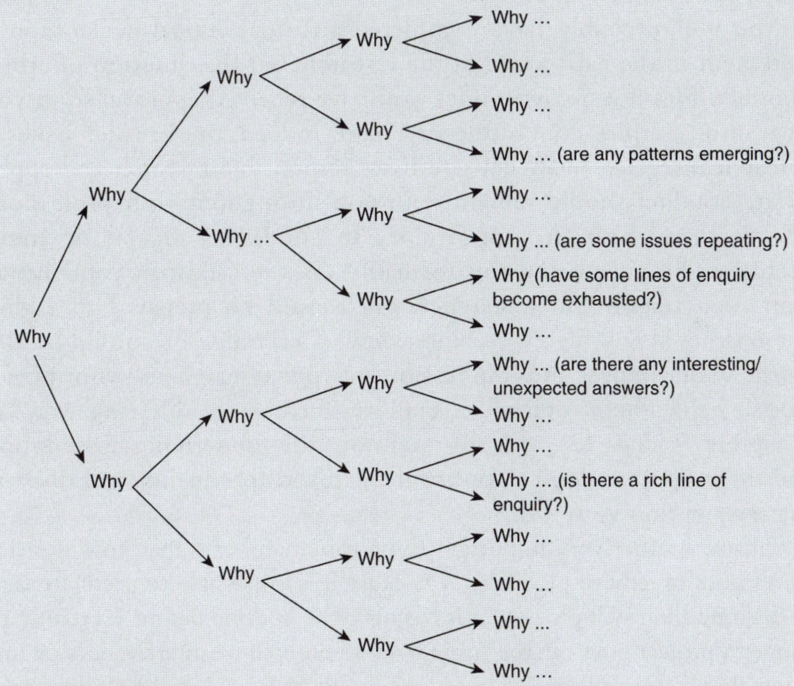

FIGURE 7.1 The 5 Whys

Mapping the journey

For any mid-stage examination that is evaluating your doctoral project proposal or interim report, a key aspect will be assessing whether the research project planning is realistic and ethical. Realistic plans are based on evidence, not wishful thinking. Therefore, you should seek advice from your supervisor and other more experienced researchers about how long various sections of your research project will take; at the same time, keep track of your own progress and how long it takes you to do various tasks. People are all different, so what takes one person two weeks may take another person a month, especially if the latter is less experienced. Equally, some people can readily cope with several simultaneous activities (multi-tasking), while others work better when focusing mainly on separate tasks sequentially. Although it may not always be possible to arrange your project exactly to suit your preferences, do try to work to your own strengths rather than mimicking others.

You will, probably, have completed a formal ethical declaration or statement in the early stage of the research, but the question of ethical conduct does not go away once you have received approval from your institution's ethics committee or board. Indeed, the broader issues of research integrity and what counts as responsible research and appropriate conduct should remain with you throughout your professional life. You may have the opportunity to conduct a regular or annual ethical audit, but even if this formality does not exist in your institution, as a responsible researcher you should be prepared to address these issues at any review (or interview). Certainly, you should be alert to the wider impact and implications of your research and your professional behaviour (topics we explore further in differing ways in Chapters 9 and 12), not to mention the underlying assumptions (be these epistemological, political or linked to equality and diversity matters) within your work.

Finally, another very important thing to remember is that novel research never goes exactly to plan. This is because it is impossible to predict exactly how something will proceed if it has never been done before. Certainly, the longer a project goes on, the more likely there will be interferences or incidents that create unforeseen situations. As we indicated in the Prologue, not only does life happen whilst you are undertaking a doctorate, but also when things go wrong this can be a cause for celebration and a benefit rather than a disaster, as the status quo or 'general expectation', is challenged. The definition of a doctorate is 'novel' or 'original' research, so a good doctoral research plan includes room for contingency. See Activity 7.3 to learn key aspects of contingency planning.

ACTIVITY 7.3 CONTINGENCY PLANNING

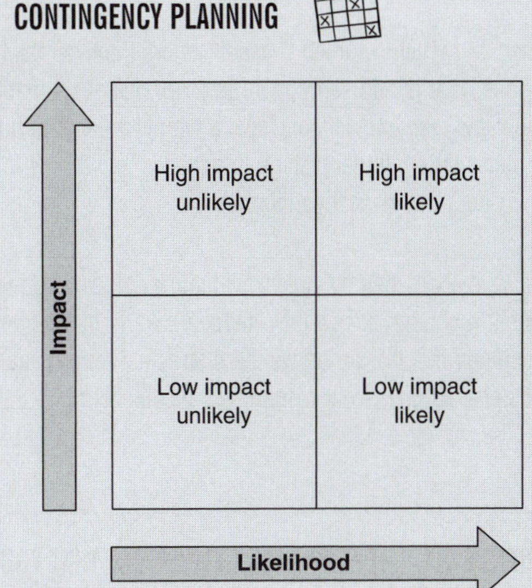

FIGURE 7.2 Contingency matrix

Using Figure 7.2:

Step 1: Think of all the potential risks to completing your research project on time. Example: Key equipment breaking down, surveys not returned, personal health problems. Try to think of as many as possible.

Step 2: Rate the likelihood of these problems happening from low to high. If you do not know, then perhaps discuss this with your supervisor or another experienced researcher.

Step 3: Rate the impact of this risk on your ability to complete your project on time from low to high.

Step 4: Starting with any risks that have both high impact and high likelihood, think about what you could do to reduce the likelihood of this happening and/or reduce the impact of it on your project. Note: sometimes, likelihood is out of your control, but you can almost always reduce impact. For example, if key equipment breaks down, you can reduce the impact by having identified in advance an alternative piece of equipment that can be used. If you suspect that the return rate on surveys may be low, you can have a plan to follow up with phone interviews or send out a greater number of surveys than you originally envisaged. If you cannot afford a transcriber for interviews, plan in

(Continued)

(Continued)

extra time for transcribing them yourself – usually, more than you think you need (this is the 'and some' rule, that is add some more to your original estimation, just in case you need it). If you know that you will only have a limited amount of time in a specialist lab or to use specialist equipment, think in advance about how to maximise your time, rather than hoping for or expecting more time.

Contingency planning is about identifying and evaluating risk, and putting plans in place to deal with potential problems before they happen. Like formal reviews, contingency planning can sometimes feel like an unwanted distraction from research in progress, but can save heartache, as one of our researchers recalls below.

VOICE OF EXPERIENCE 7.1 IT IS ONLY IN RETROSPECT THAT YOU REALISE …

I was immersed in my data collection when my supervisor reminded me that I needed to prepare a review report. What a nuisance, just when it was all flowing nicely! Begrudgingly, I set to, prepared the report and proudly summarised my results so far. I was flabbergasted when the internal assessors suggested that I had neglected to explore a recurring feature of the data. How did I miss it? The rest of the results were confirming what I had expected, but this aspect might be an aberration or something significant. I had to go back and explore it more. It turned out to be a turning point in my research, leading to a 'significant contribution to knowledge'! (*Education Researcher*)

References and further reading 

Abdul Molok, N.N., Ahmad, A. and Chang, S. (2011) 'Exploring the use of online social networking by employees: looking at the potential for information leakage', PACIS 2011 Proceedings, online at: http://aisel.aisnet.org/pacis2011/138/. A good example of an 'upgrade' or confirmation paper, with nice timeline and methods diagrams at the end.

Denicolo, P. and Reeves, J. (2014) 'How can skill development be evidenced, assessed and evaluated?', chapter 8 in *Success in Research: Developing Transferable Skills.* London: Sage.

Golding, C., Sharmini, S. and Lazarovitch, A. (2013) 'What examiners do: What thesis students should know', *Assessment and Evaluation in Higher Education*, 35 (5): 563–76.

Holbrook, A., Bourke, S., Fairbairn, H. and Lovatt, T. (2007) 'Examiner comment on the literature review in PhD theses', *Studies in Higher Education*, 32 (3): 337–56.

Also check out 'confirmation processes' at The Thesis Whisperer, online at https://thesiswhisperer.com/.

8

WHAT ARE THE CRITERIA AND HOW CAN YOU PREPARE TO DO WELL IN THE FINAL ASSESSMENT?

In this chapter, we will consider how to:

- Get into the minds of doctoral examiners so that you can prepare and respond well to the criteria they use
- Understand the criteria used when assessing the thesis
- Provide an insight into the closed room and shed light onto its secrets, for those of you who will be facing a viva voce as part of your assessment system
- Look forward to your accumulated accomplishments

We have chosen to preface this chapter with a salient reflection from a researcher.

VOICE OF EXPERIENCE 8.1 JOURNEY INTO THE UNKNOWN

In my department, there seemed to be an implicit rule that the process of the viva was not spoken about: it was a rite of passage in which candidates went off to a room, thesis under arm, only to appear later for a celebratory tea and talk of the future. As the time approached for my 'initiation ceremony' I became more and more convinced that I might be the only one of my colleagues not to deserve the special celebration. The night before my viva I had a nightmare. I stood in the wings of a brightly lit stage,

(Continued)

(Continued)

with the examiners seated at a table on the other side. When I looked down, I realised that the stage was pitted with wide holes that I must negotiate to reach the table. Just as I stepped forward with trepidation, someone placed a blindfold over my eyes. I awoke in a panic.

Fortunately, my actual experience was less traumatic and I did pass with only a few typographical errors to correct. I later understood that the secrecy was built from fear of those facing the viva, insouciance on the part of supervisors and a degree of memory loss on the part of recent successful candidates, perhaps akin to mothers forgetting birth pangs once the baby arrives. Nevertheless, that dream has recurred in my life at times of stress. However, I now see it as a helpful warning to find out as much as possible about the fear-engendering situation so that I can confront it appropriately. One more lesson from the doctorate!

(Dr Carol Boulter – science education researcher)

Carol suggests that future candidates should learn from her story, making sure that they find out in advance as much as they can about the process of demonstrating doctorateness to the examiners and prepare accordingly.

Demonstrating doctorateness

In most countries, the final examination of the doctorate consists of two components: the examination of the written dissertation and the viva voce or dissertation defence (for simplicity, we will now just use the term 'viva'). The weighing of these two components and the way in which vivas are conducted vary tremendously across countries, disciplines and even institutions. It would be wise to investigate, early in your doctoral registration, the detailed structure of the final assessment in your own context so that you can prepare for it accordingly as you proceed. However, doctoral examinations in all contexts require an **external examiner** (generally an academic from another institution). These examiners, over the course of an academic career, gain international experience, examining, presenting and working around the world. Thus, there is more international commonality and consistency about the expectations at this level than one might initially think. This is an important aspect of the doctorate, whatever its format and structure, especially in the now truly global research context.

What are examiners looking for? What are the 'learning objectives' of the doctorate? The Dublin Descriptors (Information Box 8.1) are a good place to start in answering this question, because they are an agreed set of guidelines across nations within the European context. Compare these international descriptors with the criteria laid out in your own institution's regulations in Activity 8.1.

INFORMATION BOX 8.1 DUBLIN DESCRIPTORS FOR THE THIRD CYCLE (DOCTORATE)

Qualifications that signify completion of the Third Cycle [doctoral level] are awarded to students who:

- have demonstrated a systematic understanding of a field of study and mastery of the skills and methods of research associated with that field;
- have demonstrated the ability to conceive, design, implement and adapt a substantial process of research with scholarly integrity;
- have made a contribution through original research that extends the frontier of knowledge by developing a substantial body of work, some of which merits national or international refereed publication;
- are capable of critical analysis, evaluation and synthesis of new and complex ideas;
- can communicate with their peers, the larger scholarly community and with society in general about their areas of expertise;
- can be expected to be able to promote, within academic and professional contexts, technological, social or cultural advancement in a knowledge based society.

www.vitae.ac.uk/policy/dublin-descriptors-for-doctorate-mar-2004-vitae.pdf (p. 3, accessed 27 April 2017).

ACTIVITY 8.1 YOUR INSTITUTION'S REGULATIONS

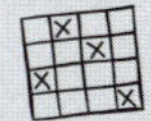

Every institution/doctoral programme should state the specific requirements to obtain a doctorate in that organisation. Look in your local handbook or university regulations to answer the questions below. If you do not know where to find these, ask your supervisor or programme administrator:

1. What are the requirements for doctoral candidates to obtain the award of their doctoral degree?
2. How do your institution's requirements compare to the Dublin Descriptors?

(Continued)

(Continued)

3 How does your institution assess the doctorate? Is there a viva or not?
4 If there is a viva, what do the regulations say about the format of the viva?
5 What are the potential outcomes of final examination at your institution? Particularly check the maximum time allowed for corrections/revisions of various kinds – see the discussion under 'Enjoying the Final Stretch'.

Once you understand what the learning objectives are, you can make sure that you clearly demonstrate that you meet them in both the written thesis/dissertation and in the viva if required. One universal requirement of a doctorate is novelty. How your work is innovative and unique should be made obvious to your examiners. Do not make them work hard to figure this out. Say it, write it. In the abstract, you may not want to give away the whole novel punch line, but you must signal to the examiners and other readers that there is an original or novel outcome, what its general nature is and where to find it in your work. This might be, for example, that a question is answered, a problem resolved, a solution found, ways forward recommended for specific circumstances. Or it may be several of these; be aware that novelty can be in many places within your research. Obviously, your main finding should contribute something new to the field, but equally, your approach/methodology/techniques may well be a key aspect of your research innovation. The way you use theory or integrate ideas from past research or draw upon literary/theatrical or musical genres for your own creative piece, may provide a unique perspective in your field, if so, this, too, is 'originality'. Identify such things explicitly; it is not the examiners' job to guess it or try to dig it out.

Something else you want your examiners to appreciate is your ability to analyse and interpret your work. The ideas that you propose based on your findings or through your arguments should show your ability to conceptualise and bring forth novel ideas. You should also then demonstrate the applicability of these ideas in relation to theory and/or practice. So, for your project, think about the various ways in which your research is adding something new to your field, and bring that contribution to knowledge to the examiners' attention.

Another consistent requirement of a doctorate is 'systematic study' and the ability to design, conduct, interpret and critique research independently. This draws on the skills of critical thinking and writing (see Chapter 4) as well as argument construction discussed in the previous chapter in relation to the work of others, but now applied to your own project. As we indicated earlier, you should be able both to give a strong and justified argument for all the choices you have made, and to identify the weakness and limitations in your own research. By the end of your doctorate you must be able to do this entirely independently, such that the examiners are convinced that you possess these abilities and you are not just doing what your supervisor has said you should do. This should be evident in your writing (see Chapter 4 for the most common problems with the written thesis), and in your viva responses. Remember that it is your work and you must be able to defend it. You also should be able to demonstrate that you can take this learning forward by extrapolating your research findings to other relevant areas of interest. A discussion of this kind of research impact (Chapter 9) is useful in your final thesis chapters and is often explored further in the viva.

The most common mistakes in thesis/dissertation writing are an overemphasis on the detailed 'whats' and 'hows' of the research, and not enough discussion of the 'whys' and 'so whats'. This is understandable to some extent because, as doctoral candidates, you spend a huge amount of time working out what you are going to do and exactly how you are going to do it. Indeed, you certainly will need to provide details of what you did and how you did it. However, examiners tend to be much more interested in understanding your thought processes behind these decisions. Therefore, for every 'what' and 'how' you write, ensure that you also include why you did this and the importance of this approach to your overall research objectives. Looking at the learning objectives for the doctorate can help you to understand why.

We provide, in Appendix IVA, a 'Summary of Criteria Used by Many Examiners for Assessing the Written Thesis', created by social science examiners with annotation by colleagues from the sciences, humanities and arts. Check with your supervisors how relevant these may be in your field – we suspect that many requirements are common across the range of disciplines.

To reiterate what we highlighted in Chapter 1, the goal of a doctorate is much more than a report about the conduct and outcome of piece of novel research; it is the development of a person who is capable of independently conducting novel research and then using that research to move their academic field forward and benefit society. A doctorate is not about the research project alone; it is about you. For us, this is the most truly rewarding part about working with doctoral researchers, watching them change and evolve over time and reflecting back with them about how far they have come. You will be amazed by how much you will develop. It is well worth reflecting on these developments along the way, as well as at the end, because how you deal with complex questions that require critical reflection is one of the criteria used by examiners in the viva. They will also be interested to explore with you further (than you can convey in the written thesis which will have word restrictions as noted in your institutional regulations) how you dealt with challenges during the research process.

Next, we try to provide insight into the viva process for those of you who will engage in such a process. For those whose doctorates are not assessed in this format, it might be worth you reading about it because the issues explored will be examined in a more implicit way through your written work. Thus, you can ensure that you answer in that written work the kinds of questions that arise in a typical viva.

An insight into the viva

Most countries have vivas as part of the final assessment of the doctorate, with the notable exception of Australia, although they do not all take the same form (for instance, some are private activities with a small number of participants, as in the UK, while others are public events with a potentially large audience, as in the Americas and many other European countries). They all do involve questioning of the candidate by at least two examiners, one of whom is not a member of the award-granting institution. Why is this kind of double assessment so popular at doctoral level? What purpose does the viva serve that is not served solely from assessing the thesis alone? The answer to this is more complicated than most doctoral researchers appreciate prior to undertaking a viva.

One interesting aspect of the process is that the examiners will have already read the thesis and come to specific conclusions about the quality and likely outcomes of the whole assessment process prior to the viva even starting. The level of certainty in this outcome does vary from country to country, depending on the formal procedures. In some European countries, for instance in some universities in Denmark, examiners provide candidates with feedback and lists of thesis revisions prior to the viva, so that the viva is simply the oral examination of the completed, polished post-revision work. In other countries, the viva is generally done prior to any feedback from the examiners and suggested revisions and corrections are based both on their reading of the dissertation and the viva itself. However, in all cases, the examiners are not entering the room without an opinion on the work. Furthermore, most research on the viva shows that these opinions are usually quite accurate reflections of the final outcomes of the viva (Trafford and Leshem, 2002). If this is true, why have the viva at all?

One critical reason for a viva is to ensure that the work done in the thesis is in fact the work of the candidate. The obtaining of a doctorate in a field is a licence to practise research. This is not something that is taken lightly by academic examiners, who are the gatekeepers of their disciplines. They must be assured that you, not your supervisor or anyone else, wrote this thesis and conducted the research. It is fine to have worked in a collaborative team and have had support and guidance from your supervisor, but by the end there should be a substantial work that was created solely by you. In this sense, the viva confirms that you are the person who should be given the title 'doctor'.

Another reason to have the viva as a form of assessment is to facilitate deeper exploration into areas that were less well developed in the thesis, to determine your understanding of them and perhaps seek to improve the final thesis document. Even the best written theses have their weaker points. When examiners are reading through this large book of work, they are looking very carefully for the parts that are weak. This may sound a bit scary; however, this is a very important piece of work, so you and they want it to be as good as possible. The examiners are, in a sense, working with you to strengthen your work and make it a piece you will always be proud of. This does mean they will ask questions about these weak points and push you to construct ever more powerful arguments, as well as to consider aspects that perhaps you overlooked. In this way, the viva is a final developmental tool.

In fact, examiners often focus quite a bit more on the developmental purpose of the viva than the simple assessment purpose. When examiners read a thesis that sparks their interest, they want to engage with you as a researcher, and to help you develop your ideas even more. Many examiners view the viva as an opportunity to see exactly how far you can go with your discussion of your work within the field, to see how well you can defend your arguments. Therefore, the best thing for you to do as a candidate in the viva is take this opportunity to stretch yourself and enjoy being able to talk in depth and at such length with experts in your field about your research. It is rare to have such an opportunity to have the undivided attention of senior academics for so long, especially as they may be among the few to have read your whole thesis thoroughly. See Voice of Experience Box 8.2 for an examiner's view on the process.

VOICE OF EXPERIENCE 8.2 THE OTHER SIDE OF THE DOCTORAL ASSESSMENT – AN EXAMINER'S PERSPECTIVE

Assessing a doctorate is at one and the same time a demanding, agonising process and, usually, a great joy and stimulation. We have the dilemma of knowing how much it means to the candidate (and their supervisor and institution) while having to ensure that standards are maintained to honour all those who have also struggled to gain this accolade.

(Continued)

(Continued)

For that latter reason, too, it is important to be rigorous, to ensure that questions are asked that challenge the candidate to deliver their best responses, either orally or in writing, while recognising that they are justifiably nervous in a viva, because this is such an important occasion.

Once a candidate has settled into a viva process the debate can be extremely stimulating. Reading about a project in the thesis that should be at the cutting edge of the field is very thought-provoking and, yes, exciting. It makes me remember why I am so interested in my field.

It is not just the candidate who has difficulty sleeping the night before a viva; I, too, worry – about whether my questions will be testing enough but clear enough to help them provide a great response; whether they will be able to 'fill in' any blanks we examiners have spotted or rise to any challenges we make to their arguments. We do know what is at stake and want to bring out the best in the candidates, especially if we have been inspired by their creativity/ingenuity or their stamina/perseverance or any combination of those things that a doctorate demands.

It is also rewarding to be able to help successful candidates to continue with their careers, perhaps suggesting what sections of the thesis will make good contributions as articles in specified journals, or inviting them to speak at conferences or contribute to a book, adding another colleague to our own networks.

(Examiner of more than 100 doctorates)

Given the importance of a viva, you can see that it is well worth preparing thoroughly for it. We suggest that you ask your supervisors to provide you with a mock viva, encourage as many friends and colleagues as possible to quiz you on aspects of your research and practise answering some of the questions we refer to below.

Questions about questions

'What are they going to ask?', 'What if I don't know the answer?', 'What if I lose the ability to speak?', 'How can I prepare?'

These are all among the most common questions we hear when we talk to doctoral researchers about the final viva examination. Of course, there is no way we can predict what questions you will be asked. However, there are some common question types, which can give you an idea of what you may expect. You are likely to be asked about why you have taken specific approaches, used specific theories, chosen specific methods. When you are asked these types of questions, the examiners are looking for your ability to justify your research decisions with a coherent and critical argument, as discussed above. Some of these decisions may have been made for very pragmatic reasons, for example resource availability, cost/practicality or supervisor expertise/direction. However, examiners are looking for a more robust answer related to rigour in the research. It is fine to be pragmatic and you can mention specific resource constraints in your answer, but, at the same time, make sure that you can make a strong and reasoned case for the advantages reaped because of your decisions. The answer 'it was all we could afford' is not going to serve you well in a viva. When finance is limited then the research questions and design should recognise that. In fact, while there are not any true 'right' answers, because there are always multiple valid arguments, there is one truly wrong answer: 'My supervisor told me to.' This is your doctorate, so even if a decision was made on the advice of your supervisor, you must be able to argue and defend the scientific (technical and/or theoretical) merits of your choices.

Two other important types of questions relate to identifying your main contributions and expanding on this to discuss the further implications of your findings. Answering these types of questions well shows 'doctorateness', which means that you meet a main criterion necessary for a doctorate. It is good advice to be able, quite concisely, to state your main contributions to knowledge, ideally in a couple of sentences. This is something you can craft ahead of time and will very likely come in handy during the viva. Also, make sure you are comfortable not only talking about the wider implications of your contribution in the context of your academic discipline, but also thinking about potential impacts on professions, industry, culture, society or the economy. The latter may not be directly relevant to all types of research, but, increasingly, this is something researchers are required to be aware of (Chapter 9) and, as examiners are fellow researchers, they may expert you to be aware, too.

Particularly challenging questions are those that require you to reflect on the weakness or limitations of your work. Inevitably there will be some areas that you are less happy with throughout such an expansive body of work. However, you do want to approach these questions with care, while still showing honest reflection. You do not want to undermine the very fabric of your thesis, although it is quite likely that in hindsight you would have done something differently, which might well improve either the research process or some aspect of the results. However, while recognising this in your response, it is also good to point out that this may not have been something you could have known without making the decisions that you did in the first place. Therefore, not only do your results progress the field but also your reflection on the process of obtaining them allows you to make suggestions about improvements in research practice in the field!

In Activity 8.2 we list some of the questions that we have gathered together from a wide range of doctoral examinations across the disciplines and in different contexts. We have amended the wording of real examples to reduce repetition and to make them more generic. Of course, you may not get any of these exact questions in your viva, though we would be astounded if the topics they represent do not emerge in some form.

ACTIVITY 8.2 VIVA PRACTICE: THEMATIC QUESTIONS FROM VIVA VOCE EXAMINATIONS

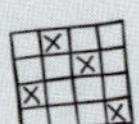

Below are some questions typically asked in a viva, designed to generically fit a range of disciplines. This activity can work any time but is ideal to practise in your final year, whilst you are finishing your thesis writing:

1 Practise answering questions from each major category, by yourself and then get others to ask you some of the questions.
2 Start thinking of other possible questions as well, including the question or questions you most dread being asked.
3 Continue to practise answering these new questions with a variety of people, ideally including your supervisor.

Introductory questions

Scene setting, allowing candidate to begin talking with enthusiasm, to explore motivation, etc.:

- What led to your interest in this topic?
- What stimulated your decision to explore this specific area?
- Why do you think this topic is important?
- What is your personal/professional position in relation to these issues?
- What did you do to ensure your personal/professional links did not bias your research?
- What is the essence of/main points about/significant aspects of your thesis?
- Talk us through your main research questions and their origins.

Literature review questions

Exploring the theoretical framework or basis of the work, how conversant the candidate is with the field and its literature. Some examples are:

- Are there any specific theorists in your literature review who stand out as particularly important? Why? How have they influenced your work?
- What is the main orientating theory for the study? Which theory or theories does your study illuminate/add to/challenge?

- What shaped/guided your literature review? Why did it cover the areas it did (and neglect others)?
- Who is the most influential writer, in your opinion, in this field and why? You don't mention the famous Dr X – why is that?

Questions about methodology and data collection

To elicit a justification for approach taken and to explore the skill with which data collection was undertaken, any opportunities and constraints encountered, how these were dealt with. Some examples are:

- What led you to decide to choose that paradigm or philosophical approach and reject alternatives?
- Talk us through the process of designing the project and what are the design's strengths and weaknesses?
- How did you select your sample, and why, and why that sample size?
- Provide a summary of techniques chosen and rejected and why.
- What were the difficulties you encountered in the data collection, how were they overcome? How did these influence your interpretation of results?
- Were there any important ethical issues or health and safety problems to handle? What were they and how were they addressed?
- How did you categorise/filter the data?
- Did the themes emerge from the data (a posteriori) or had you decided them in advance (a priori) (and why to both)?
- Were there other, alternative analysis possibilities, and why were they not included/rejected?

Questions about your findings/conclusions

- Was there anything surprising in the data, any anomalies?
- Any omissions and how do they influence the outcome?
- How do your conclusions relate to other relevant models/theories?
- Your findings are inconsistent with those of __________, how do you explain that?
- Your findings appear to be inconsistent with ______ theory or model, does that mean this theory or model is wrong?

Questions on the significance of the work/contribution to knowledge

- What is your most important contribution to your field?
- What is your contribution to knowledge; why do you think you've made a novel contribution and what is it that makes it original?

(Continued)

(Continued)

- Can you describe the most important finding of your research in one sentence?
- When you found __________, did it surprise you? How do you explain that?
- What are the important implications/key findings of the work?
- What does it suggest in terms of improvements for practice?
- What is newsworthy about it?
- How generalisable are your results and why?
- What lessons can be learnt by other researchers about the research product/process?
- If you had another chance, what would you have changed about your project, and why?
- What would you advise someone who wanted to test out your findings in a different setting or context?
- Your data show some inconsistencies. How does this affect the accuracy of your model or the confidence that you have in it?
- Please summarise for us any possible criticisms of your research.
- Are there any findings which demand urgent research attention to address them further?
- Are there any issues you had to set aside for future exploration later?

Concluding questions

- What have been some of the main things you have learned because of carrying out this piece of research?
- Which parts do you feel could make worthy publications? In which journals?
- What would you say is the greatest strength of this work? With hindsight, what are its limitations?
- What excites you most about this work?
- Is there anything that you would like to highlight from your work that we have not covered so far?
- Why did you want to do a doctorate, what benefit has your study brought you as an individual and a professional, and would you do it again?
- Is there anything you wished we asked about your thesis?

The above activity is great preparation for your viva. Similarly, having a 'mock viva' with your supervisor or other colleagues is excellent practice. During your doctorate, you should also take advantage of opportunities to give presentations of your work to others from outside your supervisory circle to find out what questions about your work arise for them and to practise answering them (Chapter 5). However, the best preparation of all would be to ensure that those of relevance to your research are answered in your thesis. If any stand out as not being addressed in that worthy tome, then expect them to be explored in some fashion in the viva. If the examiners think your answers illuminate something well or fill a gap in your thesis, then you may be asked to add them in before you are finally awarded your doctorate.

Presenting your answers

People are often worried about not being able to answer a question or freezing up during a viva. The most important thing is to remember that you do not have to answer immediately. You have time to think and to consider your answer. Breathe – then – Think. If there is something you do not understand, then by all means ask for clarification. Do interact with your examiners. You can say, 'I'm not sure if this is what you are looking for, but …' They should then be able to provide you guidance to enable you to answer their questions more fully.

It is acceptable to admit to being nervous, or say that your mind has gone blank for a minute. Examiners should understand this and allow for it. They know how important this award is to you and how much effort has gone into getting to this stage. What you want to do is then work on getting started talking again. Ask for clarification. Ask if your answer was headed in the right direction. You can say, 'I don't know exactly what you are asking, but does it relate to ________ [which you do know].' That can help move things back to your comfort zone.

Most importantly, if you honestly do not know an answer, do not make up a random answer! Be interested in the question. Say honestly, you had not thought about that but it is an interesting perspective. Perhaps ask for a reference, and write it down. As a rule of thumb in a viva situation, it is OK not to know a few of the answers, however, it is not OK not to care. In fact, some examiners will strategically push candidates to the edge of their knowledge, to see how far the candidate can go. Some people enjoy such a challenge, and so might you if you convince yourself that the professional role of a researcher is to test the boundaries of knowledge. One more thing to remember is that this is an adult, professional meeting, so you are perfectly at liberty to ask for a comfort break, even if it is simply for you to compose yourself. We have made some suggestions in Appendix IVB 'Top Tips for Preparing for the Viva' to help you present yourself and your research effectively during this special occasion.

Enjoying the final stretch

If you are one of many doctoral researchers who will experience a viva, think of it as your big day to shine. This is the day when you show off all your hard work to experts in your field. It is likely to be challenging, but by this time you should be up to the challenge. Prepare yourself, and enter the viva with a positive, yet realist, mindset. It is important to know that, in many countries, it is common to have at least some corrections after the viva, and for a fair number of people these may be substantial. However, these corrections are to make your written work even better. Your name and that of your institution is going on this thesis, and with more and more theses being available on the internet for all to read, it is important that this academic work represents you and your research in the best light. Therefore, go into the viva open to further improvement, but confident in the hard work and rationales you have put into your research already.

Each university has its own regulations and terminology about the final stage of the doctorate. Find out what terms are used in your institution so that you understand what the examiners are requiring. For instance, some may say: 'This is a pass, so congratulations Dr Z, but we will require you to ... (add the missing reference we discussed/correct the typographical errors/add a paragraph about the ethics as we discussed and so on) as a MINOR correction.' Alternatively, they may say: 'Thank you for an interesting discussion. We cannot recommend that you are awarded the doctorate just yet because we want to refer you for MAJOR corrections which will address ..., ..., and ...' The words 'minor' and 'major' are common but not universal and they or their alternatives imply amounts of corrections/amendments/additions that differ between universities. They should specify the maximum amount of time you can take for these adjustments (often, a few months for minor and a year or longer for major corrections/revisions), but remember that this is a maximum, not necessarily a required, time.

As you plan your completion stage, do have a back-up plan in mind so that you do not panic and any extension of your studies can be accommodated without putting your doctorate or your mental health at risk. It will also save you aggravation if you swallow your pride and accept and complete what examiners ask you to do, making your goal to finish this research task so you can move on. Although it seems that less than 10% of candidates pass without corrections, remember that the majority who submit a thesis do succeed in the end. Bear in mind that once achieved your title and qualification will simply (but significantly) be 'doctor with a doctorate'; there is no subscript such as 'after major amendments'.

Your supervisor should be able to continue to support you with any extra work required and will advise you on the final 'sign off' process. There will be an appeals procedure in your university and it is wise to know what it is in advance but do recognise that you generally cannot appeal on the grounds of the academic decision, nor in retrospect on inadequate support provided, but only about unfairness in the examination. It is salient and reassuring that appeals are rare, demonstrating that the process, despite its variations and challenges, works effectively for almost everyone.

By the end of your doctorate, you will have produced a substantial piece of work that contributes to your field and beyond. Reaching this academic pinnacle is an amazing accomplishment, so make sure you acknowledge this to yourself and celebrate your achievement, even if only in a modest or quiet way. Moreover, you will have grown and developed skills that will enable you to make significant contributions in whatever career you choose. Take time during this final period to reflect on this, feel pride in your work and enjoy the final steps to achieving a doctorate!

Special points for part-time and distance researchers

The assessment process has the same parameters and criteria for all doctoral researchers, whatever their mode of study, so your doctorate will be examined in the same way as all others in your university and will be equivalent to all other doctorates. You should, however, check out in advance what your university's regulations say about the time periods allowed for different kinds of amendments to the thesis. In some universities, the maximum time allowed is the same for all candidates, whereas others allow part-time candidates extra time to complete them. When you have achieved that completion, we think you deserve an extra cheer because you have demonstrated special stamina over the extended registration period. You should highlight this aspect to future employers.

Special points related to different disciplines

The general criteria apply to all disciplines but there are some differences worth pointing out. For instance, some doctorates, particularly in some arts degrees, require, in addition to the thesis, the production of an artefact/s (say, one or more art works) or a performance, which is also assessed. There are differences in the maximum and average number of words required of a thesis, with mathematics and sciences frequently requiring less than the humanities and social sciences because of different notations. How publications achieved during the research process are used within the thesis also differs both between disciplines and between universities with the same discipline, where, in some, they may be a requirement to be included and, in others, an unexpected bonus to be referenced to demonstrate that part of your work has been successfully peer reviewed. Your supervisors will advise you about such requirements but remember that these procedures serve to ensure that doctorateness, the making of an original contribution to knowledge, is achieved despite all the other differences between disciplines.

For all of you, your doctorate will make a great impact on your life. In the next chapter, we discuss how you can identify and realise the impact of your research for others.

References and further reading 

'Fake It Till You Make It', TED Talk from Amy Cuddy. www.youtube.com/watch?v=RVmMeMcGc0Y.

The Good Viva Video (2016) Angel Productions. www.angelproductions.co.uk.

Tinkler, P. and Jackson, C. (2004) *The Doctoral Examination Process: A Handbook for Students, Examiners and Supervisors*. Maidenhead: SRHE/Open University Press.

Trafford, V. and Leshem, S. (2002) 'Anatomy of a doctoral viva', *Journal of Graduate Education*, 3: 33–41.

PART THREE

PROGRESSING WITH CONFIDENCE

9

WHAT IS IMPACT AND HOW CAN IT BE BUILT INTO CURRENT RESEARCH TO ENHANCE FUTURE OPPORTUNITIES?

In this chapter, we will consider how to:

- Understand the significance of impact and its various forms
- Visualise how impact is influencing academic and research work as well as funding
- Identify the potential impact (short, medium and long term) of your own project
- Realise that potential

What is impact and why does it matter?

What is the point of research and why do we do it? If your answers include, to pursue new knowledge, to answer questions that have long puzzled you and others around you, to change the world and benefit people, sometimes in the most unexpected ways, to have fun and stimulate your interests, then you are beginning to think in terms of the professional impact of research. However, for researchers, in financially stringent times the question of who should pay for research has become a more pressing one, requiring in response a justified rationale addressing why the public should do so. Academics have always thought that their chosen research was important, wanting it to have significance and to change the world even if only in a small way. Further, as a professional obligation, leading to esteem and continued funding, researchers have always sought academic impact through publishing their work, intended to influence the discipline and shape fields of study. Thus, research impact has always been a consideration, even if expressed in different ways in different times. Nowadays, research impact has a broader remit, actively aiming to influence wider societal agendas and to contribute to greater good (for the economy, health, culture and society). There is also a political dimension that you, along with all other researchers, need to be alert to: policy makers expect funders (particularly public ones) to require researchers to demonstrate the value or worth of their research in terms readily understood by the public (including tax payers), shareholders and other stakeholders.

Up until the 1980s, research was a limited activity (MacFarlane, 2015), in contrast to the great numbers of professional researchers engaged in it today. While, in the past, being funded to research was what distinguished the academic from the hobbyist in their garden shed – now it is arguably the need to demonstrate impact that is the distinguishing criterion. If researchers want public funding (certainly in the UK, USA and Australia), then they (you) need to be able to demonstrate clearly and unequivocally the added value or benefits of the proposed research. Chandler (cited in Denicolo, 2014) differentiated other ways in which research was viewed in the past and is currently. He said that previously it was described as an end, curiosity-driven, a result of academic freedom, self-regulated, serendipitous, demonstrating academic excellence; now it is focused and forward-looking, explicit, targeted, constrained, subject to institutional governance, requiring investment and demonstrating excellence with impact.

The Research Councils UK define 'impact as the demonstrable contribution that excellent research makes to society and the economy'. For the UK **Research Excellence Framework (REF)** exercise, impact was defined as 'an effect on, change or benefit to the economy, society, culture, public policy or services, health, the environment or quality of life, beyond academia'. You can find in Appendix V a statement about impact from the 2016 Stern Review of the REF and an extract from the Research Councils UK about general 'Pathways to Impact' statements required in research proposals, while Lutz Bornmann (2012) provides a literature survey of how societal impact of research is measured and evaluated in different national contexts. Naturally, there is a lot of debate over this within the academic community, especially about whether it stifles academic freedom, creativity, long-term or 'blue skies' projects. These are indications of a fear that such constraints will result in a focus on economically productive, short-term projects, neglecting those that may eventually, or serendipitously, produce exciting new knowledge, as did the Curies' work on radioactivity and Whittle's invention of the jet engine.

While we recognise these concerns, and would regret long-term neglect of creative or blue skies research, nevertheless, we must acknowledge the environment we inhabit now, managing our research and funding in a responsible way. We also need to help newer researchers to work with this agenda so that they continue to obtain funding to do research. We do not think there is any disadvantage and, indeed, believe that a lot of good can be gained from doctoral researchers reflecting on the potential or possible impact of their research. Indeed, some universities now require their doctoral theses to include an 'Impact Statement' and some examiners, perhaps most, ask questions of a thesis or in a viva voce about the value/importance of the research. This is known colloquially as the 'so what?' question. Marini (2017) provides an indication that doctoral researchers' attention to impact also has long-term salary advantages.

Frequently, because their project necessarily deals with a restricted area and because of time limitations, doctoral candidates find it difficult to envisage the potential wider impact of their research. However, it is important to recognise that doctoral research forms a large proportion of any one university's research output and a substantial proportion of national research product. Further, doctoral research is often the seedbed or stimulus for significant future academic or commercial research. Thus, it is important that you value your doctoral contribution, recognise its potential and articulate it to others. These will be important evaluation skills for completing your doctoral research and for future work, whether it directly involves research or not. Let us begin that process in Activity 9.1 by first practising exploring the value of others' research as it impacts on our own everyday lives, next by exploring in Activity 9.2 research with impact in your academic department, and then by engaging in Reflection Point 9.1.

ACTIVITY 9.1 THE CONTRIBUTION OF RESEARCH TO IMPORTANT ASPECTS OF LIFE

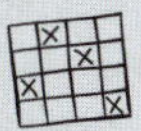

Think about some of the entities that make a positive contribution to, and impact on, the way you lead your life. For us, though we all love the feel of a new hardback book, the value of e-books is high, especially when it comes to packing a suitcase for a trip abroad. Similarly, Post-It notes have become key contributors to the smooth running of our working lives. On a serious note for one of us, the development of cardiac pacemakers has made family life much less worrisome.

(Continued)

(Continued)

Yet, downloadable books, derived from the development of computers and then the World Wide Web, originally generated some controversy. You can use the web to find the interesting story of the two serendipitous things in labs that eventually led to the development of Post-It notes. The pacemaker, as we know it now, results from findings of various research efforts in each decade of the 1900s, although the original research on which pacemakers were based was initiated by Hippocrates, then Aristotle, through Harvey, Galvani, Volta. Over the centuries scientists from a wealth of disciplines furthered the development of the tiny object inserted in the chest that keeps thousands of people alive. How is that for long-term research and development?

Now, do some desk/web research on the research origins of your personal positive entities. When you feel like a break from serious study, you might like to look up how common objects like jet engines, microwave ovens and cling-film came into being. As we have noted in Chapter 5, the researchers involved shared a common characteristic: persistence/perseverance.

For an interesting debate and more examples from experience in response to a challenge about the impact of research presented in journals, see: www.quora.com/What-are-the-real-benefits-impacts-of-academic-research

ACTIVITY 9.2 IMPACTFUL RESEARCH IN YOUR DEPARTMENT

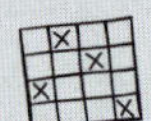

What examples are there of research that has been conducted in your department that has impact? Who or what were the main beneficiaries? Ask your supervisor and/or departmental Head or Research Director – you could use this as the basis for a seminar discussion with your fellow postgraduate researchers. Consider different kinds of impact exemplified: short and long term, as a contribution to knowledge/theory or to the economy, society, health or culture. Of course, it is likely that the research now being conducted by you and your peers is one 'academic impact' outcome of that departmental research.

REFLECTION POINT 9.1

PRECURSORS TO YOUR OWN RESEARCH

What recent previous research forms the basis of your research project? If you are following up work previously done by your supervisors, on what was their work based? Apart from your new work on the topic, what other effects did it have on theory, on practice, on individuals, on society?

One of life's little joys is seeing informative messages from Research Gate about references to, or reading of, our work by research colleagues around the globe. We encourage you to share your publications on those kind of forums, perhaps starting in the early stages by simple blogs on research interest websites.

One academic, Peter Taylor-Gooby, has controversially turned to novel writing because he believed that his research has no impact (www.timeshighereducation.com/news/professor-turns-novel-writing-his-research-had-no-impact). He told the *Times Higher Education* (1 September 2016): 'My academic output made no difference to anything.' We suspect that is not entirely true because, at least, he may have made (and we hope he did) a difference to his students. His main argument was that real impact results from a body of work rather than a single paper, though papers are used as metrics in measuring impact output of universities. We believe, like him, that even the most obscure piece of research could be turned into something else other than a classic academic publication – although the pertinent caveat here is: if one wants to or is determined enough to do so. Even blogging about your research would present it in a different format and, potentially, open your research up to a wider audience – including the world – and who knows what impact that might have.

A study by Jonathan Grant and colleagues of 6,679 impact case studies submitted to the 2014 UK Research Excellence Framework – the REF (which intends to evaluate the quality and quantity of research conducted in British higher education institutions) – revealed the kinds of impact academics had achieved, and was both inspiring and astounding for its findings (www.hefce.ac.uk/pubs/reports/Year/2015/analysisREFimpact/):

- Over 80% of the REF impact case studies included underpinning research that was multidisciplinary.
- The impact case studies were diverse and wide-ranging, with over sixty unique 'impact topics' identified.
- The reported research impacts stemmed from research in wide-ranging subject areas, with over 3,700 unique pathways from research to impact identified.
- Research undertaken in UK higher education institutions has contributed to every country in the world.

The study demonstrated that, although some subject areas exhibited a preference for or dominance in an identified area, for example the various branches of pharmacy and new drugs and their usage, all discipline areas had impact in the complete range of impact spheres. It is worth considering that assertion again – it appears that every subject area (including yours) has the potential for impact, in all the categories alluded to previously, change or benefit to: theory, economy, society, culture, public policy or services, health, the environment and quality of life. This may not be immediately obvious in relation to your specific research topic. However, by taking an interest in what kinds of impact research in general has had and engaging in discussion and activity to explore the immediate and longer-term results of research, you can be inspired by other ways of 'making impact'. Thus, your work could mark the beginnings of research impact whether you remain in academia or not; certainly, that is something worth being interested in.

What does identifying, registering and promoting impact involve?

We have noted that academics have always wanted to change the world, even if only in a small way through critique or commentary, if not by creating whole new medicinal, scientific or engineering breakthroughs. Hence, arguably, academic research has always had some measure of impact. The difference between the normal activity academics engage in daily and 'the new Impact Agenda', is that there is now a conscious and deliberate process that, ideally, is engaged with from the very conception of a research idea. That is, one would have an idea, not only about the research topic itself, but also who would benefit from the research, who might have a broader interest in the research, who might need to know about the research and how that impact might be demonstrated. There would be a plan for engaging and convincing the potential beneficiaries of the research (because this is not always self-evident as we shall discuss below), a method of capturing the evidence that the research has had impact, and a plan for promoting this activity both during the research process and at the end. This is the project management approach that you should be applying to your own research project but amended slightly to meet the stages of the impact process.

Consciously promoting and evaluating impact

The distinguishing feature for professional researchers concerning impact is the level of awareness they have about the potential and actual effects of their research, and their conscious effort to capture, record and evidence this.

How might impact affect you?

Earlier, we suggested that you may be asked to write an impact chapter or a statement as part of the submitted thesis. Furthermore, a description of likely impact, along with some evidence, is likely to become standard in the future doctoral process, at least in some countries. However, of direct importance to all doctoral researchers now is that we know that examiners in the viva often ask what the relevance (or impact) of the research work is (Chapter 8). Additionally, we would like to suggest that you think about it for future job interviews, as this question may well also appear in these situations. You could impress a prospective academic employer with your thoughts about what else you could do with your research, what publications and follow-up research, funded by external bodies perhaps, could be possible. Alternatively, if you are being interviewed for a non-academic role, you will be able to demonstrate wider thinking beyond your research project, recognition of the integration of theory and practice, and a range of skills, including the application of 'business acumen' (Chapter 11).

ACTIVITY 9.3 EXPLORING REF IMPACT CASE STUDIES

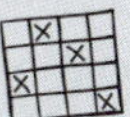

1. Go to http://impact.ref.ac.uk/CaseStudies/.
2. Go to the 'Research Subject Area' tab and pick your discipline area.
3. Read through several cases (between five and ten if possible), at least one from each 'Summary Impact Type' – see tab.
4. Make a note of the different skills and collaborations the researchers utilised to achieve this impact. (i.e., policy writing, public engagement, collaborative working with a charity).
5. This list of skills can help guide your own professional development goals (Chapter 5), helping you gain a more comprehensive view of the diverse skills necessary to be a successful researcher.

What kinds of things could you do during your registration period to promote, capture and report your research?

Disseminating your work through conference presentations and through journal articles has traditionally been the way in which new research reaches academic audiences, influencing on-going and future research and contributing to theoretical development. In areas with strong professional links, you might also be encouraged to contribute to more practice-based journals, magazines and meetings broadcasting your work more widely. These will certainly be recognised as 'impactful' activities in the academic arena and will raise your profile accordingly. But the new agenda behoves us to widen our horizons further through public engagement, outreach, public policy and enterprise activities so that research, in general and yours, gains publicity and acknowledgement of its value and, more importantly perhaps, has influence beyond the academy, affecting broader life issues and practices.

Some universities have staff who can help you with community or public engagement (PE), outreach and/or enterprise activities; many UK institutions participate in the Brilliant Club that enables doctoral researchers to teach in schools (www.thebrilliantclub.org/). Other services may be able to provide lists of schools interested in having researchers speak to pupils, local organisations or interest groups seeking speakers on interesting topics (youth groups, community groups, political meetings, environmental alliances, the University of the Third Age, for instance), businesses or industries offering short placements or longer internships or seeking consultancies on specialist issues. Some institutions have links with business parks and/or may provide advice on small company set-ups. There may even be opportunities in your area, as there are in ours, for researchers to present stand-up comedy sessions based on their research projects (www.brightclub.org/). Even if there is no official support in your institution for such endeavours, you can see that the possibilities are very wide, involving speaking to people with very diverse understandings of the world of research. You may feel more comfortable talking to well-informed people first until you develop a skill in making your research accessible or you might relish the challenge, or find less intimidating, chatting about your research in a jargon-free and technical language-free format. Many discipline-based professional bodies have support for researchers wishing to become involved in PE, and sometimes funding competitions to bid for money to support your activities. In the UK, the National Co-ordinating Centre for Public Engagement (NCCPE) supports universities to increase the quantity and quality of their work in this area and will also advise specific people interested in developing their PE profiles. Find out more about this at www.publicengagement.ac.uk/explore-it/how-we-can-help. Their definition of PE is:

> Public engagement describes the myriad of ways in which the activity and benefits of higher education and research can be shared with the public. Engagement is by definition a two-way process, involving interaction and listening, with the goal of generating mutual benefit.

One of the benefits you will gain, beyond ensuring some research impact, is the development of very saleable communication skills to enhance your CV, thus contributing to your future employment opportunities. In addition, these kinds of experience frequently force you to respond quickly to unexpected questions from the public, all of which is good preparation for the viva and may also provide you with a different perspective on your research.

Taking opportunities

It may be that, as well as public lay groups, it may be also be useful, indeed, important, for mutual benefit, to alert specific professional groups, government departments, regional assemblies, and pressure groups, to aspects of your research. It is unlikely that they will seek you out so you will need to track them down or notify them of your work through the public media (newspaper, radio, TV). Thus, you should make efforts to find out about their existence and contact details (from the web, telephone directories and the media) but also make sure that you take advantage of serendipitous opportunities (Chapter 5) to make contacts. These could be by making yourself known to key people such as those arranging campus visits for local dignitaries, by attending public council meetings or simply talking to your peers and departmental staff about who knows who (remember the 'six degrees of separation' theory – we are all linked to everyone else on the planet through a chain of no more than five intermediaries) or by joining networks such as LinkedIn. Do not give in to the misunderstanding that some people are just lucky in that they know influential people. We like the following quotation:

> Luck is what happens when preparation meets opportunity. (Seneca)

You may be lucky enough to have an influential person, your supervisor, pro-actively encouraging you to build your impact case but, if not, make your own luck by heeding the suggestions in the next section.

How can you gain your supervisor's support?

You will need to reassure your supervisor of the benefits of you engaging in any of the activities described above. They will need to be convinced that it will enhance your research rather than detract from it because they are, quite rightly, concerned with completion of the research project within a reasonable timescale so additional activities can appear as distractions from their perspectives. However, this is very much an under-researched area so, although anecdotal evidence is accumulating among the PE community that this activity is beneficial to individual researchers and their projects, you will need to consider and detail what the substantive benefits might be.

You, too, may wonder how you can fit this into a busy schedule without using your precious 'day off', as you cannot let the thesis slip. Laura Vanderkam presents 'How to Gain Control of your Free Time', an amusing but cogent TED talk, demonstrating how time can be considered to be elastic, stretching to accommodate what we want to put into it, rather than trying to 'find and save' tiny bits of time here and there. Remember that successful professionals think ahead and plan, so, you, too, can think about what you want to achieve over the next week (month, year), what you need to do to achieve that, then plan them into your diary, leaving the rest of the space for the things that matter to you less. There are, of course, some things that are essential to include (sleep, eating, refreshment and personal hygiene activities) and some that can be done less often, if at all (our personal favourites in this category are chores such as ironing and car washing).

Once you have convinced yourself of what is possible, marshal your arguments to convince your supervisors. We have provided some suggestions for you to work on in Activity 9.4.

ACTIVITY 9.4 PERSUADING YOUR SUPERVISOR OF THE VALUE OF YOUR PUBLIC ENGAGEMENT/OUTREACH ACTIVITIES

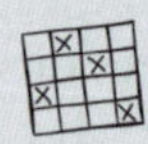

Below we present ten rationales that you might use to persuade your supervisor of the value of your plans. Choose a few that fit well with your circumstances, organise them into a hierarchy of what you think will influence your supervisor most and then weave them into a coherent, forceful argument:

1. The planned activity tests out your thinking in a variety of ways – which can only be beneficial as it will strengthen your thinking and help you to produce a more robust thesis and become good at answering questions about your research.
2. You are using it to test out specific ideas (more deliberate and targeted than no. 1 above) in the context for which they are relevant.
3. It will boost your morale at a time when you are feeling a bit jaded with the research and your thesis – so increasing your motivation.
4. If you are coming towards the end of your research, renewed interest and motivation may accelerate your submission and spur you to complete on time. (Not a good one for the disorganised, so only use this if you think you can live up to it.)
5. Your excursions may create links, leads and future projects for both you and your supervisor.
6. Tell your supervisor that you are impressed by how many Impact Case Studies, say for the Research Excellence Framework, derived from doctoral research (they may not have noticed this) and so you want to contribute, too.
7. This could be a source of some preparatory impact work, say researching policy connections, etc., for your supervisors (an appeal to their self-interest). In fact, your public engagement work may well be of benefit to your supervisor as funding bodies often strongly recommend or require research groups they fund to be involved in public engagement.

8 If you can find other postgraduate researchers in your department, school or faculty who have had success in such activities you can use these as examples, encouraging them to check with other supervisors about what are perceived to be the benefits.
9 It will add to the prestige of the department. You could present a form of business case for getting involved in something, complete with 'return on investment'.
10 It will look good on your CV – you may need to remind them that you must get a job eventually.

It is fantastic to participate in these types of activities, however to get the full benefit you need to provide evidence that your impact efforts have been successful. You should include in your plans for PE and similar activities means of capturing and recording feedback from those with whom you have interacted. This is an **evaluation activity** and so should follow traditional evaluation procedures. You can find more about this in the *Success in Research: Achieving Impact* book recommended at the end of this chapter (Denicolo, 2014), but here we will summarise questions that could guide your planning:

> How will the promotion activities support your project's potential for impact? (Are they directed to the correct audience at the right time and in the right format?)
>
> How will you demonstrate that? (What records will you keep and what evaluation tools will be used that measure, for instance, before and after event knowledge, understanding, practice, and so on?)

The answers to these questions will be useful to draw on for your thesis or viva responses but will be invaluable beyond your doctorate for demonstrating your research and professional skills to prospective employers.

VOICE OF EXPERIENCE 9.1 A RESEARCHER'S HISTORY OF PUBLIC ENGAGEMENT

At the risk of highlighting my age, I have been involved in public engagement, or public outreach as it was known previously, since the mid 1990s. The first public outreach activity I participated in was the second annual 'Brain Awareness Week' back in 1996. I was an undergraduate in a US university, who was working as a junior member on an

(Continued)

(Continued)

independent undergraduate research project in a neuroscience research lab. The head of the group arranged for us all to go to a local school to talk to 12–13-year-olds about the brain and neuroscience. The idea was to have some brain-related activities, with models and moulds of various sorts, with time for them to ask us questions. In practice, it worked, although the vast preponderance of the questions was focused on what exactly various illegal drugs do to the brain, which in hindsight we should have predicted ... but it took us a bit by surprise at the time. I remember enjoying myself, and hoping the kids we talked to enjoyed it as well. There was no evaluation; just trying to talk with different groups about research was a big thing.

I continued to participate in public engagement events over the years, talking to students in various schools and delivering exhibitions in science museums. I always got a buzz talking to different people about the cutting edge of the field and about how we might make life better in the future. I enhanced my skills by participating in these activities. I became much more confident in talking about my research to a variety of different people and became adept at tailoring activities and talking points to suit different age groups and different backgrounds. The most helpful skill I gained was being able to flexibly respond to a wide variety of questions, no matter how strange they seemed to be. I learned to be relaxed about not having all the answers and to engage in two-way discussion to help me better understand different perspectives and respond honestly. These skills were extremely helpful during my viva and now in my working career. However, these early engagement events I participated in had very little impact on my own research. Furthermore, I will never know if they had any long-lasting impact on anyone I talked with either.

Later, I had the opportunity to be involved in more 'two-way' public engagement opportunities: these events allowed for dialogue between researchers and the specific public involved. I was working on a disease-related project and as part of the funding deliverables, our research group hosted an annual members' day. During this day patients, carers and family members were invited into the university to discuss our research, funded through their memberships. I thought that if we put something together to 'wow' them, everyone would be happy. However, that is not how these days worked: the audience had some very pointed and interesting questions, which made us all think. Even more importantly, the tour and microscope demonstration sessions provoked interesting discussions, during which our guests shared valuable insights into the lived experience of the disease we were researching. This insight led us to look for pathology in different brain areas and truly enhanced our knowledge base and our research. Thus, public engagement turned into research impact, if even just in a small way.

(A neuroscience researcher)

VOICE OF EXPERIENCE 9.2 AN ACADEMIC'S EXPERIENCE OF RESEARCH IMPACT

The focus of my work is fundamental research, which is quite far away from application. So, when I was invited to a meeting with a company to talk about a potential collaboration, I thought it was highly unlikely I would have much to contribute. However, I decided to go along as a favour to the colleague who invited me and out of curiosity.

To my surprise, within that first meeting, I found there was quite a bit of my knowledge, both discipline-specific and methodological, that would be quite useful to this company. We managed to obtain funding from Innovate UK's Knowledge Transfer Partnership (KTP) scheme and from an internal university scheme. These funds enabled me to hire a postdoctoral fellow to work on a collaborative project between myself and the company. Although this project was quite far away from the research that is the mainstay of my work, I found working with industry incredibly interesting and a nice balance to the unpredictability of totally blue skies research.

That first meeting was five years ago and the collaboration is still going strong. I received additional KTP funding, have a patent, and a product line on the market as a direct result of innovation derived from this partnership. The main take-home messages I would like to share from this experience are:

1 Give opportunities a chance, even if you think it is unlikely to be of benefit to you. What is an hour or two out of your life for a meeting or event? The worst thing that will happen is you meet someone new, but nothing further comes of it. However, you never know, it could change the direction of your research or your career.
2 You don't have to be a basic/blue-skies researcher or an applied/translational researcher, you can be both. There is no reason you can't have multiple strands of research going at the same time, and in fact it is probably a good strategy to do so.
3 Most importantly, have fun. Push yourself to do different things. This is truly what drives innovation and creativity, and moreover makes the job worth doing.

More information about this collaboration can be found on the British Plastic Foundation website (www.bpf.co.uk), celebrating the opening of Plastipack new test facility and on the Plastipack website (www.plastipack.co.uk) as well.

(Dr Steve Clowes, Senior Lecturer in Physics, University of Surrey)

Stakeholders and beneficiaries

You may have previously been involved with public engagement activities or outreach work – but did you do this as a student or as an 'academic impact professional'? Many students get involved with and enjoy those activities; they have bags of enthusiasm and make a great contribution to society.

The academic impact professional will do all those things, but, in addition, they consider the bigger picture, contemplating in advance who the beneficiaries or users of research might be, and therefore targeting their outreach and engagement activities accordingly. They will also actively think of ways of capturing evidence of the value to beneficiaries and then design ways of promoting this work to influential others, their immediate and current stakeholders (funders, supervisors and institution), and potential future stakeholders, such as professional bodies, government and other policymakers, future employers and so on.

More than just getting involved, it is about considering the full round of research activity. Impact through research requires the researcher to be more strategic about what they can do with the research and how that could bring benefits not only to others, but also to the researcher themselves – for instance, could this work generate new partners, new collaborations, new ideas and research questions, and new funding opportunities. We invite you to make a start on identifying your potential beneficiaries in Activity 9.5.

ACTIVITY 9.5 POTENTIAL BENEFICIARIES AND STAKEHOLDERS

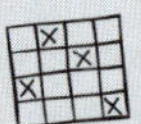

Make a list of groups of people, professional groups and areas (specific environments – built/natural; cultural, medical/healthcare; charitable; and regional, for instance) that might have an 'interest' in your research or who could benefit from it. Can you name at least one group or area for each of the categories in the boxes below? The academic category is straightforward, so we suggest that journal articles could be included here – but do you know which journals would have the highest impact in your area? It would be useful to list those journals in the relevant box below.

Academic/theoretical impact:	Political/policy impact:	Economic/business impact:
Cultural impact:	Social (including charities) impact:	Environmental impact:
Medical/healthcare impact:	Regional impact:	International impact:

This exercise may require a bit of lateral thinking and research – are there any museums, government bodies, policy areas, charities, businesses, other research institutions/departments that might be interested? Also, do not restrict yourself to thinking about your research in its entirety when it is completed: benefits may be derived from one small aspect of your research such as your unique and insightful literature review, or from your methods, or from applications that may not be in your final thesis, that may lead to a 'spin-out' activity or company, or alternative applications of an idea, perhaps in a hitherto unforeseen context, as has been demonstrated in the case studies presented to the UK REF.

Short-, medium- and long-term impact

You may not realise yet, or indeed for some time in the future, the longer-term impact or influence of your research, but it is important to publicise your ideas for future generations to reap the benefits. Even if you do not intend to remain in academia, it is worth considering publishing something for that reason alone. We encourage you to share your ideas, indeed to shout about the amazing work you have done. Even if you do that only once in the academic arena and publish one article, future readers and researchers may find it useful, as you probably have done whilst reading papers and books for your own research.

You could elaborate on your list from Activity 9.5 by considering in Activity 9.6 who might be beneficiaries or stakeholders at different times.

ACTIVITY 9.6 WHO/WHAT MIGHT BENEFIT FROM YOUR RESEARCH OR FIND IT USEFUL IMMEDIATELY AND IN THE FUTURE?

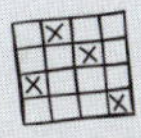

Copy the boxes below and begin to insert some ideas now, to be added to as your research develops and nears completion. Get into the habit of thinking: 'Who might be interested in this? What benefits could this lead to for myself and others?'

1	This year
2	Within 2–3 years (or when you complete?)
3	Describing impact of research beyond the completion of your doctorate will require you to have a much larger vision, even if it is wildly idealistic, of what you would like or wish to see your research leading to ...
4	Within 5–10 years
5	In 20 years' time – think big!

Of course, many of the benefits of your research will go unrealised unless you do try to disseminate your ideas and products to all the different audiences that may benefit from them. We believe that considering and communicating the wider benefit and impact of your research should be an important element in your doctoral experience, one that you should take as seriously as any member of faculty as it becomes another way of fulfilling the potential of your research.

References and further reading 

Bornmann, L. (2012) 'What is societal impact of research and how can it be assessed? A literature survey', *Journal of the Association for Information Science and Technology*, 64 (2): 217–33.

Denicolo, P.M. (ed.) (2014) *Success in Research: Achieving Impact in Research*. London: Sage.

MacFarlane, B. (2015) 'Look back in wonder: The invention of academic 'tradition', *Times Higher Education*, 25 June.

Marini, G. (2017) 'Determining PhD holders' salaries in social sciences and humanities: "impact" counts'. Accessible through: www.academia.edu.

Vanderkam, L. (2016) 'How to gain control of your free time'. TED Talk. www.ted.com/talks/laura_vanderkam_how_to_gain_control_of_your_free_time.

10

HOW CAN YOU MAKE THE MOST OF YOUR RESEARCH EXPERIENCE AT A PERSONAL LEVEL?

In this chapter, we will consider how to:

- Enjoy your research experience
- Recognise the value of diverse experience
- Use self-knowledge to gain more from your research
- Be pro-active in celebrating and sharing your achievements

Enjoying your research experience

Are you enjoying your doctoral research? This short and seemingly simple question might be more complicated to answer than it appears. If you are enjoying your research, reflect for a moment on what is making it an enjoyable experience for you. Can you distil the elements that are making it enjoyable? If you are uncertain how to answer this question or hesitate over it, are you enjoying some aspects of the process more than others? Can you identify which aspects you enjoy the most and why, and which you least enjoy and why? If you are not enjoying the experience at all, think about what would need to change to make your research experience more enjoyable for you. You may also like to ask your peers about their experiences for comparison – as we can learn much from other people's perspectives.

Reflecting on your level of enjoyment may not be an easy thing to do and, sadly, we do recognise that researchers find the process very challenging sometimes, especially in the second year or middle phase of the research, and certainly the **writing-up** stage can have its stresses, too. Stressful moments are not uncommon in life and they provide the counterpoint to happier times; we cannot understand or even recognise happiness without experiencing its contrast. The fact is that the doctorate in the UK is, by its very nature, built on a 'challenging pedagogy': the outcome is unknown, the process may change, nothing may make sense for months on end, you may change your mind about the topic, and the people involved may also change. It has been described by Dr Mark Proctor, Academic Development Officer at the University of Sunderland, as a 'risky' undertaking because it is experiential and negotiated. Knowing this and being aware of the 'risks' will enable you to anticipate them and manage them better. It would be rational and normal to expect that some things may not go quite as planned with a project extending over the course of several years. One beneficial outcome is that by its completion you should be aware of how you respond to uncertainty, change and even, at times, setbacks and disappointment. You should also be able to enjoy your achievements, noting that successful people frequently congratulate themselves and do not dwell on the negative things or mistakes for too long.

REFLECTION POINT 10.1

THE ENJOYMENT OF RESEARCH

What do you like best about research? When do you feel the most creative? What do you want to contribute to your field?

Whenever you are feeling that your doctorate is taking a bit of a dip, take time to reflect on those things you love most about your field and your research.

Yes, we firmly believe that researching for a doctorate should and can be one the highlights of your life, though none of us can change the underlying pedagogy of the doctorate or nature of the research process. We do not mean that you will feel 'ecstatic' or even enthusiastic about all your research all the time. Like all jobs and vocations, much of the research process can be dull and routine; however, it should be challenging in a good way; it should stretch your thinking, enable you to meet new people and expand your intellectual horizon. If it is not enabling any of the above or you are not enjoying your research, you need to consider why that it is and what you need to address or make happen to improve the situation. Psychologists talk about 'locus of control', whether individuals feel that they are powerless in a world in which things happen to them (external locus of control) or in one in which they can make efforts to be in control (internal locus of control). It will come as no surprise by now that we think that people who have demonstrated their intelligence sufficiently to be enrolled in doctoral study should be at least aiming for a sense of internal, personal control of their own lives, no matter how different they perceive them from 'normal' or 'wished for' lives.

ACTIVITY 10.1 MUTUAL APPRECIATION – YOUR RESEARCH AND YOU

Thinking about your research journey to date, use the table below to appreciate the positive aspects of your work and yourself.

What aspects of your research have you enjoyed the most or have given you most pleasure?	
What are you most proud of or what is your best achievement to date?	
List the moments when someone else made you feel good/proud of your research (perhaps it was feedback or a question or comment):	
What has been exceptionally good or fun that you would like to have more of in your research journey?	
How can you get more good/fun or enjoyment into your research journey?	

Appreciating the challenges of diverse experiences

Between us, we have a range of experience that illustrates the uncertain nature of the research process and how wide variation of personal experience can still lead to a positive outcome. One of us loved the research but disliked the academic environment, and found the competitive atmosphere made her feel anxious and inadequate. One of us, despite juggling for her life, found her vocation in the contrast between the dedicated support she received and the neglect she perceived other students suffering. One of us learned the true meaning of 'balance' while starting a family and completing a doctorate at the same time. Read our stories in Appendix VI.

Enjoying the research process is a complex matter. You might enjoy the research but not the environment you are working in; you might like your supervisor personally but feel unsupported professionally; your personal circumstances may support or challenge your ability to devote yourself to research. One common problem, certainly in the early stages, is that researchers underestimate the emotional impact of the journey; if researchers do anticipate problems, they tend to be of a technical kind, for instance in gathering data, finding the right interviewees or equipment. You can expect a lot of 'life' to happen in the three to four years full-time and certainly up to eight years part-time that it takes to produce a thesis. It is easy to become so absorbed by the work that you can forget two essential things:

1. You should be living life at the same time as your research (remembering others around you will be living their lives and may expect you to be present for them, too).
2. You should be enjoying your work/research; there is no honour or award for those who suffer the most.

As our stories show, the research itself can be seriously affected by events both within and outside the research and we would all acknowledge that doctoral research can be an emotional roller-coaster, but nonetheless still an enjoyable one. Certainly, by the end of the research process, you will have learned a lot about yourself, particularly which kinds of adrenalin rush provide you the most satisfaction.

Pro-actively seeking satisfaction

Research shows that we are most satisfied and productive when work does not feel like work and we are enjoying ourselves. There will always be mundane or uninspiring things to do, but they should only consume about 20% of your time, the rest being satisfying, even if demanding, engagement. Research by Kearns and Gardiner (2007) in Australia found that '[h]aving a clear sense of career purpose was most important for perceived effectiveness at work, followed by planning and prioritizing', whilst 'having a clear sense of purpose appear[ed] to boost morale and guard against distress'. Research also shows that the things that commonly throw a PhD off track are: change of supervisor and feelings of isolation and uncertainty. You can minimise the impact of these things by taking control and even artificially creating situations that will make you feel positive about your research, for instance:

- Giving a talk is one way of affirming that you are making progress (you could do this informally with your peers over lunch) and provides opportunities for feedback.
- Planning activities is one method for reducing any stress or anxiety.
- keeping a log or research diary shows the development of ideas;
- Drafting chapters clarifies your thoughts and provides tangible evidence of progress.
- Making sure that you are getting enough exercise, sleep and good food are also vital for keeping your spirits up and your brain energised.

How can I get more from my research?

Knowing what motivates you will help you get more from your research – but this means identifying what you value by reflecting on what kind of person you are and how you learn. Are you spurred on by incentives and rewards or do you respond best to threats and penalties? For instance, do you give yourself a treat, say a trip to the cinema, if you finish a piece of work, or does the impending doom of a fast-approaching deadline spur you on? Since what motivates anyone is very individual, then you need to prepare for the rough patches while enjoying the good times, choosing the incentives you know will work for you. If you work better with rewards, have a hidden stash of them (chocolate bars, silly comics or a recorded TV programme …) for emergencies. If you need deadlines, agree some additional ones, beyond the formal reviews we discussed in Chapter 7, with your supervisor or colleagues. Think about times when you have felt confident, have worked hard, felt valued and what things helped produced those results. Then consider how you could draw on similar things when needed. For example, do you feel more confident with certain people or when you received supportive comments on your work? Most people find that talking to someone helps with keeping focus on and easing the isolation of doctoral research. Your institution may provide you with a mentor or other support mechanisms, such as a pastoral care tutor or counselling service, so find out what is available. Even a peer, within or outside your discipline, with whom you can meet once a month to discuss 'life' can provide a lifeline and the stimulus of alternative perspectives.

Activities outside of the doctorate are a vital part of the research process, even if most supervisors may not be aware of how important they are. Read Dr Zoe M. Harris' thoughts about the importance of these to her doctoral experience in Voice of Experience Box 10.1.

VOICE OF EXPERIENCE 10.1 'PRODUCTIVE DISTRACTIONS'

When doing a PhD, it's sometimes hard to manage your time in a way that you don't feel guilty for not working every hour under the sun. However, working extended hours and not having a break may reduce your productivity, affect your mental health and can lead to 'burnout'. We must remember we are all different and work in different ways ... but here is a tip for avoiding that 'not-working' guilt and ways to help you take a break. I call them 'Productive Distractions'. These are fun non-work activities that, in the best cases, physically prevent you from doing work and leave little attention for feeling guilty for not working.

I worked far too hard for the first couple of years of my PhD. I felt I had to put every minute I had into it and I found it almost impossible to relax! Something had to change – Productive Distractions came to the rescue.

I undertook a range of different Productive Distractions, the easiest and most regular was the cinema, but I also signed up and paid for courses – having made a financial commitment it was harder to set aside! So I learnt to climb: an 8-week course for 2 hours in the evening. I couldn't read a paper while I was half way up a wall! I also did a course in beauty therapy – money spent meant I committed and I learnt new skills along the way. Obviously, these are things I chose to do because they interested me, but there are so many options available. For example, being part of a sports team is a commitment and it's great for your health, too; whilst a craft keeps your hands busy and requires concentration, and, as a bonus, allows some creative expression and your mind to shift away from intense academic work.

When looking for a Productive Distraction, try one that will fulfil the following things:

1 It's something you enjoy, have an interest in or are curious to try/find out more.
2 It physically prevents you from doing PhD work – like checking emails, reading papers, doing some writing/analysis in the background.
3 It occupies your mind as well as your body. Be there and be present. Allow your attention to be fully on what you are doing so you don't allow your brain to wander into guilt territory.
4 It has dual benefits – such as learning a new skill, connecting and spending time with others, or improving your health.

We have more time available to us than we think. A couple of hours spent away from your desk can be more valuable than that time spent at your desk because it refreshes your mindset and can increase productivity when you do get back to work.

(Dr Zoe M. Harris, Postdoctoral Research Associate)

Public engagement (PE), previously considered a potential distraction rather than a productive one, is now being encouraged in institutions that recognise the employability skills such activities develop. As we explored in

Chapter 9, activities such as giving a talk to the public or user group, designing a lesson for school children, teaching, delivering a stand-up comedy routine based on your research, establishing a 'research café' in a local café for the public to join in, or setting up a display based on your work in the local library or pub, is an excellent informal way of building your skills-set and CV. The world of public engagement has expanded considerably in the last decade, and it provides a real boost for anyone flagging with their research. Practitioners have commented, anecdotally, on how they notice doctoral researchers grow professionally, feel a renewed enthusiasm for their work and becoming more motivated to continue, sometimes approaching submission/completion with renewed vigour. If you have a reluctant supervisor who discourages this kind of activity, keep to a 9–5 routine during the week and deliver what you agreed to do; then, fit in the fun things at weekends or evenings, or do a time-swap, that is make up for the time 'lost' in the week at the weekend. Like Zoe, we do not believe that any time is lost; it all adds to the way you think about your research and improves your skills-set. See also our suggestions in Chapter 9 on how to gain your supervisor's support. Engaging with the public, policy-makers, business or school children, all of whom may ask awkward questions, will enable you to think on the spot, which will be excellent preparation for the viva and the world of work. It may even open unexpected, unintended possibilities for your future career. Before delving further in the next chapter about how your research experience can contribute to a satisfying career, read what one researcher has to say in Voice of Experience Box 10.2.

VOICE OF EXPERIENCE 10.2 UNINTENDED CONSEQUENCES OF PUBLIC ENGAGEMENT

I started my doctorate with a specific focus: get the top science qualification as swiftly as possible so I could get a cushy job that paid well and wouldn't be boring. My supervisors encouraged me to keep distractions at bay while working on a project close to their hearts that would lead to multiple prestigious publications. We were on the same page and all a bit annoyed when word came from on high that all of us 'lab rats' had to attend professional skills courses, so we colluded in avoiding as many of these 'opportunities' as possible. When I had to include in my annual review evidence of the required attendance, I opted for a residential school that would fill my obligations in one fell swoop, thinking that I could do a bit of writing-up while I was away. That was a mistake. We were kept so busy during the day with challenging but interesting problems to solve for some contributing employers that there was no time for skiving off.

(Continued)

(Continued)

I began to enjoy the process and then in the evening I got chatting to one of the employers, who took an interest in my research and talked about how my research skills might be valuable in his field. He gave me his card and invited me to look around his establishment. It sounded great, so I took up the offer. I was impressed – just the job and environment I would like. Then I talked to his HR folk and discovered that I would need to up my game beyond just getting an academic qualification. They want evidence of people management as well as project management skills, as well as ability to communicate to clients as well as to fellow researchers, in this country and abroad. That's why I am now grabbing every opportunity to get experience and on courses so that I can impress that employer or someone like him – I had a naïve view before – and I have a lot of catching up to do. I could moan that nobody told me, but I probably wasn't listening. The biggest surprise came from one of my supervisors, who noticed how much more enthusiastic I am about my lab work and didn't mind that it was because I wanted to create space for other development activities.

(Physics Researcher)

References and further reading 

Kearns, H. and Gardiner, M. (2007) 'Is it time well spent? The relationship between time management behaviours, perceived effectiveness and work-related morale and distress in a university context', *Higher Education Research & Development*, 26 (2): 235–47.

Whitney, D. and Trosten-Bloom, A. (2010) *The Power of Appreciative Inquiry: A Practical Guide to Positive Change,* 2nd edn. Oakland, CA: Berrett-Koehler.

11

HOW CAN YOU MAKE THE MOST OF YOUR RESEARCH EXPERIENCE FOR YOUR PROFESSIONAL CAREER?

In this chapter, we will consider how to:

- Recognise your saleable, sought-after attributes
- Be entrepreneurial, and why that matters
- Market your new potential to prospective employers and other interested parties

What sought-after personal qualities will you develop as a successful researcher?

There are five essential personal characteristics that make for a successful researcher and, we hope, a contented one:

> *Passion (or simple enthusiasm) for the topic/discipline and/or research practice is essential, especially for sustaining focus over a long period*: Although we have recognised in the previous chapter that enthusiasm can wax and wane during a doctorate, this is *the* key attribute all researchers have in common irrespective of the discipline. If you want to continue in academia, you will need such passion to sustain you through academic life. We should remind ourselves that even the most successful academics did not have a straightforward ladder to stardom, although as observers we see only the successes; often the funding and publication disappointments, failures and rejections go unrecorded. If you

are seeking a career in the wider professional world, potential employers will certainly be more impressed by an enthusiastic person than a disinterested one and they will recognise the sustaining power of a zest for life and work. Although passion cannot be faked to fool yourself, there are four other essential attributes that you can cultivate or seek help with and which are also critical to all professional success. They are open to a psychological trick, that is, we can pretend and act as though we have these attributes to convince others we possess them (as an actor tricks the audience into believing their performance) and, if we do this for long enough, we eventually also convince ourselves. It is reassuring to know that we can learn and acquire the other essential attributes; current public engagement, impact and interdisciplinary agendas make this more possible for doctoral researchers than five or ten years ago.

Self-confidence: You need to believe in yourself, and have courage, which leads to **self-efficacy**. We may all feel like imposters (see Clance and Imes, 1978) at times but (unless we are imposters, which seldom is the case), then we need to apply logical thinking and our 'rational researcher stance' to ourselves. What would a professional researcher say about you? They would notice that: you are conducting research work, probably highly complex research work; you know your subject (maybe not everything but certainly better than most); you have something to say on this subject and have communicated that in different ways, perhaps even to different types of audiences. Thus, to our observer–researcher, you look like a real researcher! An old saying is, 'Familiarity breeds contempt' – often we become so familiar with our own qualities, and the outputs of our research, that we mentally downgrade them. Outsiders looking in perceive us and our products differently, so build your confidence by talking with others about your research and seek out opportunities for public engagement or outreach opportunities.

Perseverance: One of the key academic attributes is having the determination and tenacity to see the project through to completion. You will need endurance for a thesis as the work stretches over several years, and the ability to remain motivated and focused. Indeed, we contend that you obtain a doctorate by not giving up; steadily eating the elephant/giant vegetable. That ability to keep going, even when things are not going well, is a tremendously important attribute of successful researchers; simply having great ideas is not sufficient to be a successful researcher. As Henry Ford said: 'Whether you think you can, or you think you can't – you're right,' which combines perseverance with self-belief. It also encompasses recognising what you have the power to change and prioritising those things.

Resilience: How quickly can you recover or bounce back after criticism or rejection, or do you take criticism personally? Do you look for ways to improve, or do you find it impossible to manage negative feedback or events positively? Undoubtedly, sometimes critical response to work feels like a personal attack. Certainly, some feedback could be articulated more empathically. When you receive feedback, remember that it is about your work, not about you; when giving feedback, consider how you would like to be treated and if you are being fair. This means that you need to be aware of your own unconscious bias – a human failing. What assumptions do you make about people, ideas or environments that may reveal unconscious bias? Remember to always 'review unto others as one would want to be reviewed!' Further, you can always disarm your critics by calmly recognising valid viewpoints, even if you disagree with them and intend not to use them, or by embracing a 'failure' and learning from it. To do that, you need to cultivate the virtue of being able to recognise when you need help and to ask for it.

Connectivity: At the heart of the academic profession is a paradox: researchers need people to discuss ideas with and help to move their thinking forward and, yet, academia is often thought of as a highly individuated profession. However, this may be changing, as partnership building/working increases, certainly for funding and impact purposes, whilst doctoral cohorts in specialist centres have become prevalent in the UK. One of the key attributes of successful researchers is the ability to make creative connections beyond their discipline and to gather ideas from a range of sources, including outside of academia. It is essential that you build a support network – your supervisor is the big rock but not the only one. You have friends and family who may not be in academia but certainly can listen and ask searching questions, and who may help your future career tremendously.

These five attributes complement **emotional intelligence** (**EI**) – the ability to identify your own and other's emotions and manage them, to view situations objectively and to respect alternative perspectives (see the Further Reading for more on emotional intelligence). It helps in difficult situations to recognise what you are feeling, harness any negative emotions and use them productively through your interpersonal skills. Your emotions tell you something about a situation and EI should help you identify what the real source of feeling is. Avoid letting your own anger, fear or frustration exacerbate a situation that might be resolved by considering other's positions and seeking common ground in a rational way. This is a skill you can develop as you gain experience as a researcher.

Professionally making the most of your research experience

During the research process, alongside your personal attributes, you will also develop your professional skills set. As with your personal attributes, you may need to take some time to reflect on and identify the extent and range of your professional skills-set. The full Vitae RDF will be helpful if you have access to it but see Chapter 5 for basic information and ideas. It is a well-known shortcoming of doctoral and postdoctoral researchers that, although they may have a great range of skills and knowledge, they may not be aware of what these are and, worse still, may not be able to articulate them to others.

Attributes to cultivate

The UK Roberts report (2002) found that researchers needed a lot of help with recognising and marketing their professional skills, so the most significant attribute for a professional to cultivate initially is self-awareness, followed by seven other important attributes.

Self-awareness

Aristotle said: 'Knowing yourself is the beginning of all wisdom.' Self-awareness distinguishes the professional researcher from the student. The key self-development question, to be asked of yourself each time you do something such as give a talk, teach a class and so on, is this: What would I do differently next time? This should enable you to identify both strengths, what went well and areas for improvement.

Networking

This matters everywhere but is vital in academia. The value of making the most of serendipity, chance meetings, overheard conversations cannot be overstated. It is central, also, to connectivity above.

Being entrepreneurial

The entrepreneurial spirit encompasses being pro-active and outward looking, seeking opportunities and making the best of them in every realm of work. You will need to be innovative and ground-breaking but not necessarily a mercenary capitalist. Read Dr Elaine Hickmott's views in Voice of Experience Box 11.1

Being global in your outlook

Higher education is, by nature, global – people move all around the world to work, and academic work has always crossed national boundaries. Contemporary technology and the global market of education makes it likely that you will already be in a very diverse research environment, looking forward to an international dimension to your work in the future. Do you take time to understand the lifestyles and pedagogic experiences of your fellow international researchers or departmental colleagues? Are you making the most of the global environment that you are currently working in? If not, why not? Prospective employers, both academic and non-academic, as well as funders of research expect a global mindset and outlook. Being able to at least tolerate, if not actively and constructively work in, environments characterised by diversity, is an essential attribute. Being able to actively engage with, manage and get the most from a diverse range of people is a highly sought skills-set, and universities afford plenty of opportunities for you to develop this.

Team working

Are you in a research team? If so, can you identify your strengths and contributions to the team and everyone else's as well? Reflect on your actual contribution to and your impact on the wider team (see Chapter 10 in our companion book on developing transferable skills, Denicolo and Reeves, 2014). Even if you are a lone researcher, you will be in a department and have working relationships, at the very least with your supervisor. Assess who brings what skills to the department, and how, and what your own contribution is. Seek out opportunities to work in a team and 'debrief' yourself on your strengths and weaknesses. It is easy to be a nominal member of a team, but engaging, doing what is right for the team and being a good colleague is more difficult.

Commercial awareness – business acumen

When applying for jobs, find out what the business/institution is concerned with, how it makes money and/or achieves success and what contribution to that success your potential role will make. Academia is a very mixed economy with a multitude of aims, so you can begin to build your understanding/acumen by exploring what your institution's main aims are and how your department and supervisors contribute to that. How do doctoral researchers as a group contribute to the business of the university? Revisit Activities 9.2 and 9.3 in Chapter 9, and consider this question again.

Raising your digital profile

In a world where social media dominates every aspect of life, it is critical that you control what the world knows about you. Is your digital profile fit for purpose? If we 'googled' you right now, what would we learn about you? Corporate employers have been reviewing prospective employees via the internet for some time, and academics tend to 'google' all new professional acquaintances. First, ensure that you are visible, making a digital profile of yourself if you do not have one and make sure that it is kept up to date. Second, make sure that your digital profile is what you would want people to see and matches what people are looking for. The internet provides an excellent media space for researchers to express themselves and tell the world about their work in a responsible and ethical way. Find the medium that suits you best, choosing those you have the time for and interest in maintaining. There are a huge variety of media platforms and free software to help you, so you could at least build a personal webpage, Research Gate and a LinkedIn profile for people to find out more about who you are and what you do. But be very careful over controlling the content; if you would not want the Vice Chancellor/ President, your mother or supervisor to see it, resist displaying it.

Gaining a range of experiences

It is only through doing and experiencing that you can articulate your attributes and what you can offer prospective employers. How do you know if you are leadership material if you have never led anything? Try something out – universities are opportunity-rich environments.

VOICE OF EXPERIENCE 11.1 CAREER PERSPECTIVE FROM A FORMER DOCTORAL RESEARCHER

I began my career with a PhD in Chemistry. For me, the appeal of the doctoral experience lay in developing skills and credibility. A career in industry and employability were at the top of the list and I saw a PhD as a springboard into a world of exciting career opportunities. I was right!

My favourite description is that I have gone from boiler-suit to boardroom and beyond. The PhD led me to manufacturing; manufacturing opened my eyes to business; business experience plus my doctorate helped me harness my entrepreneurial spirit and inspired me to create my own enterprise.

Looking at the world today, many sources describe how we are amid unprecedented VUCA; that is, Volatility, Uncertainty, Complexity and Ambiguity. To thrive, create opportunities and build a successful career in this environment requires the type of dexterous, expansive, innovative thinking which is developed as a doctoral researcher. Mix this with an understanding of real-world commerce and industry plus an entrepreneurial mindset, and you have a winning combination.

By understanding the truth about entrepreneurship and by developing their skills and experience beyond the research bubble, people with PhDs already create and take advantage of a plethora of opportunities; whether in academia, starting their own business or working in a corporate environment.

This is because …

- a PhD is *not* solely training to be an academic; it is development of the high-quality thinkers we need to build knowledge-based economies and solve complex global challenges;
- to achieve the level of innovation required for a PhD, researchers must be expansive and agile in their thinking abilities;
- skills developed during the doctoral experience are transferable across sectors and disciplines, bringing commercial and social benefits;
- researchers are entrepreneurial. There are many overlapping skills found in both doctoral researchers and those classified as being 'entrepreneurs'.

My top five tips for making the most of your doctoral experience are:

1. Continually explore areas outside your field of research. There are always interesting or game-changing connections to discover.
2. Keep investing in your own learning and development especially your non-technical skills, such as communication, team working, commerciality and entrepreneurship. Successful careers are built on more than the detail of your research.
3. Look beyond the perspective and opinions of your academic supervisor(s). There is an exciting world outside university walls.
4. Take time to understand how industry and business works plus explore different challenges faced by different sectors. This is important whether you decide to work in academia or industry.
5. Keep applying your ability to innovate in different scenarios and settings. The more you flex your creative abilities the more ideas with impact you will generate and be able to put into action.

Our dynamic, modern world presents interesting and exciting opportunities for those who want to get involved and add value to the economy and society. Doing a PhD makes you perfectly placed to do this. Harnessed and developed in the right way, your doctoral experience can help you change the world!

(Dr Elaine Hickmott, Development Director, EH Enterprises)

How to make the most of your experience and convince others!

You have the experience, you have knowledge and expertise (albeit in a limited area), now you find yourself looking to capitalise on these things. Several options may open to you within or outside of academia – so you should initially identify *what matters to you*; for instance, if we forced you to choose between doing research or staying in academia, which would you prefer? In academia globally, the number of academic, research and/ or teaching jobs or postdoctoral positions is limited, but there is a plethora of jobs requiring just the qualities and expertise you have gained through your doctorate. There are lots of juicy world problems waiting to be solved by amazing people like you! Having researched possible opportunities that would suit you, in and without academia, you simply need to present your carefully acquired knowledge and skilfully developed attributes in the right way to the right people, using your CV and portfolio and interpersonal skills.

Let us consider first how you might decide which areas to search, using our question above as an example in the Figure 11.1 matrix. You could produce another matrix or add a dimension to this one using other parameters important to you (high income, income not important, hours of work irrelevant, social hours required and so on.)

Once you have an idea of which direction you would like to go in, with a range of alternatives at the ready (see Contingency Planning in Activity 7.3 and Planning for the Unexpected in Chapter 3), you must align your skills-set with what your potential employer (academic or otherwise) or funder needs. Search their websites – look at previous projects

High level of need to do research	*Do research elsewhere – i.e. in industry, public or private sectors, or become an independent researcher or freelance consultant*	*Postdoc – fellowship Lectureship*
Low level of need to do research	*Use expert knowledge, interests and transferable skills in other roles outside of academia, e.g. teach in compulsory sector, become a medical writer or journalist in your field, work in problem-solving role in finance, commerce or industry*	*Take up teaching-only role, public engagement or enterprise post, researcher training, management or other position in HE*
Do you have a ...?	Low level of need to stay in HE	High level of need to stay in HE

FIGURE 11.1 Decision matrix

and key work, who are the key people in the department or organisation and how would you contribute something special to the mix. It would be naïve to think that you should be employed or funded just because you are a good researcher or have a great research idea – the truth is, the world is full of great researchers. Therefore, it is important to understand the job market both in academia and outside of it, so that you can make realistic assessments of what is best for you and what your potential 'unique selling point', what makes you a desirable employee, and how best you can bring that to employers' attention. By considering your portfolio, what it best demonstrates about your skills and attributes, you can then tailor your CV appropriately for each job. We provide a few ideas next but you should draw on advice also from your university careers service or one provided for professionals by your local authority.

Building your portfolio

A portfolio is a collection that evidences your professional development. It can be physical or virtual or both. It is more expansive than a CV, but having your professional development collected in a portfolio makes creating and tailoring your CV so much easier. As you go through your doctorate, learning new skills and enhancing others, taking advantage of a variety of opportunities and courses and developing a strong network of support, just take a bit of time every week or every month to reflect on your professional development and write down what you have been doing and how you have grown as a researcher and as a professional. Keep track of all talks you have given, courses you have taken and techniques/approaches you have learned. Keep feedback you have received, good and bad. Positive feedback is direct evidence of your skill level and your success. Critical feedback can be used to create a further development plan and to then evidence your developmental journey.

You may think that you will remember everything of importance achieved during your doctorate, but think back three years, what do you remember? Only truly major events stand out in memory, unless triggered, so record keeping of some kind is vital. In our experience, doctoral researchers undersell their skills and experience when applying for jobs because the skills they have striven to develop eventually become second nature and thus are undervalued. Consistently building a portfolio throughout the whole of your doctorate (and your professional career for that matter), will help you remember how far you have come and ensure that you are better able to represent the totality of your skills and experience when looking forward to your next career steps.

Creating a flexible curriculum vitae (CV)

Here we can only provide some brief, general guidance about creating CVs, noting some important points. There may be workshops on developing your CV provided by a Graduate School, Doctoral College or Researcher Development Team, as well as the careers service of your choice. We also provide in the further reading for this chapter some websites that provide examples of academic CVs and some that have sample CVs. However, our first piece of advice is that you should always check with any institution or organisation to which you are making an application if they have a preferred format or outline.

This hints at our second main recommendation: consider any draft CV as a flexible entity, ready to morph into a structure and content suitable for each specific employment purpose and audience. A prime example is that academic CVs tend to have different requirements to those intended for industry, commerce or the professions other than academic. For those cases, it is best to restrict your length to two pages, whereas an academic CV, which requires more information about your research and publications, might extend to four pages or more. It is simply a matter of providing what the selection committee or individual wants to know about you in relation to the post advertised.

For all CVs and application forms, think of the first stage of a selection process – putting yourself in the shoes of the person who scans your submission to see if it is worth passing on. If it is well laid out, clear, concise, legible, with consistently presented headings and no grammatical or spelling errors, it is much less likely to land in the handy wastepaper basket, real or virtual. Thus, attention to formatting forms our third recommendation, while our fourth is that the education information and career summary, that usually follow your personal details, are succinct. Education information is usually presented in reverse chronological order from your first academic degree (unless previous qualifications have professional relevance) with the names of awarding institutions. Academic CVs could include thesis and dissertation topics. Your career summary should highlight your years of experience and expertise gained, with key achievements and, for academic purposes, particularly significant publications. It is helpful if you categorise publications by type, such as books, chapters, peer-reviewed journal articles and so on. If and when your list is lengthy, you might put it in an appendix but do not forget to note the most recent and relevant publications in the main body, referring to the full list appended.

Other important sections to include are:

- research experience, methods used, key findings and accomplishments (briefly and in lay language if for a non-academic post);
- honours, prizes and recognitions;
- grants, scholarships and other funding attracted;
- teaching experience (this can be made relevant to non-academic posts as an example of leadership or ability to communicate);
- professional experience (this can be work experience, placements, internships, public engagement or previous employment that demonstrates a range of generic skills);
- administrative experience (for example, event organisation, newsletter compilation) and leadership experience (for example, posts in the student union or sports leader);
- skills relevant to the proposed work (for instance technical and practical skills, languages and so on, particularly those in which you have gained a qualification or for which you can provide evidence);
- professional affiliations and memberships that are relevant and in which you have recently been active.

For a post in academia, you might also list relevant conferences, seminars or symposia in which you presented, along with the title, again providing an appended list if you have a long list.

You will also need to provide the contact details of people, your referees, who can provide information about the quality of your work and fitness of character. For academic posts, these should usually be academics with whom you have worked; while for other professional roles, there may be other specific requirements, such as people who are familiar with your work with specific social groups. You may also need to provide evidence of eligibility to work in a country or with a specified group of people, such as children or vulnerable adults.

To return to our second recommendation, it is important to keep a draft CV to hand so that you can update it regularly, ready for tailoring as required. Tailoring for a specific occasion, which may be for a job application or to support a grant bid or to form the basis a biographic summary for a public speaking event, for example, consists of emphasising attributes that are required, reflecting the vocabulary used in the initial advertisement or call for submissions. For more information about preparing for job applications, see Top Tips 11.1.

TOP TIPS 11.1 UNDERSTANDING JOB ADVERTISEMENTS/APPLICATIONS

1. Job descriptions: these provide insight into what you would be doing if you were to be hired. You are not expected to have experience with or know how to do all the tasks listed in advance.
2. Required skills/attributes: these are the skills/attributes you need to be able to demonstrate. It is critical that you provide evidence/examples for these, so do not simply state you have these skills. Even if you do not have evidence for all required skills, it may still be worth applying, especially if you can demonstrate you have a high proportion of the requirements and a willingness to learn.
3. Desirable skills/attributes: these are not required, so do apply even if you do not have evidence of them. However, being able to demonstrate some of these may put you ahead of the game, so do include what you can.
4. Salaries can often be negotiated within reason, but get the job offer first before haggling.
5. Pay attention to any information they give about the institution or company. They will be looking for a person who not only has the skills they need, but who will fit into the environment and team as well. Ensure that in the cover letter and application you demonstrate how you match the ethos and identity of the place you are trying to work.

The importance of planning

We return to where we began – on the importance of planning. Doctoral research is a challenging experience but this does not make it impossible or not enjoyable. However, it may mean a major readjustment to the way you approach and deal with things. You will learn a lot about yourself whilst undertaking doctoral research – and this is all good for your future professional career/life. The key way to maximise your enjoyment is to take control of the process, rather than letting it (or your supervisor) control you; and the simplest way to take control is to plan.

The other way to feel in control and to enjoy the process is to share the journey – get out and share your amazing knowledge with others. In the early period, you may not think you know much but you know more than you think about your specialist topic. Other people, be they fellow PGRs, school children, the public, users, policy makers, businesses, charities – will be fascinated if you have something new to tell them, and by the middle stage you should have something relevant about your research to share. Working in isolation is not healthy for anyone, especially not for long periods, and can result in you losing the social skills required in the world of work. The relevance of this becomes obvious when you check many job advertisements: the ability to work with, lead or manage other people occurs in most. You can only produce evidence of being able to do this if you have been pro-active in grasping opportunities to lead seminars, teach undergraduates, organise workshops, explain your research in a public arena and so on as we have encouraged you in earlier chapters to do.

Check those job advertisements for other recurring professional attributes and practise mining your portfolio for evidence that you have at least the seeds of those skills ready to be grown on in a new environment. We will consider in the next and final chapter how to prepare yourself to thrive in new environments.

References and further reading 

Becker, L. and Becker, F. (2016) *Seven Steps to a Successful Career: A Guide to Employability* (Sage Study Skills series). London: Sage.

Bradberry, T. and Greaves, J. (2010) *Emotional Intelligence 2.0*. Brilliance Corporation.

Clance, P.R. and Imes, S.A. (1978) 'The imposter phenomenon in high achieving women: Dynamics and therapeutic intervention', *Psychotherapy: Theory, Research & Practice*, 15 (3): 241–7.

Denicolo, P. and Reeves, J. (2014) 'How can researchers make a successful transition to another employment?, chapter 10 in *Success in Research: Developing Transferable Skills*. London: Sage.

Denicolo, P., Duke, D.C. and Reeves, J.D. (2016) 'Researcher development and skills training within the context of postgraduate programs', in A. Hynds (ed.), *Oxford Bibliographies in Education*. New York: Oxford University Press.

Neugebauer, J. and Evans-Brain, J. (2016) *Employability: Making the Most of Your Career Development*. London: Sage.

Roberts, G. (2002) *SET for Success: The Supply of People with Science, Technology, Engineering and Maths Skills*. London: HM Treasury.

CV advice and examples on the Open University's Careers Service website at: www.open.ac.uk/careers.

CV templates can be found at: https://templates.office.com or www.livecareer.co.uk/FreeCV.

12

WHAT ARE THE KEY FEATURES FOR TRANSITIONING INTO A NEW ROLE?

In this chapter, we will consider how to:

- Reflect on what you will have achieved through researching for a doctorate
- Benefit from iteration
- Prepare to adjust to different environments
- Continue to fulfil your potential

Your final year of being a doctoral researcher, as well as being very busy with practicalities, is likely to be one that includes a range of emotions. While you complete several intended-to-be final drafts of your thesis, give presentations to practise your communication skills and disseminate your work, and prepare for the final assessment, you will also be preparing to move on and perhaps even contemplating a geographical move. There comes a point where you should pull all of your knowledge, expertise, personal and professional development together. This may be in anticipation of future employment, in preparation for job applications and interviews, or it may simply be the process of closing this phase of your life down and moving onto the next. You can expect to experience, as a natural part of this rite of passage, a considerable selection of the following:

- relief, as the end/winning post comes into view;
- trepidation, in case it is not as near as you hope;
- exhilaration, as you view all you have achieved;

- apprehension, about imminent changes;
- excitement, about imminent changes;
- nervousness, about what challenges come next;
- confidence, born from surviving several challenges;
- sorrow, about leaving friends and the comfort of the known;
- joy, that you can move on beyond the topic of your thesis.

Whatever situation you are in, towards the end of the doctoral process (perhaps six months from submission) you should recognise the amazing journey you have undertaken and take time to review it. Although it might be tempting to give your almost-ready thesis your total, undivided attention in this final phase, we do urge you to begin counting your achievements as submission time approaches, and certainly between submission and any final viva or result declaration, in readiness for the transition into your life beyond the doctorate. This will help you to maintain a positive outlook, and help convince others of your competence. If you seem not to believe in yourself, it will be hard to persuade others, whether they be examiners or prospective employers. Outwardly at least, cast off the robe of imposter (Chapter 11) and don the garb of doctor; get acclimatised to its seams of responsibilities and patches of advantages.

At the beginning of the book we suggested that there is huge potential inherent in the doctoral programme and that the process of undertaking research in a higher education institution will present you with a remarkable range of options and experiences. We recognised that making the most of such a rich opportunity required courage and self-confidence, perseverance and resilience, and above all passion and enthusiasm for your topic. We suggested that the early stages of the doctorate begin the formation of your identity as a researcher, while in Chapter 3 we advised on developing your professional voice. Now is the time to use that voice in earnest and with conviction to gain a postdoctoral post, either as a researcher in academia or industry, or a new professional role that draws on your recently acquired skills-set. We hope that you have, indeed, drawn upon that huge potential inherent in a doctoral research programme so you have a wide range of options before you. Do not feel constrained by the detailed topic of your thesis, or indeed by your discipline, because employers, within and outside of academia, are seeking people with something a lot more versatile than knowledge (which is constantly being added to and evolving). One employer/consultant confirms this in Voice of Experience Box 12.1.

VOICE OF EXPERIENCE 12.1 HOW TO MAKE THE MOST OF YOUR RESEARCH EXPERIENCE FOR YOUR PROFESSIONAL CAREER

Doctoral researchers can take many career paths, which are not necessarily linear but change dynamically as you learn new skills, develop new ideas and take opportunities as they arise. Research is at the centre of developments in many industries, government departments and institutes.

Skills developed during your doctorate include the ability to evaluate data, to communicate both in writing and orally about problems and potential solutions and to use high-level analytical thought to answer the questions posed, enabling the development of new products, appliances and problem solutions. For those in science this includes detailed, accurate work in the laboratory. These skills are highly sought in many different sectors.

To prepare yourself for a variety of opportunities, it is important to develop your transferable skills as well as your research skills. Project management is very important to make sure work programmes are clearly planned, good progress is made and that the available resources are used efficiently. General workplace skills are also important such as: team skills, time management, coaching, giving and receiving feedback, budgeting and monitoring resources, process improvement, negotiation, influencing, cultural awareness, and management and leadership. Another key skill is understanding the requirements for effective meetings. Developing these skills throughout your doctorate and demonstrating this within your CV and in interview will help you be employable in a variety of areas. Furthermore, continuing to enhance these skills continuously during your career is critical as they give additional value to the precision, detail and focus gained through your doctoral education.

A doctorate truly opens many interesting opportunities to contribute to new developments, as well as making a safer world.

(Dr Andrew Scott holds a doctorate in biochemistry, has had research, management and executive roles in large multinational organisations, employing many doctoral graduates. He now runs his own consultancy business)

Employers are seeking people who can demonstrate evidence of problem identification and solving through evaluating resources and planning in a disciplined way. Surely that describes your doctoral experience? They are also seeking people with demonstrable resilience, determination, flexibility and creativity – again the attributes honed through a doctorate. They want people whose additional skills fit their context, perhaps ability to teach, lead, communicate with a diverse range of people and in a variety of environments. One other asset you bring, which should be visible to you at this stage of the process, is experience and recognition of the value of iteration.

Benefiting from iteration

In Chapter 4, Figure 4.1 illustrated the iterative process of writing a thesis, the repeated return to successively hone your work, not in a cycle but in an upward spiral. Iteration is a facet of many aspects of research. It appears in the reading of the literature in two ways: firstly, in the experience of reading a specific book that initially might seem too complex to understand, then in rereading after further experience, when it makes more sense. We each have several books on our shelves that, on first acquaintance, were thrown down in despair of ever understanding but now are our most frequently used references. Secondly, the literature review itself is an iterative process, with a cycle of general reading to identify relevant topics, followed by cycles of refinement concluding only just before the final assessment to ensure that theories and ideas are up to date.

Data collection and analysis can be particularly iterative, indeed there is a formal process named the iterative method, in which analysis of the first tranche of data determines the nature of the next tranche to be collected and so on, with each successive understanding or interpretation derived being applied to all previous data so that there are successive refinements to solutions found. This mirrors our education, from early schooling up to and including the doctorate, as we progressively focus and gain refined understandings. For the next stage, we have become expert at iteration, which can serve us well when transferred to the world of work, if we recognise the need to translate it and our other skills to suit the new environments and tasks. This is how we achieve 'continuous improvement' professionally as individuals and in the roles we perform and the work tasks we are required to do.

Translating your transferable skills

It is common practice in higher education to refer to skills and attributes that are not purely academic or research practice as 'transferable/generic' skills because they should be useful in a wealth of contexts. However, we urge caution with this notion of transferability, as it is not as straightforward to achieve as it may appear. You may recall that, although we recognised in the Chapter 1 swimming metaphor that you brought to the doctorate a set of skills derived from previous education/work/life experience, we suggested that they would need to be applied differently in the doctoral context. This holds true also when you move on into other contexts. You will need to translate your skills into forms that fit new circumstances. Even very mundane skills such as sending emails may require some forethought in a new institution. So, you will need to be as assiduous in exploring the conventions, customs and culture in any new working milieu as we encouraged you to be when entering a doctoral programme. Eraut (2009) describes the tacit learning that takes place in the workplace as implicit knowledge, which is encountered either successfully or not. Each workplace has its own culture and taken-for-granted rules which we need to be sensitive to and navigate carefully. When we enter novel settings, we tend to make assumptions about similarities to those with which we are familiar, as the Talmud says:

> We do not see things as they are; we see them as we are.
> We do not hear things as they are; we hear them as we are.

We bring with us our understandings about how things are when we should be determined to find out 'how things are done around here'. We discussed this in Chapter 6 and you might also like to revisit Appendix III.

Plaister-Ten (2017) usefully deploys the metaphor of a cultural iceberg in business settings, in which aspects such as language, dress, emotional display, for instance, are obvious, above the waterline, and are relatively easy to recognise and adapt to. However, below the waterline are values, beliefs, expectations, attitudes and motives, which may be less easy to identify. As Eraut (2009) suggests, these are the tacit aspects that we must negotiate when we begin work in a new environment so that we do not find ourselves disorientated and unhappy, or to appear obstructive, insensitive or rude to others.

However, you have faced such an experience previously, when you entered your doctoral institution; the details are different but you can use the same tactics that we introduced you to in Chapters 2, 5 and 6 to research the customs, learn about and take advantage of opportunities and build relationships. You will continue to build networks throughout your professional life – and it may be that many of the key people in your network, those who form its cornerstone, were your doctoral peers.

VOICE OF EXPERIENCE 12.2 A NEVER-ENDING WEB

I regularly write with my former supervisor, Maureen Pope, with whom I have been friends now for more than thirty years; in turn, we share in our networks former doctoral students and their students. Though we cherish our intellectual grandparent roles, what we enjoy most is that they keep us mentally on our toes with their challenging new ideas and ways of perceiving the world.
(*Author's own experience*)

Continuous professional development

It seems, then, that although the doctorate can be viewed as being the pinnacle of educational degrees, this will not be the end of your research or learning. You will have, not only the opportunity to continue learning, but also the professional obligation to do so. Knowledge is continuously expanding (through, not the least, the contributions of doctoral researchers!) and contexts and needs/demands constantly change, too, so all professionals must keep up to date with knowledge and skills; this is good news as it means you will have many chances for stimulation. You are now entering the world of continuous professional development or CPD, in which professionals maintain their skills and knowledge levels through: self-awareness, regular reviews and reflection; coaching and mentoring; feedback from others; course attendance; and assignments or projects that stretch them or take them out of their comfort zone. All of which you will have experienced during your doctorate.

We hope that you have found many things to enjoy during your doctoral research (Chapter 10), even if you experienced moments of tedium and did not enjoy the whole process absolutely from beginning to end. How you managed the process emotionally and how you responded to any problems or setbacks will be vital resources for you to draw on in the future. As we pointed out in Chapter 11, the personal growth that accompanies your intellectual development will have enhanced your skills-set considerably and we remind you that these are all attractive and marketable attributes. In addition, as you approach doctoral status, this is an opportunity for you to consider your professional values and stance. What do you stand for, what do you care about in working terms, and what would you like your 'legacy' (even if only in a small way) to be? If you have never considered such things, now is a good time to do so as most professions and organisations have standards of behaviour that they expect, for example teaching standards in academe. Be prepared for this by reflecting on your current professional value set and how it has developed during the research process. Use Activity 12.1 to help you with the process of evidencing, which you can then add to your portfolio (Chapter 11).

Sharing experiences

We have encouraged you throughout this book to build up networks of colleagues who will support you in future roles and for whom you will reciprocate, providing assistance and encouragement. While we suggest that you continue to sustain and develop those networks as you move into

ACTIVITY 12.1 EVIDENCING YOUR ACHIEVEMENTS

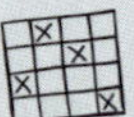

	Write your responses below:
What courses and/or professional development programmes did you attend: what did you learn and what have you gained overall from these?	
Did you have a mentor? Were you a mentor to others? If so, what did you enjoy about this experience? What did you learn and how has that changed or affected you?	
Did you get involved with any impact activities such as public engagement, enterprise or policy-influencing? What did you gain from that experience? What did other people gain from you?	
Who supported you or what 'Productive Distractions' kept you going during the process? What did you learn or obtain from them and those activities?	
Thinking back to the beginning of the process, what would you say has been your biggest personal change because of undertaking doctoral research?	
What would you like to do next and why?	

Through providing evidence for all the things you have done, your strengths and qualities, you will reach a fuller understanding of yourself as a rounded researcher, such that you can present yourself in broader professional terms – this is me, this is what I have done, this is what I am good at, this is what I can offer, and this is how I will add value to you/your workplace.

employment, may we also remind you to consider newer doctoral researchers? Remember how disorientating that first year can be. The support of more experienced researchers, who are willing to share their experiences and guidance, can be like gold dust. Many of your colleagues have contributed their experiences in this book and we are grateful to them for providing these 'voices of experience'. We urge you to add yours to them in your own contexts. Start that process by engaging with the final Reflection Point 12.1 and compare your reflections with those of others in Voice of Experience Box 12.2.

REFLECTION POINT 12.1

YOUR RESEARCH SUCCESS STORIES

As you reach the end of your doctorate, take the time to think back over your doctoral journey. What are you most proud of? Why? How have you changed as a person? What are you now able to do that you could not have before?

In our experience, the doctoral journey has a profound effect on individuals. It is important to take the time to reflect on exactly how far you have come.

VOICE OF EXPERIENCE 12.3 RESEARCHERS' REFLECTIONS ON THE DOCTORAL PROCESS

'Everyone had to start at some point, which generally means that people won't mind being asked questions. In fact, speaking now as a final year, I quite like being asked questions as it reminds me that I have actually learnt quite a bit over the years.'

'I'm a mature student so I did not expect that my doctorate would have such a huge impact on my life. Nevertheless, studying for my PhD has opened areas and opportunities that I did not think about. It is more challenging than I expected, but more rewarding as well.'

'When I started my PhD, I didn't have an idea that your PhD years were all about shaping your future. The extent to which it had taken over my life and changed the way I think has been surprising.'

(*Final year doctoral researchers – different disciplines*)

Having now shared some of our experiences, we wish you joy of your doctorate, not unalloyed joy for without contrast we cannot truly appreciate it, but joy nonetheless. We also hope that you are better able to visualise promise in uncertainty, to delight in serendipity and to believe you can realise your full potential. Finally, we share with you a quotation that we hope will inspire you as it has us:

> My mission in life is not merely to survive, but to thrive; and to do so with some passion, some compassion, some humor, and some style. (Maya Angelou)

References and further reading 

Denicolo, P. and Reeves, J. (2014) 'How can transferable skills become an integral part of life?', chapter 11 in *Success in Research: Developing Transferable Skills*. London: Sage.

Elvidge, L., Spencely, C. and Williams, E. (2017) *What Every Postdoc Needs to Know*. Abingdon: World Scientific Publishing Company.

Eraut, M. (2009) 'The transfer of knowledge between education and workplace settings', in H. Daniels, H. Lauder and J. Porter (eds), *Knowledge, Values and Educational Policy: A Critical Perspective*. Abingdon: Routledge.

Goleman, D. (1995) *Emotional Intelligence: Why It Can Matter More than IQ*. London: Bantam.

Molinsky, A. (2013) 'Common language doesn't equal common culture', *Harvard Business Review*. https://hbr.org/2013/04/common-language-doesnt-equal-c. (accessed April 2013).

Plaister-Ten, J. (2017) *Leading Across Cultures: Developing Leaders for Global Organisations*. White Paper Four, Routledge.

APPENDIX I

A SAMPLE GANTT CHART

Year 1: Aims, objectives, deliverables

Aims: By the end of Year 1, I would like to have submitted a draft chapter to supervisor.

(*Your aims are the goals for your project. They should be a high-level summary of what you wish to produce.*)

Objectives: To have located initial literature on X by 31 November; read and reviewed initial literature by 24 December and repeated process twice more by year end; begun writing first chapter by 31 October; given a paper to receive feedback on ideas in March; trained in research method Z; completed 10 days' training in transferable skills; revised chapter and submitted to supervisor before she goes on holiday in July.

(*Objectives are what enable you to achieve your aim. Objectives should be specific, measurable, attainable or agreed, realistic and timebound – SMART.*)

Key deliverables are:

1 conducted TNA;
2 attended training programme;
3 initial literature review completed and repeated (3a and 3b);
4 paper produced and delivered;
5 draft chapter written;
6 chapter submitted;
7 passed formal review.

(*Deliverables are something you produce or deliver during a project to achieve one or more objectives. Deliverables do not have to be physical things like documents; they could be understanding a method. Each deliverable should be linked to at least one objective – otherwise, why are you producing it?*)

Notice how much activity overlaps or needs to be done in parallel, as well as how deliverables may not occur in strict sequence.

		Year 1											
Activity/Task	**Duration (days)**	**Oct**	**Nov**	**Dec**	**Jan**	**Feb**	**Mar**	**Apr**	**May**	**Jun**	**Jul**	**Aug**	**Sept**
Identifying literature for review	16												
Reading – reviewing papers, making notes and adding to bibliography	80												
Meetings with supervisor	10			Vacation			Vacation				Supervisor on holiday		
Formal processes	10	Induction & TNA										Prepare for annual review	Annual review 4 September
Training - research methods and transferable skills	70												
Write draft chapter	30												
Prepare presentation	10												
Present paper in department – obtain feedback. Sub-task: make sure I am included in the programme for April	1												
Revise draft	20												
Submit draft before supervisor goes on holiday	1												
Achievement of Deliverables		1		3				4	3a, 5	6			2, 3b, 7

FIGURE APPENDIX I Sample Gantt Chart

APPENDIX II

SUMMARY DIAGRAM OF THE RESEARCHER DEVELOPMENT FRAMEWORK (RDF)

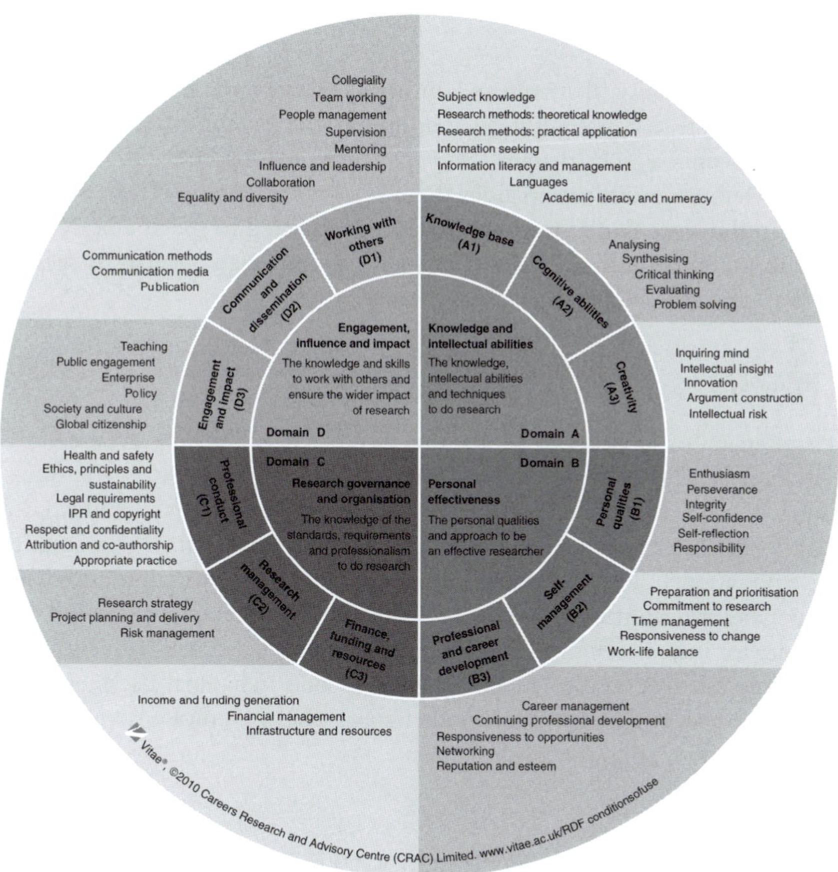

FIGURE APPENDIX II Summary diagram of the Researcher Development Framework. Reprinted with the kind permission of Vitae.

APPENDIX III
NON-VERBAL COMMUNICATION

A quick guide to some important signals

Bodily contact

This may take several forms and involve a variety of areas of the body. There are great cross-cultural variations in the extent to which bodily contact occurs, e.g. in Britain and Japan there is very little, whilst among some Mediterranean nationalities there is a lot. In Britain, it is most common in the close family, but even here it is restricted to specific body areas and in greetings and farewells. Culturally inappropriate contact is seen at best as embarrassing, at worst as aggressive.

Proximity

People stand or sit closer to people they like but, again, there is great cultural variation in what is considered a 'comfortable' proximity in any given situation. People feel uncomfortable when 'personal space' is invaded, so face-to-face meetings across cultures can elicit negative feelings that seem to have no rational cause. In general, changes in proximity communicate a desire to initiate or terminate an encounter, while increased proximity can indicate a desire for increased intimacy or aggression. In multi-national business meetings, this can give rise to much 'dancing' as one individual backs away to maintain the comfort zone and another approaches to indicate friendliness.

Orientation

This is the angle at which people sit or stand in relation to each other. The normal range is from head-on to side-by-side and varies with the nature of the situation; those who are cooperative or close friends adopt a side-by-side position, whereas in confrontation or bargaining situations people tend to use a head-on position. The main exception is that two close friends may sit head-on while eating.

Appearance

This is regarded as a special form of non-verbal communication called 'self-presentation', since many aspects of it are under voluntary control. Messages may be sent about occupation, status, competence, mood and personality, as well as the perceived importance of an occasion. There are regional and age variations in this, added to national cultural variation, so there is plenty of room to generate misunderstandings!

Posture

Distinctive postures are used to convey interpersonal attitudes, friendly or hostile. Posture also varies with emotional state along the dimension tense/relaxed. Since posture is less well controlled than face or voice, there may be 'leakage', for example anxiety may not be seen in the face but can be seen in posture. A relaxed posture indicates self-assurance and can promote confidence in both parties of an interaction.

Head nods

These play an important part in relation to speech. Slow nods indicate a listener's understanding; more frequent nods encourage the speaker to continue; rapid nods indicate the listener's wish to speak.

Note that head nodding or shaking varies between cultures in whether they indicate agreement – yes – or disagreement – no.

Facial expression

This is used to modify or 'frame' what is being said. It is usually well controlled, negative attitudes and emotions usually being suppressed, but some aspects are difficult to control, e.g. perspiration and pupil dilation and contraction. The latter can indicate dislike, fear or pain under steady light conditions.

Gestures

Movements of head, feet and other parts of the body are used to communicate. The hands are the most expressive but are also most under conscious control. Hand gestures may also replace speech, which is physically or emotionally suppressed. They may be used to deliberately replace speech but they do not always mean the same thing in different cultures. Some gestures, such as finger pointing, can be common and innocuous in some cultures but very rude in others. Feet, being the least under conscious control, often 'leak' information while the rest of the body is under control.

Looking

Eye contact plays an important role in communicating interpersonal attitudes and establishing relationships. Looking and proximity can substitute for each other in signalling degree of intimacy. In the UK the length of gaze from no eye contact to long eye contact signals disinterest, low intimacy, clinical interest to sexual attraction or aggression – the latter depending on other non-verbal signals. There are large cultural differences in the meaning of lengths of eye contact and between whom it can take place. For instance, in Western cultures, 'looking someone in the eye' is considered a sign of honesty, whereas, in other cultures it is considered rude to look a person of higher status in the eye.

Non-verbal aspects of speech

Pitch, stress, tone and timing convey many kinds of information – about emotions, personality, group membership, etc., for instance an anxious person speaks rapidly, 'breathily' and with many speech errors, while an angry or dominant person speaks loudly and slowly.

Equilibrium processes

There is more to interaction than individuals responding to each other: they must behave in a highly co-ordinated way. There must be co-ordination over:

- the nature of the activity
- the role relationship

- how intimate the encounter is
- the dominance relations
- the emotional tone and
- the proper sequence of acts.

This pattern is mainly worked out using non-verbal cues to synchronise the interaction, to establish the intimacy and dominance levels and to reward the other person for sustaining the interaction. However, once equilibrium is established, it is very resistant to change.

APPENDIX IV

ADVICE ON FINAL ASSESSMENT

A. Summary of criteria used by many examiners for assessing the written thesis

Overall requirements

A thesis should have:

- A careful, clear presentation that has the reader's reading and understanding needs in mind.
- If necessary, or helpful, a glossary of terms and/or of acronyms preceding main text and succeeding Contents list.
- The contribution to knowledge expected and achieved made explicit.
- Chapters that are coherent in themselves and which contribute to an integrated whole which follows a consistent argument.

Sectional attributes

The following sectional attributes are sought.

Abstract

- Clearly describes main aspects of the thesis (purpose, theoretical and methodological base and general outputs and outcomes).
- Stays within the word limit.

Introduction

- Rationale for undertaking study clearly explicated.
- The appropriateness of the researcher conducting this study made clear. (*Science note*: This is less applicable to the sciences, where the positivist framework requires a design that supports researcher neutrality.)
- A brief overview of thesis provided, demonstrating the 'storyline', chapter by chapter.

Review of relevant literature

(*Science note*: Often, the introduction and literature review chapters are integrated as one.) (*English Literature note*: Often, the entire thesis is in essence a critique of literature, and so detailed and sophisticated argumentation relating to the literature will be evident in the majority of chapters.):

- Succinct, penetrating, challenging, critical, analytical approach.
- Demonstration of thorough knowledge of field.
- Primary rather than secondary sources used.
- Recent references, except where older seminal work is acknowledged.
- Quotations (NB: page numbers required) used to illustrate or exemplify rather than substitute for own words in argument.
- Organised to show a developing argument for the hypotheses/research questions.

Statement of research problems or plan for development of a creative piece

- Clear and succinct hypotheses or questions or basic plan derived from/ revealed by the literature review.
- Should have a novel theoretical or methodological or creative slant and/or bring together previously unrelated fields and/or a new area of application.
- Well-articulated rationale for 'worthwhileness' of research.

Approach and methods of enquiry adopted

Theoretical argument – methodology rather than 'methods':

- Rationale for general approach closely argued, giving reasoned case for rejecting other possible approaches.
- Justification of research design presented, taking account of potential advantages and limitations.

- Research techniques argued as theoretically and practically relevant to research problem.
- Reasons given for rejection of possible alternatives.
- Rationale provided for amendments to standard tests and procedures or for detailed design of innovative techniques.
- Rationale provided for the selection of the analysis procedures, choice of statistical tests, etc.

Data collection

Description of actual process where appropriate.

(*Arts note*: If a piece is being created [performance, a book, an artwork] or an extended argument based on the literature, for instance, being prepared, then data collection, analysis and presentation may not apply. They would be replaced by the artwork or argument with a description of how they emerged.):

- Clearly set out and easy to follow, possibly including a flowchart, Gantt Chart or similar.
- Relevant details included (how access was achieved, number of subjects/respondents).
- Relevant profiles, timing of interventions, duration of interventions, etc. (or what materials and equipment were used, what procedures were followed, etc.).
- Ethical issues – what permissions were obtained, what guarantees were given, how ethical issues have been acknowledged and dealt with.
- Difficulties encountered and how they were dealt with so that the research was not compromised.

Analysis of data (where appropriate)

(*Science note*: Sometimes, statistical expertise is utilised to analyse scientific data. This does not mean that you do not have to understand your data and what the analysis entails. Make sure that you work with an expert, so that you can answer any questions about the analysis of your data.):

- Mode of analysis theoretically justified.
- Any assumptions stated and justified.
- Congruent with research questions/hypotheses and approach adopted.
- Details of procedure clearly presented.

Presentation of data (where appropriate)

(*Science note*: Graphs, tables and figures are extremely important in a science thesis. These should be clear, well labelled and self-explanatory, with just the legend. Examiners spend a good deal of time looking at figures; ensure that there are no mistakes.):

- Clearly structured.
- Data 'trail' evident.
- Details of why, who, what, when and where provided.
- Tables, figures, diagrams to summarise data clearly numbered and titled and referred to in the text.

Discussion of outcomes or conclusions of argument

- Main points summarised and evaluated, interpretations made of raw data.
- Links made to literature previously presented, e.g. what previous research/theory has been supported, substantiated, challenged, amended, rejected, etc.
- Reflections on the research process – limitations addressed and consequent implications for results.
- Suggestions for repeat or further research based on this research.
- Implications of results for theory and for practice.
- Clear articulation of contribution to knowledge.

References

- All references in the text included in an appropriate style.
- No references included that do not appear in the text.
- But a separate, short bibliography of influential texts is sometimes (in some institutions/disciplines) acceptable.

Appendices

- All appendices clearly numbered in the order of appearance in the main text.

B. Top tips for preparing for a viva

Throughout your doctoral registration

Take every opportunity possible to talk to people in formal (seminars and conferences) and informal (with researcher colleagues over coffee, friends over lunch, interest groups at meetings, neighbours over the fence) settings. The more varied your audiences, the better able you will be to articulate your ideas in a range of ways and the more confident you will become. Public engagement activities are very useful in this respect.

Pre-viva weeks

Make sure that you are well prepared for the viva by:

- Encouraging your supervisor to provide you with a mock viva.
- Arranging for the proof-readers (essential contributors to thesis preparation process) of your final draft to ask you as many questions as possible about your work, its purpose and process and to have you elaborate on what you said about it in the written version.
- Thinking of the most awful, difficult question that anyone could ask you and formulate in advance the main points that you would include in your response (facing your worse fears diminishes them!).
- Drawing up a list of any typing errors you noticed since you handed in the bound/online thesis so that you can confess these to examiners before they bring them to your attention (NB: there are ALWAYS some!).
- Ensuring that you know your written version thoroughly and can find specific sections easily (you can take your hard copy thesis into the viva with you, so you might want to put some [only a few] Post-It notes down the side so that you can turn to main sections easily).

These tips will help you to speak fluently and confidently about your work. This ability is something that the examiners are looking for.

The night before

- If it helps your confidence, have one last skim through the thesis but do not stay up long and late to do this. Getting some sleep is much more important.
- You may find that taking some physical exercise in the fresh air helps with your nerves. Tempting though it may be, try not to resort to sleeping medicines or alcohol because these frequently lead to a fuzzy morning head!
- You could prepare by learning some relaxation techniques in advance.

On the day

- Dress smartly, as befits the dignity and importance of the occasion, but comfortably, remembering that it is a work occasion! Choose clothes that you will not be tempted to fidget with or worry about but that help you feel confident.
- Bring with you:
    - a copy of your thesis;
    - a pen and notebook;
    - a prepared list of typographical errors that you found after submission;
    - personal necessities, e.g. tissues, bottle of water.
- If you tend to have physical symptoms when you are nervous, then you may like to persuade a good friend to be your chauffeur for the day. You can also reduce adrenalin levels (that make your tongue dry) by going for a brisk walk in the fresh air or by at least a bit of 'on-the-spot' jogging in the nearest private place!
- Make sure that you leave more than enough time to reach the appointed place punctually – allow for transport delays and parking problems. Make every effort to avoid arriving late and/or flustered.
- Before you go into the room, try some 'power posing', in a quiet place. For about five minutes or so, make yourself as big as possible, standing up straight and tall, and stretching out your arms. Be positive, walk in proudly. This is your big day to shine.

What will probably happen

- Your examiners will have met to discuss your work and to organise the viva by preparing questions and the order of asking them. Remember, though, that they are human, too, and may not have left enough time for transport problems and so on – so do not assume that there is a problem with your thesis if they are not quite ready at the appointed start time.
- You should be introduced to the external examiner by the **independent chair**, if there is one, or by the **internal examiner**. They should tell you what mode of address they prefer (Jack/Gill/Doctor/Professor) but, if they forget to, do ask rather than worry throughout the viva whether you are being rude.
- Very, very rarely the examiners will tell a candidate the expected outcome at the beginning – this is not good practice for many reasons but it does sometimes happen. If it is good news, do not let this relax you so much that you lose the sharpness of mind required. Some experienced examiners might reassure you that they have found the thesis interesting and enjoyable so that you know there is some value in it. Thereafter, your task is to reassure them that you, too, value the research process and results and, furthermore, you can convince others of their merit. It would be very

unusual, indeed, for examiners to indicate at the beginning that there are major flaws but many do commence by suggesting that there are several issues they want to explore in depth – this is more frequently a compliment rather than a complaint.

- If an examiner says, for example, 'on page 167 you say …', then take the time to look up that page to see what you did say, in its context, before leaping in with an answer.
- If you don't understand a question, say so politely (examiners can ramble on sometimes!). Say something like: 'I'm not sure what you mean exactly – could you repeat/rephrase the question?'
- However apparently basic or even idiotic the question seems (remember, you are now the expert in the area and are very familiar with the work), respond politely!
- Allow yourself some thinking time: it is OK to say, 'That is a good point … let me think about it for a moment …' Breathe – then – Think.
- Defend your work firmly but calmly. Show that you are prepared to learn but believe in what you have done, considering the circumstances. For instance, you can say something like, 'Yes, that is a valid criticism but at the time, the materials/equipment/resources were the only ones available and, as I explained in Chapter 5, the ones I used did have other benefits …' Or, 'I'm afraid I can't agree. Atkin's work is interesting but it is not relevant in the particular context of my work for the following reason …'
- Be careful to avoid undermining your work by agreeing with every criticism the examiners may put forward. It may invalidate your 'contribution to knowledge' or they may have simply been testing your ability to formulate verbally a cogent argument.
- Do not ramble on for too long in response to any one question; the examiners will still want to explore some specific issues, no matter how long it takes, so do not try to fill up the time in an attempt to avoid more questions. If the answer is complex, you can respond by saying, 'The answer to that is complex but, in summary, it involves X, Y and Z. Would you like me to elaborate on all or some of those aspects?'
- A viva can take any length of time – there are no rules to guide examiners about length- but an average time is 1.5 to 3 hours (while the range can be from 30 minutes to 5 hours – both extremes being very unusual, though sometimes discipline-dependent – check in your department about past vivas).
- At the end of the discussion, you may be asked to comment on the quality of your support at the university. You will probably have to wait then while the examiners review your responses and formulate their verdict. If they do not indicate how long they need for this, ask if you will have time to take a 'comfort break' so that you are not worrying about whether you have time to visit the toilet, etc. Equally, if you need such a comfort break during the viva, it is better to ask than to be distracted – the examiners may need one, too, and be relieved that you asked!

The finale

You will generally be given the result on the day of the viva and have explained to you, if only briefly, any requirements for amendments and the time in which you will be allowed to make them. Good examiners will tell you clearly the reasons for their decision and all examiners should ensure that you will be supplied with a written version of their requirements within a short period (a week or so).

In summary

- Avoid being dogmatic, overly defensive, rude, long-winded, laid back or blasé, apologetic for your work or obsequious.
- Do be thoughtful, reflective, honest, direct but not rude, concise and specific (but do not give one-word answers!), prepared but not rigidly so, confident but not overly so, and do your homework on the examiners (what their main research interests are and what they might like or find challenging about your thesis).
- Enjoy your viva – and good luck!

APPENDIX V

POLICY INFORMATION ABOUT IMPACT

Guidance on the REF

The Stern Review of the Research Excellence Framework (2016) makes this Recommendation:

> Guidance on the REF should make it clear that impact case studies should not be narrowly interpreted, need not solely focus on socio-economic impacts but should also include impact on government policy, on public engagement and understanding, on cultural life, on academic impacts outside the field, and impacts on teaching.

For more information about the REF and proposed changes to future REF exercises, see the Stern Review, found on the UK government website (www.gov.uk/government/uploads/system/uploads/attachment_data/file/541338/ind-16-9-ref-stern-review.pdf).

Guidance from Research Councils UK

Research Councils UK gives this guidance on Pathways to Impact (see www.rcuk.ac.uk/innovation/impacts/):

> **A clearly thought through and acceptable Pathways to Impact statement**
>
> A clearly thought through and acceptable Pathways to Impact [statement] is an essential component of a research proposal and a condition of funding. Grants will not be allowed to start until a clearly thought through and acceptable Pathways to Impact statement is received.

A clearly thought through and acceptable Pathways to Impact statement should:

- be project-specific and not generalised;
- be flexible and focus on potential outcomes.

Researchers should be encouraged to:

- identify and actively engage relevant users of research and stakeholders at appropriate stages;
- articulate a clear understanding of the context and needs of users and consider ways for the proposed research to meet these needs or impact upon understandings of these needs;
- outline the planning and management of associated activities including timing, personnel, skills, budget, deliverables and feasibility;
- include evidence of any existing engagement with relevant end users.

It is expected that being able to describe a Pathway to Impact will apply for the vast majority of proposals. In the few exceptions where this is not the case, the Pathways to Impact statement should be used to fully justify the reasons why this is not possible.

APPENDIX VI

AUTHORS' DOCTORAL EXPERIENCES

Pam's story

Although I had a full-time scholarship, a combination of the fear of having no job at the end of my studies making me reluctant to give up entirely my FE teaching post, the need to play the hostess to support my husband's business and the multifarious demands of two young teenagers, all made for a frantic lifestyle. It included manually crunching data (no handheld computers then) while under a hairdryer, mentally drafting chapters on the way back from the school run and trying out emerging ideas on college teaching colleagues and students. My university colleagues, a tightly knit group of departmental staff dedicated to the whole group of doctoral researchers, were, to me, an exotic bunch but kind and generous with their support and advice. With new ideas and perspectives, they made my studies challenging but stimulating. We were all shocked, during my final year, when we encountered the first of what was to be almost a quinquennial 'university restructuring exercise'. Our cosy, research-oriented department amalgamated with a larger, much more political, entity which had no methods training for doctoral students or supervisor training for staff. Before my own viva, having been lucky to gain an academic post in the new structure, I took on my first doctoral student … a baptism of fire. These contrasting experiences engendered my career-long passion for developing better support for both supervisors and their doctoral students. Decades of lobbying and fighting with fellow enthusiasts for these improvements within my employing universities, and through national and international committees, make it deeply saddening when academics and doctoral researchers short-sightedly dismiss the widening opportunities now available to focus solely on research projects.

Dawn's story

Overall, I enjoyed doctoral research. The times I was happiest were when I had a colleague to bounce ideas off and to come up with crazy hypotheses with. I am an extraverted thinker and thrive on discussion, challenge and debate. I also like puzzles and working with data to find interesting patterns. So, for much of my doctoral career, I was quite happy. I worked hard and often found myself working with other members of my research team on 'extra' projects. I liked to be busy and did manage to get a fair number of co-authorships for my efforts.

This changed quite a bit when I got pregnant, a little more than halfway through my doctorate. To be fair, my supervisor was fantastic about it. He had a professional wife and children and he understood that there is 'no good time' for professional women to start a family. If it is something you want and the time is right personally, you just should go for it. Go for it I did. However, pregnancy and looking after a baby took a lot more out of me than I expected, even though, by all accounts, I had a very healthy pregnancy (despite horrible 'all-day' sickness for three months) and was lucky enough to have a wonderfully healthy baby girl. I did find I couldn't do quite as much as I did before, even in pregnancy. I would get tired. I also found that the work I thought I would get through while on maternity leave, didn't quite happen. Being a natural overachiever, I had to work to forgive myself this and allow myself to concentrate on me and my baby for this period.

However, going back to the lab after maternity leave was another big blow. I felt looked down upon because I could no longer work late into the evening and do all the 'extra' things I used to do. I needed to focus on moving my doctorate forward and balancing my family life, and, because of that, I was not so much a part of the research group community anymore. It was lonely. And there were people who made insinuations that I was less dedicated to my field and to research because I chose to have a family. Nonetheless, I worked through it all, making time to enjoy my baby and I successfully passed my viva, with ten publications to boot. In hindsight, I would not change a thing about starting my family or doing my doctorate. My baby daughter gave me perspective. For those of us who now work to support researchers, one thing I certainly have taken from the experience is the importance of supporting the diverse and changing needs of researchers throughout the entire doctorate journey, which takes place in the context of complex adult life.

Julie's story

I had great supervision but didn't appreciate that until the thesis was completed and the dust had settled on the whole experience, about two years after my graduation. The research process itself had been extremely stressful, both personally and intellectually. Personal tragedy happened very early on in my research and continued right up to my graduation, with several family deaths, including those of my mother and both grandmothers. I received an intellectual blow when my supervisor moved to another university at the end of the second year and at a key moment in the research. In addition, the topic I had chosen, and which I loved, proved controversial, so I had a lot of criticism from within my discipline. When my first supervisor moved on, I was unable to move institutions because of my personal circumstances, but I was mature enough to realise that, to succeed, I would need someone locally I could discuss things with. I was in a small department, which could have restricted my options, but it was a very supportive one, both personally and professionally. I approached someone who was not an obvious choice as a supervisor, yet whom I thought could help me through the process. Indeed, on giving him a sample chapter, he said: 'I don't agree with a word you have written, but don't let someone like me put you off!' This demonstrated that he was the perfect person to supervise me and my thesis! We still drew on the subject expertise of my first supervisor and I learned two lessons from the change in supervision: first, the intellectual support needed may not be the only form of support one needs to get through the PhD process. Second, given my personal circumstances, I needed a wider support network of buddies to bounce ideas off and to help me feel good about the work and myself – and I found them among my department peers, and other colleagues I met on training courses, at internal seminars and external conferences, as well as my friends and family. I learned that it is essential to be acutely aware of what help one needs and to know when and how to get it; and, like Dawn and Pam, this experience has driven my passion for supporting researchers ever since.

GLOSSARY

Abstract A summary of the main contents of a book, thesis or article.

Advisor *see* Supervisor

Citation styles These are methods of acknowledging the sources of information within the text and in reference lists. They differ in the location, order and structure of references and there are conventions linked to disciplines and writing genres within them.

Completion The point when all the requirements of a doctorate have been successfully achieved and the award confirmed.

Credentialism The need for certificates, degrees and other formal qualifications that evidence the acquisition of knowledge and skill.

Critical feedback Responses that note quality aspects of a piece of work, including what was good and what could be improved.

Critical mass A term borrowed from nuclear physics, meaning the amount of substance required to make a reaction happen, this is now used as a (disputed and notional) number of researchers required to provide for a rich and creative research environment.

Cultural sensitivity Knowing, being aware and accepting that cultural differences and similarities between people exist, without assigning them a value, positive or negative, better or worse, right or wrong.

Culture An active process of meaning-making; the sum of attitudes, customs and beliefs that distinguishes one group of people from another.

Dissertation A written report about a project carried out at master's level in the UK, for instance, and at doctoral level in the USA, for instance.

Doctoral College Part of a university devoted to doctoral researchers as a focal point for a range of support and other services.

Doctoral programme All the learning and research experiences that make up doctoral study.

Doctoral researcher Someone engaged in pursuing a doctoral qualification. Previously/sometimes known as a doctoral student or candidate.

Early career researcher Generally, a postdoctoral researcher in the first stages of their career but, in some literature, doctoral researchers are also subsumed into this grouping.

Emotional intelligence (EI) The ability to be aware of, control and express one's own emotions and be sensitive to and handle well those of others.

Epistemology The branch of philosophy concerned with the study of knowledge, its nature, justification and rationality of belief. An individual's epistemology is what s/he believes are the limits of truth and proof and what is recognised as only opinion.

Ethics The moral principles that guide and govern a researcher's behaviour in the conduct of their research projects.

Evaluation activity A process undertaken to judge the quality of a process and its products.

Exclusion criteria The strategy used in a systematic review or a narrative synthesis for deciding which articles to exclude from the analysis of the literature.

External examiner An academic from a different university to the candidate's who assesses the doctorate products, ensuring that they meet the criteria recognised as universal for such an award.

Graduate School Part of a university devoted to either all postgraduates or to doctoral researchers as a focal point for a range of support and other services.

HASS Acronym for humanities, arts and social sciences.

Inclusion criteria The strategy used in a systematic review or a narrative synthesis for deciding which articles to include in the analysis of the literature.

Independent chair An academic who manages the process of the viva voce but who has no role in the assessment of the doctoral research under scrutiny.

Impact (with research) The demonstrable contribution that research makes to society, its culture, health, wealth and environment.

Inter-library loan A system or scheme, whereby researchers can request literature and other resources from other libraries or repositories.

Internal examiner An academic who works in the same university as the doctoral candidate but who has made no direct contribution to the research process other than to an assessment of its outputs. The examining role includes ensuring that the doctoral products fit the regulations of the university for that award.

Iteration Repetition to develop successively closer approximations to a desired state or solution. The results of one iteration is the starting point for the next.

Literature review A critical summary of key themes and an evaluation of important studies within the body of literature relevant to a piece of research.

Massification The process of increasing access to a wider, and therefore more numerous, section of the population.

Mock viva An exercise in which candidates are asked questions about their research as a practice for the formal final viva voce.

Narrative review A summary of key themes and evaluation of key studies relevant to a specific research topic. The review is deliberately structured by the author to guide the reader from the broad research context down to limitations in the field relating to the specific focus of the author's research. The structure is used to help the author present a clear line of argument or storyline that runs through the review.

Narrative synthesis A summary of key themes or key patterns that emerge from a body of literature which has been reviewed in a systematic way using a formal procedure. Important in a narrative synthesis is the need to minimise distorted analysis resulting from the subjective choices of the researcher. For this reason, a narrative synthesis often forms part of a systematic review of a body of literature in which procedures are in place to ensure objectivity.

Ontology The branch of metaphysics dealing with the nature of being.

Paradigm A philosophical and theoretical framework of a scientific school or a discipline within which theories, laws and generalisations, and the research methods performed to produce them, are formulated.

Pedagogy The method and practice of teaching, especially as a theoretical concept.

Peer review Evaluation of scientific, academic or professional work by others working in the same field and therefore conversant with its paradigm/s.

Plagiarism The practice of using other people's work as if it were your own. It is a form of stealing and includes copying other's work without references to credit the source.

Postdoctoral researcher (postdoc) Someone who has successfully achieved their doctorate and is working as a researcher, usually in a university or research organisation, in a paid position.

Project The bounded research, starting with a research question or hypothesis and culminating in a completed report, known in some countries as a thesis and in others as a dissertation.

Research Excellence Framework (REF) UK A five- to six-yearly UK national ranking of all higher education institutions to determine core funding. Ranking involves peer review of submissions and not simply metrics such as research income, publications, citations, student numbers, the environment and impact. The process was recently reviewed by an independent authority, led by Lord Nicholas Stern, published by the UK government (www.gov.uk).

Research methodology An argument presented about the selection of approach and methods for a research project that demonstrates the study's validity by explaining the reasons for that selection and for rejecting alternatives.

Researcher bias The presence of subjectivity within a literature review arising from the researcher's choices about how to present the literature to further a specific argument. Also, the potential for results to be skewed, usually inadvertently, because of the presence of a researcher in the system.

Researcher Development Framework (RDF) A tool indicating the main attributes/skills of a researcher over a working life, developed under the auspices of Vitae amongst other things to aid researchers identify areas for further development.

Self-efficacy The extent to which you believe you can determine an outcome, can complete tasks and fulfil goals.

Seminal research A piece of work/research that is ground-breaking, pivotal and/or inspirational and that exerts influence over the discipline.

SRHE Society for Research into Higher Education – UK based.

STEMM Science, Technology, Engineering, Maths and Medicine.

Submission The point when a thesis/dissertation is presented for formal final assessment.

Supervisor A person charged with guiding and supporting a doctoral researcher from induction to completion, sometimes known as an 'advisor'. Any researcher may have several supervisors, although one should be recognised as the principal or main supervisor.

Systematic review A summary and evaluation of all studies available to date relating to a specific research question. The evaluation is achieved using a procedure that is explained so clearly that other researchers could replicate it if they wished.

Thesis A written report about a project carried out at master's level in the USA, for instance, and at doctoral level in the UK, for instance. Also, a proposition or argument.

UKCGE UK Council for Graduate Education.

Vitae A UK-based organisation for developing the careers of researchers, with links worldwide.

Viva voce An oral examination for an academic qualification. It typically involves the candidate responding to questions about his/her study area and sometimes involves a presentation by the candidate. A closed viva refers to one conducted in private involving only the candidate, examiners and perhaps a chair person, and, less frequently, one observer, say a supervisor, or note-taker. An open viva can involve any number of observers.

Widening participation Making accessible opportunities to study at higher educational levels to those, perhaps from socio-economic or ethnic groups, who have traditionally not participated.

Writing-up The period towards the end of the research process where the complete version of the thesis is compiled. Even 'completed' chapters will need to be edited together to make an elegant, flowing and readable whole.

INDEX